# Estimating the effects of
# social interventions

# Estimating the effects of social interventions

CHARLES M. JUDD
*Harvard University*

and

DAVID A. KENNY
*University of Connecticut*

CAMBRIDGE UNIVERSITY PRESS
Cambridge
London   New York   New Rochelle
Melbourne   Sydney

Published by the Press Syndicate of the University of Cambridge
The Pitt Building, Trumpington Street, Cambridge CB2 1RP
32 East 57th Street, New York, NY 10022, USA
296 Beaconsfield Parade, Middle Park, Melbourne 3206, Australia

First published 1981

Printed in the United States of America

*Library of Congress Cataloging in Publication Data*
Judd, Charles M.
Estimating the effects of social interventions.

1. Social science research – United States.
2. Evaluation research (Social action programs) – United
States.  I. Kenny, David A., 1946–      II. Title.
H62.5.U5J83    361'.973               81–2405
ISBN 0 521 22975 8   hard covers      AACR2
ISBN 0 521 29755 9   paperback

To Liz and Mary Ellen

# Contents

vii

# Preface

In the fall of 1977, we jointly offered a graduate course in the Department of Psychology and Social Relations at Harvard University. That course, "Psychology and Social Relations 2570: Methods of Applied Social Research," was based on two convictions that we shared. The first was that our graduate students were likely sometime in their professional careers to engage in applied social scientific research. At some point they would all be called upon to evaluate a social intervention. Our second shared conviction was that although the research methods we normally teach to social science graduate students are relevant to applied social research, a different general orientation toward these methods is necessary.

As we attempted to prepare and organize the course, it became apparent to us that our own orientation toward applied research methods was not reflected in the textbooks that were available on research methods. Hence, at the conclusion of the course, we made the fateful decision that we would really organize it and turn it into a book. The few students who enrolled in our course might have been better instructed had we succeeded in organizing the material prior to offering the course, rather than subsequently. Had we been able to do that, however, this book probably would not have been undertaken. In a sense, then, we owe a great deal to those students. Only as we came to understand that the course readings were not entirely what we wanted, and to realize that our course structure left something to be desired, were we motivated to write the book. Those students, when they read it, are likely to be pleased to see that we have finally organized the course they took.

One of the advantages of the low enrollment in that course was that the two of us spent nearly as much time talking to each other as we did talking to our students. In the subsequent years, as this book progressed, most of our time together was spent discussing what we were writing rather than actually writing it. In a very real sense, all of the ideas in these pages are joint products. We each learned a great deal from the other, and our separate ideas grew into a common set as the book was written. Surprisingly, in the process of arriving at this consensus, our friendship remained intact and even grew.

Our intention in writing this book was to provide a tool that would be useful to those actually conducting applied research, regardless of the substantive domain in which they work. We believe that the problems of research design and validity that we address appear whenever social interventions are evaluated, regardless of the nature of those interventions.

Because of this intention, we have attempted throughout to discuss on an intuitive level issues that in a more formal treatment might have required much more lengthy statistical arguments. In other words, at times we provide guidance to the researcher without elaborating upon the statistical proofs that support our conclusion. We have chosen this path in the interest of brevity and in the hope of keeping the arguments comprehensible to a wide range of active researchers. The statistical proofs that we omit are generally available elsewhere. At the end of the book we have suggested supplementary readings that present more technical material.

Just as we do not burden the reader with statistical proofs, so also we have avoided an exposition of the basic statistical procedure, multiple regression, that underlies the analyses we discuss. This book should not be seen as a textbook on statistics. We presume that the reader is already familiar with the basics of multiple regression. Fortunately, excellent texts already exist.

Although we have attempted to write a clear, straightforward exposition for the practitioner, it has been occasionally necessary to introduce rather complicated material. We present such material not for its own sake, but because the task facing the researcher is complicated. Complications arise in many ways. First, applied research involves inherently "noisy" data: Relationships among variables are inevitably weak, and measurement error is a constant problem. We have tried to emphasize these topics when discussing the precision of the estimate of effects. Second, in order to know whether the estimate of a program effect is biased, one must make a careful analysis of the reasons why persons are assigned to treatment and comparison groups. Thus, we continually refer to the assumptions made about this assignment process throughout the book. Third, researchers are continually making implicit causal assumptions in their analyses of data. We have tried to spell out some of these assumptions, as well as to present methods to estimate more complex but more realistic models. Fourth, any discussion of methods for applied social research must include a consideration of the reality of complex issues that the investigator can and should face. We have included a discussion of the complicating issues of nonindependent observations, covariates, and multiple treatment and outcome variables.

The organization of the book is as follows: The first three chapters are introductory and explain the key concepts that are discussed throughout the book. Chapters 4 through 9 form the heart of the book and present a discussion of the various research designs used to evaluate social interventions. Generally we first present the design; then we elaborate the traditional statistical analysis procedures used to analyze the design; and finally we discuss complications in the analysis and solutions to these complications. The last two chapters discuss general issues in the evaluation of social interventions. The book can be used both as a textbook and as a reference book. If used as a textbook, the chapters should be read consecutively. If used as a reference book, the first three chapters should be read before reading about any particular research design.

Although this book is a joint product hammered out during extended discussions, it also reflects the influence of many others on our thinking. We owe these others, both separately and jointly, many thanks. One of us, Charles M. Judd, owes much to his parents. His father's commitment to improving human welfare has been a constant reminder that all endeavors ultimately need an application. Morton Deutsch, Judd's dissertation advisor, has also been instrumental in his interest in applied social science. The depth and seriousness of Deutsch's thought continue as an example. As a graduate student, Judd took a course on the general linear model from John Hammond, who was then in sociology at Columbia University. Although Hammond is probably not aware of his influence, that course has shaped much of Judd's subsequent thought on statistical issues. Finally, a number of others have also been influential, among them R. Gary Bridge, Peter Moock, and Janice Steil.

In the case of David A. Kenny, his interest in the effects of social interventions stems from many sources. His father, Thomas P. Kenny, has been actively involved in public policy as a labor and community leader. It is to him that Kenny owes his initial interest in the topic. His undergraduate advisor, Robert Sommer, showed him that social science could be used as a vehicle for positive social change. In his graduate training, he learned from Donald T. Campbell, Thomas D. Cook, Robert Boruch, Albert Erlebacher, and Lee Sechrest. Campbell's towering intellect and constant encouragement shaped and guided Kenny's graduate education. Cook, who was at the time beginning his secondary evaluation of *Sesame Street,* provided him with concrete experience in the evaluation of social interventions. After Kenny received his degree, others, especially Marcia Guttentag, encouraged his applied interests.

Jointly, we wish to thank a number of colleagues and friends. Pierce Barker, Peter Bentler, Charles Reichardt, and Robert Rosenthal provided excellent critical reviews of portions of the manuscript. Although we did not always follow their advice, their comments were exceedingly helpful. A number of other reviewers remain anonymous to us. We hope they will realize their influence when they see the portions of the book they reviewed. In addition, James Dalton, Jon Krosnick, Lawrence La Voie, Dean Simonton, Merle Sprinzen, Gail Tomala, Rebecca Warner, and Stephen Zaccaro made valuable contributions. Our editor, Susan Milmoe, has also been of great help to us. She has given us the freedom to write the book we wanted to write and, at the same time, has been of assistance in providing a grant and arranging for chapter reviews. Finally, we thank those who assisted by typing the numerous chapter drafts: Jean Brumbaugh, Bev Douhan, and Mary Ellen Kenny. Blair Boudreau deserves special mention for her excellent and efficient typing of the final manuscript.

There were a number of fortuitous events and circumstances that made this book possible. We acknowledge the help of the housing shortage in California, the postwar baby boom, lunches with Reid Hastie, and three-handed hearts games.

On a more serious note, it is to our wives, Elizabeth Judd and Mary Ellen Kenny, that we are most grateful, and to whom we dedicate this book. We thank them for their companionship, their encouragement, their assistance, and their patience.

Charles M. Judd                     David A. Kenny
Cambridge, Massachusetts            Storrs, Connecticut

# 1
# Introduction

One of the original and enduring goals of the social sciences has been to generate knowledge and information that can be used to guide social policy. For instance, many of the concerns and interests of sociologists grew out of the discipline's original efforts to ameliorate the social conditions brought on by the industrial revolution and the subsequent urbanization of America during the last half of the nineteenth century (Lazarsfeld & Reitz, 1975). Likewise, psychologists have long been concerned with a variety of applied issues; for example, personnel selection and training and the diagnosis and treatment of mental illness have been central interests of psychologists since the last century. Finally, and perhaps most clearly, the modern study of economics grew out of efforts to understand how government policies (or the lack thereof) affect the economic well-being of the country, with the aim of providing guidance to economic decision makers.

Although the interest in generating information for applied purposes is a long-standing one in the social sciences, it has, if anything, grown in recent years. Three separate but interrelated forces have been responsible for this growth. First, newly trained social scientists are facing a shrinking academic job market and are therefore seeking employment in government and private agencies whose purpose is to conduct research to guide social policy. Second, in the last twenty years social welfare programs have grown enormously. As more and more money has been spent on those programs, administrators and policy makers have increasingly realized the need to evaluate them. Hence, increasingly the government and private agencies have hired social scientists to conduct evaluation research. Finally, as increasing amounts of money have become available from the federal government for applied evaluation

1

research, funds for the conduct of basic social research have been drying up. Among academic social scientists, it is common knowledge that research into basic social processes is not being supported at the level it had been in the recent past.

Although opportunities for young social scientists are increasingly applied in nature, and therefore their interests are more applied, social scientific training has by and large been slower to change in this direction. Many social scientists are currently finding employment in the area of policy and evaluation research. Few of them, however, receive graduate training designed explicitly for such careers. They therefore find themselves inadequately prepared in the methodological skills necessary for applied research.

This book grew out of the authors' belief that research in applied settings presupposes an orientation to data, research design, and statistical procedures that is different from the orientation conveyed in most books or courses on basic research methods. The difference between these orientations is, however, a difference of degree rather than one of kind. Applied researchers use the same set of methodological and statistical skills as basic researchers, but they use these skills with a different perspective than that of basic researchers. Our purpose in this book is to review a set of research designs that are particularly useful in applied research settings. We discuss both the merits and problems of these designs as well as strategies for analyzing the resulting data. Our discussion is oriented particularly toward the applied researcher. Thus, although what we have to say is likely to be informative to the basic researcher as well, our orientation on the methodological issues we address is quite different from that encountered in most basic research methods books.

We can be somewhat more explicit concerning how our emphases in this book differ from what they would have been had we written a book on the design and analysis of basic social research. First, applied social researchers tend to employ different types of research designs than do their colleagues in basic research. They are perhaps less likely to use what we call randomized experimental designs because of the control of the treatment necessitated by such designs. Applied researchers are more likely to use quasi-experimental designs, where the need for control over the treatment is somewhat reduced. Hence, we emphasize the design and analysis of quasi-experiments to a greater extent in this book than we would in a book on basic research methods.

More generally, the settings in which applied research is conducted are likely to have an impact on the research design that can be employed. Hence, in some contexts it may make sense to do a randomized experiment; in other contexts such designs are not feasible, and a quasi-experimental design should be used. Thus, the choice of research design is to some extent dictated to the applied researcher, whereas in basic research the choice is determined primarily by the researcher's predilection. An applied researcher must therefore be familiar with a variety of different designs and their analysis, whereas a basic researcher may be able to pursue his or her research interests effectively using a very few techniques.

Another difference in emphasis between applied and basic social research emerges from differences in the type of intervention or program whose effects are assessed in the research In many applied research projects, the social program that is evaluated is relatively massive. It is difficult and expensive to set up, many people are involved in administering it, and its effects are likely to have both social and political consequences. The size and importance of independent variables in basic research are perhaps at a more modest level. Because of this difference, there may be more at stake in reaching valid conclusions in applied research, in the sense that it would be extremely costly to conclude that some social program had no effect when in fact it did. Thus, in the language of statistical analysis, the power or precision of the statistics employed is probably of greater concern to the applied researcher than to his or her basic research counterpart.

Just as the size of interventions in applied research may motivate the researcher to pay increasing attention to the power of statistical procedures, so too the complexity of such interventions may introduce a great deal of extraneous variation that renders conclusions more difficult. For instance, if we are evaluating the impact of a social welfare program that has been instituted on a massive scale, it may be quite difficult to argue that the treatment received by each person in the study is identical. Different individuals receive slightly different treatments because they deal with different staffs, remain in the program for different intervals, and so forth. In other words, in applied social research extraneous and uncontrolled variation may exist in the treatment or independent variable that would normally be controlled in more basic research. Because of this, it may be more difficult to detect the effects of interventions in applied research, and when they exist, it may be difficult to determine what factor in a multifaceted intervention is responsible for those effects.

Another difference in orientation between applied and basic researchers concerns the emphasis typically placed on the ability to generalize from a research study. We might reasonably expect a social welfare program that shows positive effects in an evaluation to be implemented more widely, based on the recommendations of the evaluation. If such dissemination of the program is likely to result from the evaluation, then the researcher should have some confidence that the results of the evaluation research are generalizable to the new population who will be exposed to the program. In basic research, it typically is not the case that the treatment becomes more widely distributed following the research. Hence, the question of generalizability may be less salient to the basic researcher.

As part of the concern with generalizability in applied research, researchers are typically quite interested in how the intervention operates differently in different settings or on different populations. In statistical terms, applied researchers may be more interested in assessing interactions between the treatment variable and characteristics of the sample than more basic researchers.

All of these different emphases imply that researchers in applied settings must differ from their basic research colleagues in the breadth of concerns and methods that occupy them. They are more likely to encounter diverse research designs, are more likely to be concerned with statistical precision, deal with more multidimensional treatments, and must be more concerned with generalizing effects than basic researchers. All of this operates to increase the complexity of the applied researcher's task. We believe that the methodological concerns of the basic researcher are fundamental to the conduct of applied research and that, in addition, the applied research setting imposes many new concerns that may safely be ignored in a great deal of basic research.

Given all this, the task of this book is to familiarize the reader with the complexity of conducting research, using many different research designs, in applied settings. What we have to say is likely to be informative to the basic researcher as well. The concerns we raise are relevant to basic research; they are simply more demanding of attention in applied contexts. Our book differs from other books that consider the design and analysis of social research in that we hope to acquaint the reader with the complexity, the uncertainties, and the importance of design decisions in applied settings. The applied researcher faces a formidable set of tasks. Most books and courses in research methods, because they are oriented toward basic research, do not appreciate the complexity and diversity of these tasks.

### The plan of the book

The basic model for the research designs presented in this book is one of program evaluation. That is, the type of applied research we shall be discussing is the evaluation of some intervention or program, delivered intentionally or not, that is expected to have social, economic, or psychological consequences on those exposed to it.

Although the evaluation model is the basis for the research designs discussed in this book, evaluation constitutes, in fact, only one type of applied social research. Social researchers frequently collect data to diagnose some social problem. Such research, although related to the evaluation model, is not quite the same. Applied diagnostic research attempts to identify what treatments or conditions are responsible for a given outcome or situation that is observed. In essence, then, diagnostic research is evaluation turned around. In evaluation we seek the outcomes of a treatment or condition; in diagnosis we seek the treatment or condition that produces the outcome we observe.

In addition to evaluation and diagnosis, some applied research is conducted in a placement model, where the goal is to match some treatment or person to a situation where the most beneficial outcomes can be obtained. In the placement model, the researcher is aware of the treatment (this may be a person as in personnel placement) to be delivered and the outcome that is desired. Data are gathered to locate the precise conditions under which the treatment is most likely to achieve the desired outcome.

In the next chapter the basic model for the conduct and analysis of evaluation research is presented. This model, which holds in general, regardless of the specific research design employed, is one in which persons or other units that the program is expected to affect have been assigned to levels of the treatment (including, perhaps, no treatment) and subsequently some outcome variable or variables are measured that are expected to show the impact of the treatment. Within this general model we can differentiate between specific research designs by considering three factors:

1. The first factor is the way in which assignment of units to treatment conditions has been or is conducted – in other words, what rule or variable has determined treatment assignment. Essentially there are three sorts of assignment rules or variables: a random assignment rule where each unit has a known probability of assignment to each treatment condition; a known but nonrandom assignment rule where assignment is based on some known variable such as a pre-treatment measure of the unit; and an unknown assignment rule where the variable that determined assignment is not only unmeasured but unknown.

2. The second factor for differentiating among research designs concerns the presence or absence of a pre-treatment measure or pretest.

3. The third factor refers to the manner in which comparisons between treatment conditions are made. We can either observe different persons in the different treatment conditions or we can expose everyone to all of the treatment conditions. In the former situation, treatment effects are estimated by comparisons between persons. In the latter case, treatment effects are estimated by comparisons within persons.

Having discussed the basic evaluation model in Chapter 2, we proceed in Chapter 3 to identify a set of criteria, called research validities, that can be used to evaluate the quality of information generated by social research designs.

Chapters 4 through 9 present the research designs that are the heart of the book. The discussion of each design is roughly broken into three parts. First the design is defined and decisions that must be made by the researcher in using the design are identified. Next we discuss how each design has been classically or traditionally analyzed. This discussion includes what we see as being the major problems or oversights of the traditional analysis. The third part presents some complexities of analysis and design or alternative analysis procedures to the classic strategies, which at least in part eliminate the problems of the classic strategies. In each of these chapters we discuss the advantages and disadvantages of alternative analysis strategies in terms of the criteria identified in Chapter 3.

The design discussed in Chapter 4 is the randomized experimental design, where units have been randomly assigned to treatment conditions.

Chapter 5 discusses the regression discontinuity design. In this design, the assignment rule is known but nonrandom, and pre-treatment measures are gathered. In fact, the assignment variable is a pre-treatment measure.

Chapter 6 discusses the nonequivalent control group design, which is probably the most widely employed quasi-experimental design. It is defined by an unknown and nonrandom assignment rule coupled with pre-treatment measures of the outcome variable.

Interrupted time-series designs are discussed in Chapter 7. Unlike the other designs, time-series designs make treatment comparisons within a unit across time rather than between units. The assignment variable for this design can be random, known, or unknown.

Chapter 8 discusses miscellaneous quasi-experimental designs. For all of these designs the assignment rule is unknown and a pre-treatment measure is gathered. Chapter 8 also presents a series of issues that affect design and analysis decisions in quasi-experiments.

Chapter 9 concludes the discussion of designs with the post-only correlational design. Here, the assignment variable is unknown and pre-treatment measures are not taken. The data are thus exclusively cross-sectional.

In a more traditional nomenclature for these designs, Chapter 4 covers experiments, Chapters 5 through 8 cover quasi-experiments, and Chapter 9 discusses correlational designs. Quasi-experiments differ from randomized experiments in that the assignment rule is not random. In quasi-experiments the researcher has access to the units prior to the treatment. Correlational designs are similar to quasi-experiments in that the assignment rule is not random. Unlike quasi-experiments, however, in correlational designs the researcher has access to the units at only one point in time.

In Chapter 10, having presented our basic discussion of the various designs, we consider a variety of further issues that often confront the applied researcher regardless of the specific designs that he or she employs. These issues include the process of identifying and probing for mediating and interacting variables in treatment effects, the need for and techniques of secondary analysis of applied research data, and procedures for generalizing effects across repeated independent evaluation studies that all examine similar treatments.

Chapter 11 closes with a review of the major themes that have occurred throughout the book. Here we also review the research designs we have covered and provide some final comments on their strengths and weaknesses.

Our intention in writing this book has been to construct a text that could flow with a course. Thus, the topics we develop at later points in the book in some sense build upon what has preceded them. At the same time, we hope that this book can be used as a reference source, so that a researcher who, for instance, is designing a nonequivalent control group study can refer to the appropriate chapter for guidance. If the reader plans to use this book more for the latter purpose than for the former, we nevertheless encourage him or her to read at least the next two chapters before skipping on to designs of particular interest.

# 2

# The basic evaluation model

In the first chapter we defined the basic evaluation model as

> one in which persons or other units that the program is expected to affect have been assigned to levels of the treatment (including, perhaps, no treatment) and subsequently some outcome variable or variables are measured that are expected to show the impact of the treatment.

The purpose of this chapter is to discuss this basic model in more detail, to present its rationale, and to provide an overview of how treatment effects in general are estimated. An understanding of this basic model and its estimation is central to the rest of the book, in that nearly all we discuss subsequently is a variant of it.

To define the model in more detail and present its rationale, we shall use an example of an applied evaluation that might be conducted: the evaluation of the impact of day care on the emotional development of children. Suppose that we were hired as researchers to estimate this impact. If we knew little about the design of social research, we might decide to evaluate the day-care program by putting all the children available to us into day care and subsequently keeping track of their emotional development. The problem with such a study, of course, is that we have no idea of how the children would develop if they had not been put into day care. Hence we are unable to determine whether the emotional development we see in day care is different from what it would have been had the children been left in their homes.

We thus must include some sort of other treatment in our research in order to establish a baseline comparison group with which to compare the children receiving the day-care treatment. This alternative treatment condition is frequently called a comparison or control group. For purposes of comparison with the treatment group, we frequently want the comparison group to receive exactly the treatment that would have been received by all children had the day-care program not been instituted.

Now that we have decided that both treatment and comparison groups are necessary to assess the impact of day care, the next step is to determine how the children might be assigned to one or the other condition. Sometimes this decision can be made by the researcher; more often it is made by some other agency or some process outside of the researcher's control. Ideally, we would like children to be assigned to conditions in such a way that, *in the absence of treatment effects,* the children in the treatment and comparison conditions do exactly the same on measures of emotional development that are subsequently administered. How might we do this?

It might seem that one way would be to measure all the children on emotional development prior to treatment administration, then to match children who score similarly, and to divide them, once matched, into treatment and comparison groups. For instance, we might decide to match boys with girls on initial development and then, within each male–female pair, the boy would be assigned to the treatment condition and the girl would be assigned to the comparison condition. All unmatched children would be omitted from the study.

Although this assignment procedure would seem to accomplish the desired result of assuring comparable groups, in fact it probably would not. Even if initially each of the boys were matched with a girl, boys and girls might be developing at different rates. Hence, in the absence of treatment effects, the boys in the treatment condition would be expected to differ from the girls in the comparison condition on a test of emotional development administered at a later point, after the treatment had been delivered.

The only way to be certain that the children in the two conditions would score the same on this post-treatment measure in the absence of treatment effects is to make the assignment on the basis of some variable that is unrelated to the subsequent outcome or post-treatment measure. However, because assignment is determined well before the outcome measure is taken and because we hope to observe treatment effects, there is no actual characteristic of the children that we can be sure would be uncorrelated with the outcome in the absence of treatment effects. Hence, to achieve the desired result with any certainty, assignment should not be based on any characteristic of the children. In fact, the only way to have confidence that the variable used for assignment will be uncorrelated with the outcome in the absence of treatment effects is to use a variable that, within the limits of probability, is uncorrelated with *all* other variables: a variable whose values are randomly generated. This, then, is the rationale for randomized experimentation, in which subjects are assigned randomly to treatment conditions.

Frequently researchers are not able to employ a random assignment rule because of constraints in the situation where the research is conducted. For instance, in our example, it may be that day-care centers cannot afford to take as many children below the age of 2 because younger children require more attention and hence increase the day-care center's costs. A random rule might put more young children in the center than could be afforded. Nevertheless, the administrators of the center may want some younger children in the research because they are interested in day care's effects on them as well as on older children. Hence the researcher is faced with the need to assign children to the treatment and comparison conditions in part on the basis of age. He or she divides all the children into two groups above and below age 2, and within each group randomly assigns children to conditions using different probabilities of assignment. For the younger children, 30% are in the day-care treatment, 70% are in the comparison condition. Among the older children, 80% are in the day-care treatment, 20% are in the comparison condition. This assignment plan is depicted in Table 2.1. With this assignment plan we would not expect children in the treatment and comparison groups to score equally on the outcome measure even in the absence of treatment effects, *unless we first equated children on age.* We would expect that the children in the two conditions would score the same in the absence of treatment effects so long as we looked at only one age group at a time. Thus, valid comparisons can be made between the two conditions if we first equate for age, which is the variable on which assignment was probabilistically based. As in Chapter 1, the variable on which assignment is based is called the assignment variable or the assignment rule.

The general principle from this example is that when the assignment rule is other than random, we need to control for it in order to make valid comparisons between the treatment groups. If we control for the assignment variable, whether statistically or by making comparisons only within its levels, then we can have

Table 2.1. *Probabilistic assignment to treatments based on age*

| Age | Treatment group | Comparison group | Total |
|---|---|---|---|
| Less than 2 years | 30% | 70% | 100% |
| Greater than 2 years | 80% | 20% | 100% |

confidence that the comparison of treatment and comparison groups would show no difference in the absence of treatment effects.

Sometimes the researcher is faced with a situation in which the assignment rule is neither random nor based on some known variable. For instance, in the day-care example, if the researcher could not control assignment and therefore did not know on what basis children had been assigned to treatment groups, it would be extremely difficult to equate groups on the basis of the assignment variable. In such cases, we frequently attempt to equate on the assignment variable indirectly, by using pre-treatment measures as statistical controls. Such a procedure approximates controlling for the unknown assignment variable when various assumptions are met concerning the relationship between the unknown assignment variable and the pretest and concerning the expected growth between the pre- and posttests.

If the assignment variable is unknown and no pretest measures are taken, as in the post-only correlational design, approximating control over the assignment variable becomes very difficult, though still worth attempting.

This example, as we have presented it, parallels the presentation of research designs in this book. The basic problem in nearly all of these designs is the problem of defining and controlling the assignment variable. If it is random, as in randomized experiments, it does not need to be controlled, for it is uncorrelated with the outcome. If it is known, it is relatively easy to control, although further complications arise. If it is unknown, we approximate its control either by using pretest measures or by making assumptions about the posttest measures when pretests are not available.

### Estimation

Although there are differences among the designs in this book, we shall employ what is called the *general linear model* throughout to estimate treatment effects. We shall usually present this general linear model in its multiple regression form, although analysis of variance and analysis of covariance are also subsumed under it. Because multiple regression is the general technique for estimating effects under the general linear model, in the pages that follow we present an overview of it and the relevant terminology. This section of the chapter should not be assumed to substitute, however, for a more formal exposure to multiple regression and analysis of variance that we presume the reader has already received.

In the estimation of treatment effects we are interested primarily in estimating relationships between variables and then making causal inferences about those relationships based on other pieces of information. There exist a variety of techniques for calculating the relationship between two variables. One common way to estimate the relationship between two variables is to collect data from a number of units ($N$ of them) on the two variables ($X_i$ and $Y_i$) and plot the resulting points on a graph. An easy way to summarize the resulting scatter diagram, as it is called, is by fitting a straight line to the points in such a way that deviations of the points from the line are minimized.

The formula for a straight line is

$$Y_i = b_0 + b_1 X_i$$

where $X_i$ and $Y_i$ are variables, $b_0$ is the intercept of the line on the $Y$ axis, and $b_1$ is the slope. We wish to fit a straight line to the data points of the scatter diagram so that deviations of points from it are in some way minimized. In other words, we shall fit the equation

$$Y_i = b_0 + b_1 X_i + e_i$$

where $e_i$ represents the deviations between each $Y_i$ and $\hat{Y}_i$, where $\hat{Y}_i$ is defined as

$$\hat{Y}_i = b_0 + b_1 X_i$$

We wish to solve for values of the coefficients $b_0$ and $b_1$ in such a manner that $e_i$ across all $N$ observations is minimized. If we simply decided to minimize the sum of $e_i$ across the observations, an infinite number of coefficients is possible. What is usually done is to solve for the coefficients that minimize the sum of $e_i^2$ across all the observations. The resulting solution for the coefficients is called the *least-squares* solution.

Simple and multiple regression yield these least-squares coefficients. In the case of multiple regression, where we have three or more variables, one dependent ($Y_i$) and two or more independent ($X_{1i}$, $X_{2i}$, and so on), we solve for the values of the coefficients in the equation

$$Y_i = b_0 + b_1 X_{1i} + b_2 X_{2i} + \cdots + e_i$$

that minimize the sum of the squared deviations.

The interpretation of the coefficients in this equation is straight-forward: The intercept $b_0$ represents the expected value of $Y_i$ when all of the independent variables, $X$'s, equal zero. Each of the slope coefficients, or the regression coefficients ($b_1$, $b_2$, ...), indicates the predicted change in $Y_i$ associated with a one-unit change in its independent variable, *with all other variables-held constant*. It is this last phrase that renders multiple regression quite powerful. Suppose that $X_{1i}$ were defined as the treatment variable and $X_{2i}$ was the known assignment rule in a study where randomized assignment was not employed. The coefficient of the treatment variable then estimates the treatment effect with the assignment variable held constant, even though $X_{1i}$ and $X_{2i}$ are correlated.

In this example, we have defined $X_{1i}$ as the treatment variable. This may be done in the case of two conditions, a treatment group and a comparison group, by setting $X_{1i}$ at one if an individual is in the treatment condition, and at zero if an individual is in the comparison condition. Independent variables that have this sort of dichotomous nature are commonly called *dummy variables*. A more extended discussion of them is given in Chapter 4.

Because the regression coefficient for the treatment variable, $b_1$, is the best estimate of the treatment effect, researchers usually want to determine whether it is statistically different from zero. Tests of statistical inference are used to achieve this purpose. These tests require assumptions about the nature of the residuals. One assumption of particular importance in applied social research is that these residuals are independent. In other words, any residual does not give any information concerning the magnitude of any other residual. This assumption is particularly crucial in time-series designs (Chapter 7).

The interpretation of regression coefficients depends on the units in which the independent variables and the dependent variable are measured. If two predictors are measured in different units, then it is difficult to compare the magnitude of their coefficients. Occasionally, when such comparisons are informative, the regression equation may be computed with all variables standardized $[(X_i - \overline{X})/s_x$, where $\overline{X}$ is the mean of $X_i$ and $s_x$ is the standard deviation]. In such cases, the resulting coefficients (standardized regression coefficients or $\beta_i$'s) are interpreted in units of standard deviations. Although these standardized coefficients are useful for comparisons among predictors within an equation, they render interpretation more difficult than the unstandardized coefficients in other cases. For instance, if we are comparing effects between two different samples, the standardized coefficients should not be used because their magnitude depends on the standard deviations of the variables within the two samples. With only a few exceptions, we shall prefer the unstandardized or raw regression coefficients in this book.

The regression coefficients enable us to predict each $Y_i$ from any combination of values on the independent variables. In this sense they are informative about the linear relationship between the dependent variable and the independent variables. They do not, however, succinctly inform us of how accurate our predictions are. Some multiple regression equations may generate quite accurate predictions, whereas others may not. An index of the accuracy of prediction would be quite helpful.

It is quite easy to calculate the degree to which our predicted $Y_i$ or $\hat{Y}_i$ diverges from the actual $Y_i$ for each observation. The difference between these two is the residual in the regression equation, the sum of the square of which is minimized by the least-squares solution. Hence, we might use, as an index of the accuracy of the regression prediction, the sum

$$\sum_{i=1}^{N} (Y_i - \hat{Y}_i)^2$$

The value of this sum is quite variable, because it depends on the units in which $Y$ is measured. Therefore, we need to compare this sum with an index of how good our prediction of $Y$ would be if we did not take into account the relationship with the $X$'s. If we knew nothing about the predictors, our predicted value of $Y$ for every case would be the mean of $Y_i$, $\overline{Y}$. If we square and sum across observations the deviation of observed $Y_i$ from $\overline{Y}$, we have an index of quality of prediction given no information concerning the $X$ variables.

In light of this, the ratio

$$\frac{\sum_{i-1}^{N} (Y_i - \hat{Y}_i)^2}{\sum_{i-1}^{N} (Y_i - \overline{Y})^2}$$

can be interpreted as the degree to which errors of prediction of $Y_i$ given the set of $X_i$'s are smaller than errors of prediction given no information about the $X_i$'s. The lower limit to this ratio is zero, in which case the numerator is zero and we perfectly predict $Y_i$ given the $X_i$'s. The upper limit of the ratio is one, where $\hat{Y}_i$ equals $\overline{Y}$, in which case we have gained no predictive power from the set of $X_i$'s at all.

As an index of the degree to which our use of the $X_i$'s to predict $Y_i$ improves our prediction from that made without the $X_i$'s, it makes sense to compute the difference between the above ratio and one. This difference score is what is traditionally referred to as the squared multiple correlation coefficient:

$$R^2 = 1 - \frac{\sum_{i-1}^{N} (Y_i - \hat{Y}_i)^2}{\sum_{i-1}^{N} (Y_i - \overline{Y})^2}$$

This coefficient tells us the proportion of the total variation in $Y_i$ that can be "explained" by the relationship between $Y_i$ and the predictors. It can be rewritten as

$$R^2 = \frac{\sum_{i-1}^{N} (\hat{Y}_i - \overline{Y})^2}{\sum_{i-1}^{N} (Y_i - \overline{Y})^2}$$

The square root of this is called the multiple correlation coefficient.

At times, we present in this book equations in which some variables are unmeasured or hypothetical. For instance, if the assignment variable is unknown, we may nevertheless wish to include it in an equation. Whenever hypothetical or unknown variables are included in an equation, the equation is known as a *structural equation.* Multiple regression analysis cannot ordinarily be used to estimate the coefficients of such equations. They generally require other procedures, known as structural modeling techniques, as discussed in Chapter 9.

### Conclusion

In this chapter we have presented the basic evaluation model and developed the rationale for controlling the assignment variable in estimating treatment effects. We have further presented the basics of the general procedure used throughout the book to estimate treatment effects. In the next chapter, we define a set of research validities that can be used to discriminate among research designs and analysis strategies.

# 3
# Validity in social research

The goal of both the applied and basic social researcher is to generate information that is as accurate, generalizable, and otherwise valid as possible. The purpose of this chapter is to discuss the ways in which research is valid or invalid. In other words, we review criteria by which we can evaluate the information gathered and conclusions generated by social research. Without such criteria it would be difficult to choose among research designs or among analysis strategies.

Four different types of research validity are reviewed. The fourfold division and the names we employ are borrowed from Cook and Campbell (1979). Our definitions of the four validities, however, are substantially different from those that have been given elsewhere. Thus, although this chapter owes much to others, it incorporates our own interpretations.

The chapter is organized in six sections. In the first we define the four types of research validity. In each of the next four sections we discuss threats to each type of validity as well as ways to overcome the threats. In the final section interrelations among the four validities are presented.

### The definition of research validities

The conduct of social research under the general evaluation model that was presented in the last chapter begins with a causal hypothesis. For instance, any of the following might constitute a hypothesis underlying some research project:

1 Rehabilitation programs in prisons can lead to less recidivism among first-time offenders.

2 Crowded classrooms in inner-city schools hinder the educational achievement of disadvantaged pupils.
3 Public-appeal campaigns are effective in decreasing smoking among highly educated people in metropolitan areas.

In form, each of these hypotheses posits a causal relationship between a treatment and an outcome for some population in some setting. All causal hypotheses that are the basis for social research incorporate these four components, at least implicitly.

The hypotheses posit a causal relationship between some general theoretical treatment (e.g., rehabilitation programs, crowded classrooms, and public-appeal campaigns) and some general theoretical outcome (e.g., recidivism, achievement, and smoking). Likewise, hypotheses discuss these causal relationships for a theoretical population and setting. When the research is actually designed, all of these general theoretical constructs or ideas need to be translated into specific instances or operations. Translating the theoretical constructs of the hypothesis into the specific instances of the research design is commonly known as *operationalizing* the constructs. Thus, to pick our first hypothesis as an example, the theoretical outcome, recidivism, must be operationalized, perhaps as number of felonies committed in the 2 years after release. In a parallel manner, to conduct the research we need to identify specific instances of the setting (prisons in general) and population (first-time offenders).

Once the constructs of our theoretical hypothesis have been operationalized, and once the research has been conducted, we must determine if there are any effects of the operationalized treatment. This involves two issues:

1 Are the effects of sufficient size to be detectable?
2 Are detectable effects in fact due to this treatment, or are there competing causal explanations?

Finally, after we have answered these questions, we may want to know if the causal effects we observe among the operationalized constructs may be generalized to other theoretical treatments, outcomes, populations, and settings that are of interest.

Conclusions of social research may be questioned at any of the four points we have just outlined. We might doubt the conclusions of social research for any of the following reasons:

1　The theoretical constructs of the hypothesis are not adequately operationalized.
2　The research design employed is not sufficiently precise or powerful enough to enable us to detect causal effects among the operationalized constructs.
3　The detected effects on the operationalized outcome are in fact due to factors in the research other than the treatment.
4　The generalizations from the research to other constructs, those not operationalized, are inappropriate.

Each of these four concerns can be called an aspect of the validity of social research.

We shall refer to the first as *construct validity,* the second as *conclusion validity,* the third as *internal validity,* and the fourth as *external validity*. For our purposes, following the above discussion, they can be defined as follows:

1　Construct validity: the extent to which the theoretical constructs of treatment, outcome, population, and setting have been successfully operationalized.
2　Conclusion validity: the extent to which the research design is sufficiently precise or powerful for us to detect effects on the operationalized outcome should they exist.
3　Internal validity: the extent to which the detected effects on the operationalized outcome are due to the operationalized treatment rather than to other competing causes.
4　External validity: the extent to which the effects we observe among operationalized constructs can be generalized to theoretical constructs other than those specified in the original research hypothesis.

In essence these four types of validity concern different sorts of relationships in the research enterprise. Construct validity refers to the relationships between theoretical constructs and their operations. Both conclusion and internal validity refer to the relationship between the operationalized treatment and operationalized outcome: Conclusion validity concerns our ability to detect that relationship; internal validity concerns whether that relationship is a causal one. External validity concerns the relationship between the hypothesized constructs that were operationalized and other constructs of interest that were not.

In the paragraphs that follow, we discuss each of these validities in more detail. We identify the major ways in which each is threatened, as well as strategies to overcome these threats.

### Construct validity

We defined construct validity as the extent to which the specific outcome measures, treatments, samples, and settings employed in the research represent the theoretical constructs of interest. In the paragraphs that follow we elaborate on this definition, point to the two major threats to construct validity and specify procedures for maximizing it.

The reader is probably most comfortable thinking of the construct validity of tests or measures of attributes, for that is the context in which the term is most widely used (Cronbach, 1970; Cronbach & Meehl, 1955; Nunnally, 1978). Discussing the construct validity of outcome measures in social research, therefore, is a relatively familiar task, because outcome measures are typically tests that attempt to locate persons on attributes. The construct validity of an outcome measure is the extent to which that measure assesses the theoretical attribute we seek to measure.

Every variable we measure is likely to reflect a variety of constructs as well as purely random error. The following equation illustrates this fact:

$$Y = C_1 + C_2 + \cdots + C_r + E$$

where $Y$ refers to some measured variable, the set of $C$ refers to a set of unmeasured theoretical constructs that contribute to variation in $Y$, and $E$ refers to random error or simply "noise" in the measurement of $Y$. As an example, suppose that we are interested in identifying the effect of some civics education program on a political attitude. We might construct an attitude measurement scale and administer it to both treatment and comparison subjects. It is likely that individual scores on the attitude scale reflect at least three different constructs: the true underlying attitude we hope to measure ($C_1$), the degree to which subjects seek to project socially desirable images of themselves ($C_2$), and the degree to which subjects have sufficient verbal skills to understand what is being asked of them ($C_3$). In addition to these three systematic sources of variation in the measure, there is also inevitably random noise or error that contributes to the scale responses ($E$). The question of construct validity of our measure, $Y$, refers to the extent to which each of the constructs accounts for variation in $Y$. The question of reliability refers to the extent to which $E$ accounts for variation in $Y$. Reliability will be discussed in the next section of this chapter under conclusion validity.

If our measure $Y$ has high construct validity, that is, if it truly measures the underlying political attitude we want it to measure, then the contribution of $C_1$ to $Y$ should be substantial. However, this is only a necessary, but not a sufficient condition for high construct validity. In addition, we wish to be assured that the contribution of constructs that are not of theoretical interest for the research at hand, $C_2$ and $C_3$, are relatively small. The two necessary and sufficient conditions for construct validity are thus (Campbell & Fiske, 1959):

1   Convergent validity: the extent to which variation in the measure is a result of variation in the theoretical construct of interest; and
2   Discriminant validity: the extent to which variation in the measure is *not* a result of variation in other constructs of little theoretical interest.

In the example of our political attitude scale, convergent validity refers to the extent to which variation in the scale is a result of variation in the true, underlying political attitude that is of theoretical interest. Discriminant validity refers to the extent to which variation in the scale is *not* a result of variation in the social desirability and verbal skills constructs that are of little theoretical interest.

Just as we can discuss the construct validity of a measure that seeks to locate subjects on some attribute, so also we can speak of the construct validity of treatments, subjects or samples, and research settings. In any given piece of research, each of these can be thought of as representative of some theoretical larger class of treatments, samples, and settings. We may also speak of the convergent and discriminant validity of treatments, subjects, and settings.

A specific treatment administered in a study is an attempted operationalization of some theoretical treatment that is the researcher's real interest. Thus, in the evaluation of day-care centers, the treatment received by children in the treated group is a specific day-care center, staff, and schedule. It is extremely important for the researcher to believe that this specific treatment is representative of the generic treatment of interest. Likewise the researcher must be convinced that theoretical constructs of little interest have not been operationalized in the specific treatment employed. For instance, the researcher is hopeful that any effects observed as a function of the day-care treatment are effects of day care per se and not of some idiosyncracies of the specific day-care center staff employed.

Another well-known example illustrates the two conditions of treatment construct validity. Robert Rosenthal and his colleagues (Rosenthal & Rosnow, 1969; Rosenthal, 1976; Rosenthal & Rubin, 1978) have repeatedly shown how experimenters' expectations or hypotheses may influence the outcomes of social research. In nearly all social research, experimenter expectations are a construct that we hope is not operationalized by the treatment that is actually administered. This is done by using researchers who are unaware of the research hypotheses. Thus we hope to deliver a treatment with high convergent validity (it operationalizes the theoretical treatment) and high discriminant validity against the experimenter expectation artifact.[1]

Just as we can speak of the construct validity of outcomes and treatments, so too we can discuss the construct validity of subjects or samples. The issue here is the extent to which the specific subjects who are measured in a study represent the theoretical population of interest (convergent validity) and do not represent populations of no theoretical interest (discriminant validity). As an example, suppose that we were interested in the effects of a mental-health treatment on schizophrenia. Patients diagnosed as schizophrenic had been assigned to treatment and comparison conditions, and subsequently treatment effects were observed. At a later date, rediagnoses of the subjects indicated that some of them were not schizophrenic but rather manic-depressive, and it further appeared upon reanalysis of the research data that if the manic-depressives were eliminated, no treatment effects were observed. In this case, we wished to generalize to the theoretical population of individuals suffering from schizophrenia. Because of the inexactness of clinical diagnoses, however, our sample has quite low

---

[1] Sometimes experimenter expectation effects are not a concern in applied research, because the treatment delivery in the research may be carried out by the staff who would regularly deliver the treatment even if research were not being conducted. In this case, staff expectations constitute part of the theoretical treatment of interest.

discriminant validity. We therefore are able to generalize the treatment effects not to the population of theoretical interest but rather to a population of less interest, individuals who are manic-depressive.

The standard procedure for ensuring the construct validity of subjects is to select them by random sampling from the population of interest. Sampling procedures have been developed to accomplish this purpose (Sudman, 1976). Researchers are also well advised to gather demographic data on their subjects in order to describe adequately the population from which they come.

We can also speak of the construct validity of the situation in which research is conducted. Suppose that we conducted research on doctor–patient interactions in hospital settings. We would like our chosen setting to be representative of the theoretical construct of interest: the stereotypic hospital setting. It may be that the setting chosen for research is not a hospital setting, but rather an outpatient clinic. We would then want to make sure that our setting had construct validity, that our effects are not exclusively generalizable to the population of outpatient clinics rather than to the intended population of hospital settings.

### Threats to construct validity

There are two types of threats to construct validity. First, we may encounter low construct validity because we have failed to develop a construct theory. That is, we may not have defined the theoretical constructs in enough detail to operationalize them successfully. Second, even if we have a well-developed theory concerning the theoretical constructs, we may fail to examine empirically the interrelations among successive operationalizations. Such a failure can lead to quite low construct validity in spite of a well-developed construct theory.

Developing an adequate construct theory means that we have thought about the "nomological net" in which the construct is embedded (Cronbach & Meehl, 1955). This nomological net represents the way in which the construct relates to other constructs and to potential operationalizations. Linkages among the theoretical constructs need to be considered for the following two reasons. First, we would like to achieve high discriminant validity and so our construct theory must tell us that the construct and some other construct of little interest are not the same. Second, we may wish to operationalize a construct other than the one of theoretical interest, if the original one is relatively inaccessible and if our theory indicates that the original construct is caused by the more accessible one. To use an example from marketing research, telephone surveys typically assess liking for a product. This construct is assumed to cause the construct that is of more interest to the researchers, that is, purchasing. Liking is simply easier to operationalize.

Linkages between constructs and potential operationalizations are of practical importance, because they guide the researcher in the choice of what to measure. Every measure or operationalization represents a theoretical hypothesis concerning the relationship between the unmeasurable construct and its indicators. Hypotheses about the validity of an operationalization should be based on experience, convention, common sense, and prior research.

A well-developed construct theory, including a precise theoretical definition of the construct and the specification of the nomological net in which it lies, should give rise to a number of potential operationalizations. By employing a few of these simultaneously and by examining the relationships among them we can gain confidence in the construct validity of our measures. Unless we operationalize constructs in more than one way, we cannot examine our construct theory empirically.

If we employ multiple operationalizations, or *indicators* as they are also known, we should expect them to correlate with each other. This is so because we believe them to correlate highly with the unmeasured construct. Given certain assumptions, it is possible to estimate the correlations between the indicators and the unmeasured construct from the observed correlations among the indicators. In certain cases, then, by examining the relationships among multiple indicators we can infer the relationship between each indicator and the construct of interest. This relationship is of fundamental importance, for it represents the convergent construct validity of the indicators.

Suppose, for instance, that we have two outcome measures, $Y_1$ and $Y_2$, which we assume to be indicators of the unmeasured construct of interest, $C_1$.[2] We assume that variation in each $Y$ is in part caused by $C_1$ and in part is due to a host of other factors, including random error. In addition, we assume that all causes of variation in $Y_1$, other than the construct of interest, $C_1$, are uncorrelated with all other causes of variation in $Y_2$. In essence, we are then

---

[2] In the following models we assume that all variables and constructs have been standardized.

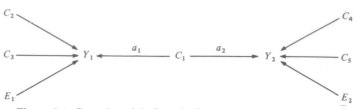

Figure 3.1. Causal model of two indicators.

assuming the causal model for our two measures depicted in Figure 3.1. The constructs $C_2$, $C_3$, $C_4$, and $C_5$ represent unmeasured sources of systematic variation in $Y_1$ and $Y_2$ in addition to the common cause $C_1$. Random error in $Y_1$ and $Y_2$ is represented by $E_1$ and $E_2$. The effects of the construct of interest on the indicators are represented by $a_1$ and $a_2$, which we might call the "validity coefficients." These are simply the correlations between the construct and the indicators, $r_{Y_1C_1}$ and $r_{Y_2C_1}$.

Given the causal model of Figure 3.1, it can be shown that the correlation between $Y_1$ and $Y_2$ equals the product of the two validity coefficients, or

$$r_{Y_1Y_2} = r_{Y_1C_1} r_{Y_2C_1}$$

If we assume that both $Y_1$ and $Y_2$ are equally good indicators of $C_1$, then we can estimate the magnitude of the validity coefficients as

$$r_{Y_1C_1} = r_{Y_2C_1} = \sqrt{r_{Y_1Y_2}}$$

If we have three indicators of $C_1$, assuming that all causes of each, other than $C_1$, are uncorrelated, we can estimate the validity coefficient for each indicator without assuming that they are equally good indicators. For the model in Figure 3.2, it can be shown that

$$r_{Y_1C_1} = \sqrt{\frac{r_{Y_1Y_2} r_{Y_1Y_3}}{r_{Y_2Y_3}}}$$

$$r_{Y_2C_1} = \sqrt{\frac{r_{Y_1Y_2} r_{Y_2Y_3}}{r_{Y_1Y_3}}}$$

$$r_{Y_3C_1} = \sqrt{\frac{r_{Y_1Y_3} r_{Y_2Y_3}}{r_{Y_1Y_2}}}$$

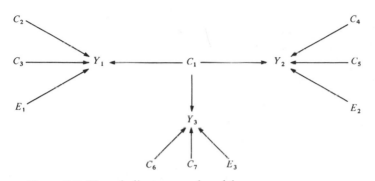

Figure 3.2. Three-indicator causal model.

With more than three indicators of a single construct, not only can we estimate their correlations with the construct, but also the adequacy of the assumptions behind the causal model can be tested (Kenny, 1979).

Multiple indicators of a single construct can thus enable us to estimate the relationships between the construct and its indicators. They enable us to estimate the convergent validity of an operationalized variable. The second half of construct validity, discriminant validity, can also be estimated by multiple indicators when we can define and operationalize the construct against which we seek discriminant validity. Suppose, for instance, that we seek to measure social development as an outcome in an evaluation of day-care centers. We develop multiple indicators of it to assess their convergent validity. Further, we decide that it is important to be sure that our measures assess *social* development, and not development in general or *cognitive* development. So we seek discriminant validity against the cognitive development construct. We might then develop three indicators of social development and three more indicators of cognitive development. If we intercorrelated all six indicators, the resulting matrix of correlations is a form of what is called a multitrait-multimethod matrix (Campbell & Fiske, 1959) and can be used to estimate both the convergent and discriminant validity of our measures.[3] The former is indicated by high intercorrelations among the measures of social development. The latter is

[3] Traditionally, the multitrait-multimethod matrix has been defined as the correlation matrix between indicators of different constructs measured by the same set of methods. In other words, methods are factorially crossed with constructs. In our example, methods are nested within constructs.

suggested by what we hope will be relatively low correlations between indicators of the two different constructs. In other words, we want an indicator of a construct to be more highly correlated with other indicators of the same construct than it is with indicators of the other construct. In addition to simply checking the relative magnitude of the correlations to assess both types of validity, more formal modeling procedures have been developed to estimate convergent and discriminant validity from this multitrait-multi-method matrix (Alwin, 1974; Kenny, 1979).

Our discussion of multiple indicators has focused so far on the correlations among them and how these correlations can be used to estimate their construct validity. There is also another source of information concerning the construct validity of multiple outcome indicators. If they all represent the theoretical construct of interest, they all might be expected to show roughly similar effects of the treatment. In other words, we can use the magnitude of treatment effects on multiple outcome measures to inform us about the construct validity of those outcome measures. If we find treatment effects for one indicator, we should expect them on another indicator of the same construct (convergent validity), and we might not expect them on indicators of a different construct (discriminant validity). The simultaneous analysis of treatment effects on multiple outcome measures is thus an important procedure for ascertaining construct validity. In each of the subsequent chapters, where we discuss the analysis of specific designs we shall devote attention to the analysis of multiple outcomes.

All of the examples we have given of multiple operationalizations of constructs to assess construct validity have concerned outcome variables. The same logic, however, if not quite the analytic rigor, can be used to assess the construct validity of treatments, samples, and settings through multiple operationalizations. For instance, suppose that we have a theoretical population of interest. If we took multiple samples that we believe represented that population, we could examine if treatment effects were similar in each and thus gain some assurance of convergent validity. Likewise, discriminant validity could be assessed by comparing effects on samples from the population of interest to the effects on samples from another theoretical population.

In sum, there are two fundamental steps for maximizing construct validity in social research. The first step consists of the development of a precise and well-defined construct theory. The second step is to employ multiple indicators of treatments, outcomes, samples, and settings wherever possible. This latter step may involve a trade-off with efficiency (and perhaps other trade-offs as well), but it is the best way of assessing the adequacy of the construct theory.

### Conclusion validity

Conclusion validity was defined earlier as the extent to which the research is sufficiently precise or powerful enough to enable us to detect treatment effects. In fact, however, there are two types of conclusion errors that can be made concerning the presence of treatment effects. The first type of error is to conclude that treatment effects exist when in fact they do not. The second type of error is to conclude that treatment effects do not exist when they in fact do. This distinction is identical to the Type I versus Type II error distinction that is a fundamental part of most introductory statistics textbooks.

Our definition of conclusion validity focuses on the second type of conclusion errors: the extent to which we can detect treatment effects should they exist. This focus is due to two factors. First, most social researchers are routinely trained to be sensitive to Type I errors, concluding that treatment effects exist when in fact they do not. Methods courses usually are geared toward the use of inferential statistics to estimate the probability of Type I conclusion errors. We routinely fix $\alpha$, the probability of Type I errors, at some value, and then report the presence or absence of treatment effects given this probability. The second reason for focusing on Type II conclusion errors is that they acquire more importance in many applied research settings than they perhaps have in more basic research settings. All too often in the last 20 years, evaluations of education, rehabilitation, and social welfare programs conclude that these programs have little effect. In part this may be due to failures to detect effects when in fact they exist. Given the expense of putting together and administering these social welfare programs, it is crucial that any effects that they engender be detected.

In discussing conclusion errors, it is important to distinguish these errors from what we might call *bias* in the estimate of treatment effects. In the case of bias, we misestimate the magnitude of treatment effects because for some reason or another we have failed to control adequately for some competing causal explanation. Bias occurs when threats to internal validity have not been effectively eliminated, with the result that treatment effects are either over- or underestimated. In the case of conclusion errors, we properly estimate the magnitude of treatment effects, but we reach inappropriate conclusions about their presence when they are compared with other sources of variation in the data. Conclusions about the presence or absence of treatment effects are always made by comparing some measure of effect size with other sources of variation in the data. In conclusion errors, we correctly calculate the treatment effect size, but we inappropriately conclude that the effect is not reliable when compared to other variation in the data.

In order to identify the sources of Type II conclusion errors, it is helpful to return to the model of sources of variation in indicators developed earlier. In that model, variation in an indicator was due to (1) variation in the theoretical construct of interest; (2) variation in other constructs; and (3) random error variation. The model was illustrated by referring to a political attitude scale as the measure, the true underlying political attitude as the construct of interest, and social desirability and verbal ability as other systematic sources of variation. We assume that the treatment, if it was effective, affects only the theoretical construct of interest, the underlying true political attitude, and not the other sources of variation in the measure.

Conclusions about the presence or absence of treatment effects compare variation in the outcome measure due to the treatment with other sources of variation in the measure. To the extent that variation due to sources other than the construct of interest is substantial and uncontrolled, nonsignificant treatment effects will be reported. In other words, as irrelevant sources of variation in the outcome measure get large, so treatment effects look relatively small. Hence we may conclude that they do not reliably exist.

The choice of procedures for overcoming the conclusion validity threat of irrelevant sources of variation in the outcome measure depends on whether the irrelevant variation is systematic or random. If we suspect that constructs other than the construct of interest are substantially responsible for variation in the outcome, and we wish to improve our precision or conclusion validity, then we should attempt to control statistically for the irrelevant variation. Control over irrelevant but systematic variation in the outcome measure can be achieved either through the use of a blocking variable or through the analysis of covariance. These procedures are discussed in detail in the next chapter. If we suspect that the irrelevant sources of variation in the outcome measure are due primarily to random noise or error rather than to systematic sources, we might attempt to derive an outcome measure from multiple indicators that is more reliable. Alternatively, we might use structural modeling procedures, discussed in Chapter 9, to estimate treatment effects on the unmeasured construct, removing irrelevant error variation from its indicators.

Conclusion errors may also be caused by the use of insufficiently powerful treatment variables. Suppose, for instance, that we are interested in evaluating the effect of psychotherapy on depressed patients. It may be that those effects reliably emerge only when patients are in psychotherapy for an extended period of time. If the treatment condition exposed patients to only a single or a few psychotherapy sessions, effects of the treatment might not be found. We would then mistakenly conclude that psychotherapy does nothing for depression, when in fact the evaluation has not been sufficiently sensitive to demonstrate its effects. The solution to this sort of threat to conclusion validity is to employ treatment levels that are relatively extreme if we wish to detect treatment effects. A more extended discussion of the choice of levels of the treatment variable is included in the next chapter. Although extremity tends to enhance conclusion validity, it makes little sense to employ more extreme levels than are ever likely to emerge outside of the research. It may not be worth much to find out that psychotherapy affects depressive patients if that effect emerges after 10 years of intensive therapy.

In addition to a lack of precision due to irrelevant sources of variation and insufficiently powerful treatments, conclusion errors can also be made if we have not gathered data from enough observations and if those observations are quite heterogeneous. It is a well-documented fact that statistical precision or the ability to detect effects increases directly as the number of subjects increases (Cohen, 1969). In fact, if a researcher can estimate in advance the magnitude of the expected treatment effect, a "power analysis" can be conducted to determine the sample size necessary to ensure that a Type II error is avoided. Such a procedure is strongly recommended for all who engage in evaluation research. Where there is disagreement about the expected magnitude of treatment effect, the conservative strategy (although also the most costly strategy) is to calculate the needed number of observations based on the smallest estimate.

Just as using too few subjects can lower conclusion validity, so using subjects who are quite heterogeneous can have the same effect. In essence this is a cause of Type II errors because it increases irrelevant variation in the outcome variable. One source of heterogeneity of subjects' outcome scores can arise if the treatments that are delivered to them are not uniform within any condition. Hence, heterogeneity of treatment is also a threat to conclusion validity.

A final source of conclusion error in social research occurs when inappropriate assumptions are made concerning the independence of observations. Statistical tests are routinely based on the assumption that observations are independent. Frequently, however, this assumption may be questionable. For instance, if we are examining children in a classroom for the effect of some curriculum treatment, the inevitable and intense interaction among those children throws into question the independence assumption, if the children are the unit of analysis. Usually the effect of inappropriately assuming independence is on Type I conclusion errors: We may report treatment effects when in fact they do not exist. In some cases, however, the inappropriate assumption of independence can lead to Type II conclusion errors. A more extended discussion of the independence assumption is included in Chapter 8.

### Internal validity

We earlier defined internal validity as the extent to which detected treatment effects on the outcome variable are due to the treatment of interest rather than to other competing causes. In other words, internal validity concerns the adequacy of the *causal* conclusions that are reached from the observed relationship between treatment and outcome. It concerns not only the question of whether or not such a relationship is causal, but also whether our estimate of its magnitude is unbiased, in the sense discussed in the previous section.

There are a variety of threats to internal validity that have been enumerated by Campbell and Stanley (1963) and by Cook and Campbell (1979). In the following paragraphs we review some of these threats. Before doing so, however, it is worth noting that the presence of different sorts of threats depends on the nature of treatment comparisons. As we discussed in the first chapter, and as we shall highlight again in Chapter 11, comparisons between treatments can be made either within the same subjects or between subjects. Some of the threats that we review below are threats when comparisons are made within subjects. Others are threats when comparisons are made between subjects. It is helpful in discussing these threats to identify how they are dependent on the nature of the treatment comparisons.

1. Selection: If different subjects are assigned to the treatment and comparison conditions or, equivalently, if treatment comparisons are made between subjects, and if a nonrandom assignment rule is used, then we can expect to observe differences on the outcome measure even in the absence of treatment effects. Selection is a source of bias whenever treatment comparisons are made between subjects and a nonrandom assignment rule is used. Because this combination of between-subjects comparisons and nonrandom assignment is frequently the basis for quasi-experimental research, examples of selection as a source of bias are easy to find. Deutsch and Collins (1951) attempted to demonstrate that interracial housing projects led to a decrease in racial prejudice and discriminatory behavior. They thus compared prejudice outcome measures between those living in interracial housing and those living in segregated housing. In spite of the authors' valiant efforts to eliminate the competing cause of selection, it is probably the case that some of the differences found between the two groups were due to the fact that the people in them were different. Those who decided in 1950 to live in an interracial environment were without doubt different sorts of people from those who lived in a segregated environment.

2. Maturation: If treatment comparisons are made within subjects and if subjects are first observed in the comparison condition and then in the treatment condition, it is likely that any subject's two outcome scores will differ because he or she has matured during the interval between the comparison and treatment observations. Maturation is a potential source of bias whenever treatment comparisons are made within subjects and the order in which subjects are observed under the treatment and comparison conditions is nonrandom – for example, subjects are first observed under the comparison condition and then under the treatment condition. To illustrate the threat of maturation, suppose that we were interested in the effects of an alcohol education program on

drinking. To observe subjects' drinking prior to the treatment, or under the comparison condition, all subjects kept a record of their behavior over a 3-year period. After exposure to the education program, a record was again kept of the subjects' drinking over a 3-year period. Because the 3-year observation in the comparison condition was recorded prior to the 3-year observation in the treatment condition for all subjects, maturational differences in drinking are confounded with treatment effects.

3. History: Whenever maturation is a source of bias in estimating treatment effects, history is likely to be as well. In the above example, all subjects matured from the comparison condition observations to the treatment condition observations. In addition, various historical events occurred that potentially affect the outcome variable of interest. For instance, the price of alcohol may increase dramatically during the course of the research, resulting in a general decrease in drinking throughout the population. Just as with maturation, history is a potential source of bias whenever treatment comparisons are made within subjects and whenever the order of observation of individual subjects under treatment and control conditions is not determined randomly.

4. Mortality: If subjects drop out of the research for some unknown reason, then subject mortality is a potential source of bias in designs where treatment comparisons are made within subjects. Suppose that subjects were observed first under a comparison condition and then only a subsample was observed under the treatment condition. That subsample is likely to differ in unknown ways from those who dropped out after the comparison observations. This difference is a source of bias.

5. Testing: It has been shown that simply asking a subject's opinion may influence that opinion or its centrality to the subject at a later point in time. For instance, Bridge, Reeder, Kanouse, Kinder, Nagy, and Judd (1977) found that subjects who had previously been interviewed about cancer were subsequently more concerned about cancer than respondents whose previous interview did not refer to cancer. In research designs that involve within-subject treatment comparisons and a nonrandom order of treatment exposure, such testing effects are a potential source of bias in estimating treatment effects.

6. Regression artifact: It is a well-known fact that extreme observations tend to be less extreme if remeasured. A trivial example illustrates the point: Suppose that we compute the week-

by-week batting average of some baseball player who has a lifetime average of .300. If, for a given week, the computed average is .170, the chances are excellent that the average the following week will be closer to .300. This phenomenon, known as *regression toward the mean,* may be a threat to internal validity in research designs that involve within-subject treatment comparisons. An example from Campbell (1969) illustrates the potential bias. In 1955 the State of Connecticut observed a sharp increase in traffic fatalities and hence introduced a vigorous law enforcement program to reduce speeding. In 1956, there were many fewer traffic fatalities than in the previous year. In this example, the treatment comparison is made within the same subject (i.e., Connecticut) and there exist two competing causal explanations for the 1955–6 fatality difference: (1) an actual treatment effect, and (2) the tendency for an extreme observation to regress toward the mean.

Although it may be clear from this example how regression to the mean can be a source of bias, the nature of the regression artifact is often a source of confusion. A more detailed discussion of the phenomenon appears in Chapter 8.

7. Instrumentation: If different outcome measures are used for gathering the observations in the various treatment conditions, then the treatments may look different in the absence of treatment effects. Instrumentation in this sense is a threat to internal validity regardless of whether treatment comparisons are made within or between subjects.

As should be clear from our discussion of construct validity, outcome measures can differ from each other in two ways. They may be different indicators of the same underlying construct. They may also be indicators of different constructs. Each of these differences may be responsible for an instrumentation threat to internal validity. If the measures given to the different treatment conditions are all indicators of the same construct but employ different metrics or use different scales, then metric differences are confounded with treatment effects unless transformations are used to derive a common metric. If the outcome measures assess different constructs in the different conditions, no transformations can render them comparable. An additional instrumentation threat can also arise when a measure has floor or ceiling effects, that is, when it lacks interval properties.

As we have defined the above threats to internal validity, selection is a threat only when between-subject treatment comparisons are made; and maturation, history, mortality, testing, and regression are threats only when treatment comparisons are made within subjects. However, if subjects have not been assigned randomly to the different conditions of a between-subjects design and these subjects are observed over time, then *differential* maturation, history, mortality, testing, and regression all become potential sources of bias. In other words, selection can interact with the within-subject threats.

1. Selection by maturation: Whenever selection is a threat, it is likely that the treatment groups differ not only initially but also in their rate of growth or maturation. Differential maturation between treatment conditions is a common source of bias.

As Campbell and Erlebacher (1970) point out, a selection by maturation interaction frequently leads to the erroneous conclusion that a compensatory treatment (one designed to help a population that is disadvantaged in some way) has a negative effect. It usually is the case that individuals who receive lower scores on measures of learning or achievement are growing at a slower rate than individuals who score more highly. A compensatory educational program might be given to these slower learners after a pre-treatment test and their post-treatment scores compared with the scores of a group of faster learners who received no treatment. If the compensatory treatment had no effect at all, the difference between the pre-treatment and post-treatment scores for the untreated faster learners would be greater than the same difference for those who learn more slowly and received the ineffective treatment. Because the group receiving the treatment grew less, one might conclude that the treatment had a negative effect. In fact, however, differential growth rates explain the difference, and the treatment had no effect at all.

2. Selection by history: Treatment groups that are formed by a nonrandom assignment rule may be affected differently by experiences and historical events occurring in the pretest–posttest interval. They also may be expected to be exposed to different events during the interval. Differences that exist between groups on the outcome measure may be attributable, therefore, to different histories to which the groups are exposed.

3. Selection by mortality: Treatment groups that differ prior to the treatment as a result of employing a nonrandom assignment rule may show differential mortality rates. That is, more subjects may

drop out in one condition than another because different types of subjects are included in the various conditions. Estimates of treatment effects that do not take account of this differential mortality will be biased.

4. Selection by testing: Treatment groups that differ initially as a result of nonrandom assignment may be affected to different degrees by taking a pretest. They thus may show different testing effects, which become a source of bias in estimating treatment effects.

5. Selection by regression artifact: Treatment groups that differ initially as a result of a nonrandom assignment rule may be differentially extreme on their pretest scores and thus may exhibit differing degrees of regression to the mean.

In addition to interactions between selection and the within-subject threats, the treatment itself may interact with various threats, with the result that treatment effects are estimated with bias. As will become clear, however, these treatment interaction threats may be alternatively seen as problems of construct validity, or more specifically as problems of the construct validity of the treatment, instead of problems of internal validity. The line between construct validity and internal validity becomes hazy at this point.

1. Treatment by mortality: Of the treatment interactions, this one is probably most clearly a threat to internal validity rather than a construct validity problem. It may be that the different treatments cause differential mortality in the treatment groups, even when a random assignment rule has been used. When subjects drop out of one group but not out of another, or when different sorts of subjects drop out in the various treatment conditions, then subsequent treatment effects that are estimated on the remaining subjects are biased.

Because this threat is a problem even in randomized experimental designs, we discuss it in more detail in the next chapter. It is worth noting here, however, how this treatment by mortality threat can be looked upon as a problem of construct validity rather than as a source of bias. It may be that the treatment exerts its effect by selecting out those individuals who can potentially be affected. For instance, suppose that we were evaluating a drug rehabilitation program. The program may be effective by providing an incentive to drug abusers who are already motivated to change their drug usage. Those who are not so motivated will drop out of the rehabilitation program. If the treatment exerts its effect in part through subject selection, then differential mortality can be seen as a part of the treatment program rather than as a source of bias.

2. Treatment by testing: It may be that the presence of a pretest sensitizes subjects to the treatment they are about to receive. In such cases, the treatment effect can be said to depend on the presence of the pretest. If we wish to generalize the treatment effect to a situation where a pretest would not normally be included, then a treatment by testing interaction is a source of bias. Equally plausibly, however, we could argue that the treatment had low construct validity because we wish to generalize to a treatment that does not normally include a pretest. This treatment by testing interaction is discussed further in the next chapter where we suggest procedures for estimating its magnitude.

There are a series of other problems that can also be seen either as threats to internal validity or, alternatively, as problems in the construct validity of the treatment. For instance, individuals in a control group where no treatment is received may realize that they are receiving no treatment and may be motivated to try harder or otherwise compensate for their lack of treatment. Cook and Campbell (1979) label this threat *compensatory rivalry*. Administrators of the experiment may also feel a need to compensate "deprived" comparison groups, a threat that Cook and Campbell name *compensatory equalization of treatment*. It may also be the case that a treatment is never delivered, or is delivered very incompletely. Further, if subjects in the comparison group are in close proximity to treated subjects, there may be some diffusion or contagion of the treatment, such that the desired differences between the groups are minimized. Just the opposite may also occur: Treated subjects may end up receiving more than just the treatment, they may be accorded more attention, and other experiences may happen to them as a group. All of these threats to internal validity concern the nature of the treatment variable in the experimental setting. The treatment may be less than intended; it may be more or different than intended; the untreated group may not be untreated. Threats of this nature have been seen as threats to internal validity in that they constitute competing causes for obtained posttest differences. They are better seen as construct validity threats, however, because they concern the nature of the treatment variable and its relationship to the theoretical treatment construct.

Most of the threats to internal validity are eliminated as competing explanations for treatment effects when a random assignment rule is used. Certain of the threats are not, however, taken care of through the use of a random assignment rule. The two threats that were described as treatment interactions remain potential sources of bias in randomized experimental designs. Differential mortality (a treatment by mortality interaction) is a source of bias even with random assignment. Likewise, a treatment by testing interaction remains a threat unless subjects are also randomly assigned to pretest/no pretest conditions. In sum, any of the threats to internal validity that are not likely to be eliminated through the use of a random assignment rule can be alternatively seen as threats to construct validity, and therefore not as threats to internal validity.

### External validity

External validity, as we have defined it, is the most difficult of the four validities to achieve. It has been defined as the extent to which the effects observed in a study can be generalized to theoretical constructs other than those specified in the original research hypothesis. Just as construct validity concerns the relation between constructs and operationalizations for outcomes, treatments, samples, and settings, so too we can speak of the external validity of each of these. In other words, we might seek to generalize from the outcomes, treatments, samples, and settings in our original research hypothesis to others that were originally unspecified.

The definition of external validity that we have given differs in two major ways from the usual notion. First, we are defining it as generalization from construct to construct rather than as generalization from various observed samples, outcomes, treatments, and settings. Second, although social scientists are quite comfortable discussing the external validity of samples, or even of settings, our definition includes its relevance for treatments and outcomes.

We normally think that the demands of external validity are met by engaging in some form of random sampling from a known population to ensure that we can generalize observed relationships from our sample to the population of interest. As we have defined the four validities, however, sampling procedures that enable us to generalize from an observed group of subjects to a population of interest are relevant to construct validity rather than to external validity. They enable us to have confidence that the theoretical construct of interest is represented or adequately operationalized in the research at hand. Although generalization from observations to theoretical populations of interest is the domain of construct validity, generalization from the theoretical population or construct that was operationalized (or sampled) to other populations or constructs of interest is the domain of external validity.

An example illustrates the distinction. The television program *Sesame Street* was evaluated by researchers at Educational Testing Service (Ball & Bogatz, 1970) who decided to examine its effect on the cognitive development of disadvantaged preschool children. The theoretical population of interest to which they wished to generalize consisted of preschool children from poor families. To achieve this generalization they engaged in a fairly elaborate sampling procedure. Through this sampling they could have confidence that the theoretical population of interest was represented in the study. According to our definition, this sampling procedure is designed to maximize the construct validity of the sample, that is, to enable the researchers to generalize from a specific operation to a theoretical construct of interest. The procedure to ensure the construct validity of the sample is exactly parallel to what is to be done to ensure the construct validity for outcome measures: Define the construct or theoretical population of interest and then choose multiple examples of it for actual measurement.

The external validity concern in the *Sesame Street* evaluation is not whether we can generalize to disadvantaged preschoolers, but rather whether we can generalize the observed effects to other populations (e.g., *advantaged* preschoolers) that were not actually operationalized in the research.[4] Likewise, the external validity of outcome measures concerns the confidence with which we can generalize from the construct measured (e.g., reading readiness) to other unmeasured constructs (e.g., cooperative play).

According to this definition, the only tool to increase external validity is theory that defines the relationships between constructs, theory validated by prior research, experience, and common sense. In the example above, researchers who wish to generalize the observed effects of *Sesame Street* to advantaged preschoolers must engage in theoretical speculation on the way in which social and

---

[4] In fact, a small sample of advantaged preschoolers was included in the research so that, strictly speaking, generalization to this population was also a construct validity task. To illustrate the distinction between construct and external validity, however, we are pretending that this small sample was not included in the research.

economic status should, or should not, interact with the television program. This speculation is informed by prior research and experience. We might conceive of different theoretical populations as departing from the sampled population along a gradient of similarity. Some theoretical populations are quite similar to the sampled population; others are less similar. Generally the confidence that we have in generalization to populations not operationalized depends on the population's location on this gradient of similarity. Such gradients of similarity can also be used for generalization to outcome, treatment, and setting constructs that were not operationalized in the research.

If the theory and experience that guide external validity are inadequate, that is, if the construct to which we wish to generalize is too far removed from the construct that was operationalized, then the only option open to us is to transform a concern of external validity into a problem of construct validity. In other words, if we wish to generalize to a construct that was not operationalized in the research, and we do not have confidence in the theory and experience that should guide the generalization, then our only option is to conduct more research, operationalizing the new construct to which we wish to generalize. For example, to be confident in the generalization to advantaged children in the evaluation of *Sesame Street,* the researcher would need to conduct more research using a sample of children from the advantaged population. In this research, what used to be an external validity problem is now a construct validity problem.

Occasionally it happens that researchers wish to engage in generalizations to many different populations or constructs. They may be fearful about engaging in theoretical generalization and hence simultaneously sample from all the different populations of interest. In other words, in one piece of research they attempt to operationalize simultaneously many different constructs so as to generalize to them all. This response to external validity concerns, turning them into many simultaneous issues of construct validity, has a price in that it usually lowers the conclusion validity of the research. Instead of a sample of $N$ units from a single population, the research may employ six samples, each of $N/6$ units, from six populations. In this case, the confidence that Type II conclusion errors have been avoided in the case of any one of the populations is substantially lower than if the full sample, of $N$ units, had been chosen from the population.

## Relationships and priorities among validities

The reader will probably have noticed that our recommendations for valid research contradict each other at various points. For instance, if generalization to all members of a population is desired, then the researcher is advised to sample from the diversity of that population. On the other hand, a diverse and heterogeneous sample will increase the probability of Type II conclusion errors unless steps are taken to control statistically for the diversity.

The purpose of this final section is to make explicit some of the interrelations and conflicts between the various validities. Once that is accomplished, we close with a few comments concerning priorities among the validities and the ways in which competing claims on social researchers make their tasks anything but simple. The following pairs of validities may conflict.

1. Construct and conclusion validities: In order to maximize construct validity, we have advised the researcher to take two steps. First, he or she must develop a definition and theory of the construct. Second, it is wise to sample multiple and diverse instances of possible indicators of the construct. This second recommendation often may, and usually does, conflict with the need to reduce irrelevant variation in outcome measures, a prerequisite for avoiding Type II conclusion errors. For instance, if the researcher wants to generalize effects of a treatment to all members of some population, he or she should sample the full range of that population. The heterogeneity of the resulting sample is likely to introduce substantial unexplained variation in the outcome variable, which in turn may swamp relatively small treatment effects. In a parallel manner, conducting research in a variety of settings also introduces irrelevant variance, as does operationalizing the treatment in a variety of ways. Occasionally the irrelevant variation in the outcome measure that these multiple operationalizations introduce can be controlled statistically so that there is no loss in conclusion validity. The researcher is strongly advised to search for characteristics of the sample or settings that explain variation in the outcome and that can be controlled.

2. Construct and internal validities: As we argued in both this chapter and the last, the most effective procedure for maximizing internal validity is to conduct a randomized experiment in which subjects are assigned randomly to the treatment conditions. Experimental research designs are most easily accomplished in special

settings where strict control can be maintained over factors that might constitute competing causes to the treatment. Thus, for instance, in such settings we can make sure that the only differences between various conditions are intended differences. Because the need for such control implies a special setting, it may also necessitate the use of a set of volunteer subjects who interrupt their regular schedule to participate and the use of a treatment specially constructed so that it may be manipulated effectively. As a result, the construct validity of setting, sample, and treatment may be compromised as threats to internal validity are eliminated.

3. Conclusion and internal validity: Suppose that we are interested in showing the effects of higher levels of self-esteem on academic achievement among secondary school children. We may decide that internal validity is extremely important and therefore we conduct a randomized experiment. We want to assign children randomly to different levels of self-esteem. To accomplish this, we must manipulate self-esteem in some way; we must have an experimental treatment that affects self-esteem. In whatever way we decide to carry out this manipulation, it will probably be the case that the manipulated levels of self-esteem will not be very extreme. Try as we may, we probably will not be very successful in causing large changes in subjects' self-esteem. We have seen that with nonextreme levels of the treatment we may make Type II conclusion errors; we may decide that treatment effects do not exist when in fact they would be found if we measured the full range of naturally occurring self-esteem. Hence, by seeking to manipulate self-esteem we may gain internal validity at the expense of a decrease in conclusion validity. Randomized experiments require that we manipulate the treatment. Ethical and practical considerations may require that we limit the range of the treatment variable.

The potential conflicting claims of the various validities necessitate priority decisions among them. Is the researcher more concerned about sound generalizations to the population of interest, or is he or she more concerned with avoiding a Type II conclusion error and so wishes to restrict the heterogeneity of the research sample? Is internal validity to be maximized at the expense of construct validity, if manipulating the treatment means transforming it to something different than it usually is? Decisions such as these are always made by researchers. All too often, however, they are made without a great deal of thought and reflect research traditions as much as the necessary priorities for a specific research problem.

Laboratory, experimental research has traditionally placed internal validity at the top of its priority list. If causal statements cannot be made, research that attempts solely to verify theory may be of little value. Construct validity has also been important to laboratory research, with particular attention being given to the construct validity of the independent variable. External and conclusion validities have traditionally been relatively neglected. The probability of committing Type II conclusion errors has usually not even been assessed.

Researchers in applied settings, evaluating the effects of some social program, must emphasize conclusion validity and the construct validity of samples and settings to a greater extent than in laboratory research. Conclusion validity is important for applied research, we have argued, because of the number of studies that have found little or no effects for large social programs. Construct validity of populations and settings is important, for the purpose of such research is to gain knowledge about an effect in a specific setting for a given population rather than to gain more basic theoretical knowledge of causal relationships in the abstract.

Although conclusion validity and the construct validity of samples and settings may be more important in applied research than in basic laboratory research, internal validity and the construct validity of treatments and outcomes are not less important. Clearly the researcher wishes to eliminate competing causes for any treatment effects observed. Likewise, it is important that the treatment as delivered and the measured outcomes represent the theoretical constructs of interest.

Therefore, we suggest that the applied researcher is more subject to the conflicting claims of research validities than his or her colleague in laboratory research. The latter scientist can rely on the priorities among the research validities that have been established by a research tradition. For the applied researcher, on the other hand, there is no tradition-given set of priorities. There may be occasions or situations where conclusion validity is supremely important. At other times, issues of construct validity may be paramount. More likely than not, all of the conflicting claims will seem to be undeniably important to the applied social researcher. We take no final position concerning which of these claims should be heeded most closely.

# 4

# Randomized experiments

In the last chapter four sources of invalidity in social research were identified. Much of the rest of this book details the ways in which various research designs and strategies of analysis affect the validity of applied social research. In the present chapter we are concerned with randomized experimental designs, designs that are maximally efficient at eliminating threats to internal validity.

Randomized experiments are defined by the use of a random assignment rule in assigning experimental units to treatment conditions. Because of its importance, discussion of the definition of a random assignment rule is in order. A random assignment rule is one in which the probability that any subject receives any given treatment is known and is other than one or zero. It is sometimes mistakenly thought that a random assignment rule requires that the probability of a subject's assignment to one treatment is equal to his or her assignment to any other treatment. In fact, it is entirely possible to engage in random assignment with the additional condition that the number of subjects in one treatment is different from the number in some other treatment. The best-known applied example of such unequal random assignment is the New Jersey graduated work incentive experiment (Rees, 1974), where the experimenters decided to ensure that more subjects received some treatments than received others.

In order to carry out a randomized experiment, it is usually necessary for the researcher to control and actively manipulate the treatment or independent variable of interest. There may be instances where the researcher believes that a random assignment rule has been used, but the researcher himself or herself has not had direct control over assigning units to treatment conditions. In fact, however, it is quite unlikely that a truly random assignment rule has been used unless the researcher assures randomization through the use of a table of random numbers, flipping coins, or some similar procedure.

Randomized experiments are the research design of choice if the goal is to maximize internal validity. The reader will recall from the preceding chapter that internal validity is the extent to which we can reach *causal* conclusions about treatment effects. In a general sense, there are three conditions that are necessary for asserting causality between two variables (Kenny, 1979): (1) covariation or correlation between them; (2) time precedence of cause to effect; and (3) lack of spuriousness. Most of the threats to internal validity concern this third condition, our ability to rule out spuriousness, where spuriousness is defined as covariation between treatment and outcome due to shared common causes. For example, if subjects in the treatment and comparison groups differed prior to treatment, as in the nonequivalent control group design (Chapter 6), then those differences may be responsible for both treatment assignment and any observed differences on the outcome measure. Hence, covariation of treatment and outcome would not be due to a causal effect but rather to a shared common cause: selection.

Randomized experiments maximize internal validity by ruling out spuriousness through the use of a random assignment rule. Without delving into the theory of randomization, its rationale is intuitively reasonable. In order to rule out spuriousness, we need to be assured that no characteristics of the subjects (e.g., personalities, backgrounds) are correlated with the treatments received by them. Randomization, correctly carried out, assures no such correlations on the average. If the assignment rule is random, then subject characteristics cannot be expected to correlate with treatment more than one time in twenty (given an $\alpha$ level of .05).

The organization of the remainder of this chapter is as follows. First we discuss issues of design in randomized experiments. In particular, we focus on three design issues. The first concerns the selection of treatment levels and control or comparison groups. We then discuss the issue of the unit of analysis in randomized experiments. The final design issue we discuss concerns aspects of the research design that can increase conclusion validity. Following this elaboration of design issues, we devote most of the remainder of the chapter to the statistical analysis of randomized experiments. In the analysis section we discuss the traditional use of analysis of variance and analysis of covariance in experimental designs. We then show

how these analyses are subsumed under the general analytic procedure of multiple regression that we discussed in Chapter 2. Finally, we discuss problems that typically emerge in the use of randomized experiments in applied social research.

## Experimental design issues

Before conducting any research, three questions should be answered:

1 What is the nature of the program or treatment to be evaluated?
2 What are the relevant outcomes to be assessed?
3 What is the population to be examined for treatment effects?

There exist considerable differences of opinion concerning how researchers should answer these questions. One major part of this controversy is the degree of independence of the researcher from the staff of the program to be evaluated. At one extreme is Michael Scriven (1974), who argues for *goal-free evaluation.* According to Scriven, the researcher should not even ask the program staff or administrators about outcomes or the treatment. At the other extreme, Edwards, Guttentag, and Snapper (1975) present an elegant procedure that quantifies the opinions of program administrators about relevant outcomes and control groups.

Once general answers to these questions have been reached, the researcher must make a decision about the overall type of design that is both feasible and informative. A great deal of information must be weighed in reaching this decision, information about both the feasibility of maintaining a research design in a given applied setting and the validity of the conclusions that are likely to emerge. Randomized experiments may be more feasible in some types of settings than in others. For instance, there may be lotteries, in which the distribution of some resource is naturally randomized (e.g., Staw, 1974). Whenever the resource or treatment is scarce (i.e., demand is greater than supply), experiments may be feasible if administrators can be convinced that a random distribution is as fair as any other sort of distribution rule. Cook and Campbell (1979) have discussed other conditions under which randomized experiments may be feasible.

Once a general decision has been made about the use of a random assignment rule, a series of more specific design decisions must be made. These design decisions can be grouped into three sets:

1 Decisions concerning treatment presentations and combinations
2 Decisions concerning the experimental unit to be observed
3 Decisions to increase conclusion validity

We discuss these three sets in detail below.

### *Treatment selection and presentation decisions*

There are a series of interrelated issues concerning treatment selection and presentation that are discussed below. First, we define factorial designs and distinguish between crossed and nested designs. Next, we focus on issues in selecting treatment levels to be observed. The use of repeated measurement designs in which units are exposed to multiple treatments is then discussed. Finally, the important issue of defining what constitutes an adequate control or comparison group is elaborated upon.

*Factorial designs.* In experiments there exist one or more experimental factors, each of which has at least two levels. Each subject in the research receives one or more combinations of levels of each of the different factors. For example, the graduated work incentive experiment conducted in New Jersey to evaluate the effects of a negative income tax (Rees, 1974) manipulated two experimental factors: the "basic benefit" or amount paid to a family with no other source of income, and an "implicit tax rate" or rate at which benefits were reduced as family income rose. The families that were the subjects in the study were assigned to a treatment condition that was defined by a specific combination of the two factors. Four different levels of the "basic benefit" and three levels of the "implicit tax rate" were combined or crossed to create the twelve experimental treatment conditions. The four levels of the basic benefit were defined by the percentage of "poverty-level" income provided to the family: 125%, 100%, 75%, and 50%. The three implicit tax rate levels, rates at which the benefit declined as earned income rose, were 30%, 50%, and 70%. Crossing these two factors yields twelve treatment conditions to which subjects could have been assigned. This fully crossed factorial design is depicted in

Table 4.1. *Crossed factorial design employed in the graduated work incentive experiment*

| Basic benefit | Implicit tax rate | | |
|---|---|---|---|
| | 30% | 50% | 70% |
| 125% | x | x | x |
| 100% | x | x | x |
| 75% | x | x | x |
| 50% | x | x | x |

From Rees, 1974.

Table 4.1. Each family, or experimental unit, was randomly assigned to a cell of the factorial design and observed under only that one specific treatment combination. In experimental terminology, families were nested within treatments.[1]

It might seem that a crossed factorial design is more complex than it need be if our purpose is simply to assess the effects of the two factors. Might it not be simpler to conduct two studies, one on the effect of the basic benefit factor, using four treatments, and one on the effect of the implicit tax rate, using three treatment conditions? The disadvantage to conducting these two studies, as compared with using a crossed design, is that the effects of one factor may differ depending on the level of the other factor. For instance, variations in implicit tax rate may have different effects depending on whether the basic benefit is high or low. If the effect of one factor does in fact depend on the level of another, we have what is known as a statistical interaction between the two. Only in crossed factorial designs can such interactions be detected. So the first decision concerning the design of treatment conditions concerns whether in fact interactions between factors of interest are important to detect. If they are, as is usually the case, then we should use a crossed factorial design.

In addition to crossing experimental factors to produce treatment conditions, there may be occasions when factors are nested within other factors. For instance, suppose that we were engaged in high

[1] In fact, families were not assigned to some of the cells in this fully crossed design. Some treatment combinations were considered quite improbable and hence were omitted from the design, e.g., 125% basic benefit with a tax rate of 30%.

school curriculum evaluation, where one of the experimental factors is the type of curriculum (old versus new) taught to students. Teachers might then be nested within levels of the curriculum if some teachers were best prepared to teach the old curriculum and others best able to teach the new. The teacher-by-curriculum interaction cannot be assessed with such a nesting procedure. Only if teachers and curricula are crossed is the interaction testable. In addition to not being able to test interactions between nested factors, the effects of one factor are confounded with the effects of the other under which it is nested. In our example, different teachers teach the different curricula. For instance, only the older teachers may teach the old curriculum, whereas only the younger, more recently trained teachers may teach the new curriculum. If such is the case, then observed outcome differences between subjects in the two curricula may be due either to teachers' experience or to curricula. To overcome this confounding we might randomly assign teachers to levels of the curriculum factor. This randomization procedure would be in addition to that used to assign students to the treatment conditions. If teachers have been randomly assigned to levels of the curriculum factor, the curricula are unconfounded with teacher characteristics by the same logic that treatments are unconfounded with subject differences in any randomized experiment.

If we can randomly assign teachers to the different curricula, then in all probability we can cross teachers with curricula. Randomization of teachers to curricula means that every teacher has the capacity to teach every curriculum. Therefore, we might have each teacher teach them all. Such a crossed design is preferable to a nested design, because the interaction between teachers and curricula can be tested.[2]

*Selection of treatment levels.* The researcher must inevitably decide on the number and extremity of levels of an experimental factor to be observed in the study. Suppose, for instance, that we are examining the effects of length of psychotherapeutic treatment on emotional adjustment. We might imagine two different research

---

[2] Not all nested variables can be made to be crossed with the variable that they are nested within. For instance, classrooms that are nested within schools cannot be crossed with schools.

plans. Under plan A we include five levels of the treatment: 0 hours, 25 hours, 50 hours, 75 hours, and 100 hours of psychotherapy. Under plan B we include only two levels: 0 hours and 100 hours. If the total number of subjects in the two designs is equal and if the longer a subject is in psychotherapy the stronger the effect, then design plan B has substantially more conclusion validity than design plan A. The disadvantage of choosing design plan B over A is that nonlinear effects of duration of psychotherapy cannot be assessed. If, for instance, psychotherapy has no increased effect after the initial 25 hours, we would be unable to detect this with plan B. The decision of which plan to use, of how many and which levels of a factor to examine, must ultimately depend on a theory or prior research that leads us to expect treatment effects of a particular sort. Decisions concerning the levels of a factor to be included are ultimately construct validity decisions.

*Repeated measurement designs.* Up to this point we have assumed that subjects or experimental units are assessed under one and only one treatment condition. In the terminology of analysis of variance, subjects are nested within levels of factors. It may be appropriate in some settings to cross subjects with the levels of an experimental factor. For instance, if we had access to only a very few subjects, we might decide to administer all levels of an experimental factor to each of them in order to assess the effects of the factor on as large a sample as possible. Such designs, where subjects are crossed with a factor, are called *repeated measures designs,* in that the same subject's outcomes are repeatedly assessed under different treatment conditions. In repeated measures designs, treatment comparisons are made within units rather than between units, as was described in Chapter 1. These designs are relatively rare in applied social research, because the treatments typically take a long time to deliver and their effects may not be immediately observable.

There are a variety of advantages and disadvantages to using designs where subjects are measured under more than one experimental treatment. The first major advantage concerns conclusion validity. If the experimenter has access to only a very few subjects, it is to his or her advantage to measure them all under all of the treatment conditions. In addition, conclusion validity is enhanced in these designs by our ability to subtract out variance due to differ-

Table 4.2. *Example of a repeated measures design: subjects nested within factor A with repeated measurements on factor B*

| Factor A | | Factor B | | |
| | | Level 1 | Level 2 | Level 3 |
|---|---|---|---|---|
| Level 1 | subj. $1_1$ | x | x | x |
| | subj. $2_1$ | x | x | x |
| | . | . | . | . |
| | . | . | . | . |
| | . | . | . | . |
| | subj. $n_1$ | x | x | x |
| Level 2 | subj. $1_2$ | x | x | x |
| | subj. $2_2$ | x | x | x |
| | . | . | . | . |
| | . | . | . | . |
| | . | . | . | . |
| | subj. $n_2$ | x | x | x |
| Level 3 | subj. $1_3$ | x | x | x |
| | subj. $2_3$ | x | x | x |
| | . | . | . | . |
| | . | . | . | . |
| | . | . | . | . |
| | subj. $n_3$ | x | x | x |

ences between subjects in their average responses. In essence each subject serves as his or her own control, and thus variation between subjects can be removed in testing treatment effects.

The other advantage to repeated measures designs is that some treatments in their usual settings may happen in sequence. Generalization of treatment effects in such settings may be easier if their effects have also been assessed in sequence. For instance, students in high schools typically are taught by five or six different teachers during the school day. If we are interested in examining the effects of teachers' experience on the level of students' academic interest, we might prefer a repeated measures design because such repeated exposure to different teachers is the setting to which we wish to generalize.

The disadvantages of repeated measurement designs arise from certain assumptions that must be made to analyze the resulting data successfully. First, it must be assumed that the effect of any treatment does not persist or carry over past the administration of a second treatment. Given the size and complexity of most interventions in applied social research, it is probably unsafe to assume the absence of carryover effects. Second, the analysis makes a more technical assumption that is called the homogeneity of covariance assumption. The condition for meeting this assumption is that the correlations between all possible pairs of outcome measures are all equal. Unfortunately, this assumption is seldom examined. Failure to meet its conditions can result in biased inference tests (Harris, 1975).

In addition to these two problems in repeated measurement designs, treatment differences may also be confounded with the order in which the different treatments were administered. Suppose that we used the repeated measurement design of Table 4.2. In this design subjects are nested within levels of factor A and crossed with levels of factor B. All subjects receive level 2 of factor B after level 1. Differences in levels are confounded with the sequence in which treatments are received. In order to overcome this confounding between sequence and levels of a factor, it is necessary to assign subjects randomly to different sequences. A design with three different sequences to which subjects might be randomly assigned is depicted in Table 4.3. The numbers in the body of this table refer to the order in which levels of factor B are received by subjects in the various sequence conditions. Thus, in sequence 3, subjects first receive level 2 of factor B, then level 3, and finally level 1. This design, a Latin square design, unconfounds sequence and levels of factor B, and thus permits their simultaneous assessment, although various interactions are confounded (Winer, 1971).

*Control or comparison groups.* One of the most complex decisions facing the researcher concerns the nature of an appropriate comparison group or groups. If we have a series of treatment conditions, we may need to assign subjects randomly to a condition in which no actual treatment is received. But because "no" treatment is technically impossible, as all subjects are exposed to some set of social and psychological variables during the course of the research, it is important to decide what constitutes the comparison condition. For instance, suppose that a researcher is evaluating a day-care curriculum. He or she may be interested in manipulating experimentally both the size of the center and the extensiveness of planned activities for the children in the center. If the researcher

Table 4.3. *Latin-square repeated measurement design*

| Factor A: Sequence | | Factor B Level 1 | Level 2 | Level 3 |
|---|---|---|---|---|
| Sequence 1 | subj. $1_1$ | $1^a$ | 2 | 3 |
| | subj. $2_1$ | 1 | 2 | 3 |
| | subj. $n_1$ | 1 | 2 | 3 |
| Sequence 2 | subj. $1_2$ | 2 | 3 | 1 |
| | subj. $2_2$ | 2 | 3 | 1 |
| | subj. $n_2$ | 2 | 3 | 1 |
| Sequence 3 | subj. $1_3$ | 3 | 1 | 2 |
| | subj. $2_3$ | 3 | 1 | 2 |
| | subj. $n_3$ | 3 | 1 | 2 |

[a]The numbers in the body of this table refer to the order in which a level of factor B was received. Thus, under sequence 1, level 1 is received first, then level 2, and finally level 3.

seeks to determine the effects of day care, in addition to the effects of variations within day care, then he or she needs to designate a non-day-care comparison group. Children who are randomly assigned to this non-day-care group may in fact be in a variety of different "treatments." They may be at home with a parent, they may be at home with other children for whom the parent babysits, or they may be with a babysitter. Deciding which is the appropriate comparison "treatment" is a construct validity task. Two questions should be thought through in defining the comparison condition. First, what would subjects in the experimental groups be receiving as "treatment" if in fact no experiment were being conducted? Second, to what future situation or setting do we want to generalize results, or, in other words, what construct is being operationalized as the independent variable? For instance, in our day-care example, if "at home with parent" is defined as the comparison condition, then one aspect of the independent variable is being away from parent, whereas if the comparison condition is "with a babysitter," the independent variable operationalizes a somewhat different construct. Researchers should never choose a comparison group *only* for reasons of convenience or just for the sake of having a comparison group. A comparison group should provide a conceptually meaningful baseline.

### Experimental unit decisions

We are acting on the assumption that the researcher has already decided in a general manner on the population affected by the treatment to be evaluated. There remains, however, a number of crucial decisions to be made concerning the level at which the affected population enters the research as experimental units. In more concrete terms, we may be interested in the impact of a community mental health program on the mental health of residents. We know in a general way that the residents constitute the affected population. However, they may participate in the research at a variety of different levels or degrees of aggregation: We may randomly assign individuals to the treatment and measure their outcomes; we may randomly assign blocks of households; or the experimental unit may be entire communities of the affected population. Deciding which level is the most appropriate in any piece of applied research is a fundamental and frequently difficult problem.

In theory, there is one central issue here: At what level do we wish to generalize our effects? In practice, however, there are three different, though related decisions to be made concerning the levels at which the affected population serves as experimental units. First, the experimenter must decide at which level he or she randomly assigns units to treatment conditions. In a curriculum evaluation, does the researcher randomly assign classrooms or individuals to curricula? Second, the researcher must decide at which level outcomes are to be measured, regardless of the level at which randomization took place. Third, the level of the experimental unit to be analyzed must be decided.

Unfortunately, it is frequently not realized that the first and third decisions, concerning levels of randomization and analysis, are inevitably linked. Once the level of randomization of units to treatments has been decided, so too has the analysis level. If classrooms have been randomly assigned to different curricula, if communities have been randomly assigned to different community mental health programs, then, statistically speaking, there exist only as many degrees of freedom in the data as the number of experimental units assigned. An analysis that treats the individual as the unit when aggregates have been assigned to treatment conditions inappropriately overestimates the amount of information in the data. (See Chapter 8, however, for an exception to this rule.)

The level of analysis decision is dictated by the randomization level, but the level at which measurement is conducted may be independent of the level of randomization. Although we may randomly assign aggregate units to experimental treatments, and hence base the analysis on aggregates, we may measure individual as well as aggregate outcomes. The reverse of this, however, is frequently not possible. If we randomly assign individuals within aggregates to different experimental treatments, then the measurement of aggregate outcomes is meaningless for purposes of treatment comparison. The example of the community mental health evaluation clarifies this. If we randomly assign communities to types of community mental health centers, we can still assess individual as well as community level outcomes. That is, we can measure both individual measures, such as mental health attitudes of residents within the communities, and community measures, such as the extent to which community governing bodies discuss mental health issues. With both levels of measurement we can assess effects of type of center on individual and aggregate outcomes, provided, of course, that the analysis uses communities as the experimental unit.

If, on the other hand, individuals within communities are randomly assigned to one type of community mental health center or to another, we are unable to measure the impact of treatment on aggregate or community level outcomes, even though the individual outcomes may be measured quite well.

In light of this discussion, three conclusions can be reached. First, it makes sense to measure outcomes on the finest levels possible, or unaggregated levels, as well as aggregate outcomes. This is true regardless of the unit of randomization and analysis. Second, if we are interested in aggregate level outcomes that are meaningless at the individual level (e.g., community governing bodies' reactions), it makes sense to assign aggregate units to treatments randomly and, hence, to analyze on the aggregate level. Third, analysis should be based on the unit that was randomly assigned. If aggregates have been randomly assigned, but outcomes are measured at the individual level, aggregate averages or other summary statistics should serve as dependent measures in the analysis.

There is a qualification to be made to the second conclusion, where we recommend randomly assigning, and hence analyzing aggregates if the researcher is interested in aggregate outcomes. The qualification concerns the interpretation of aggregate analyses of individual outcomes. There is an extensive literature (e.g.,

Goodman, 1959; Hammond, 1973; Robinson, 1950) on the pitfalls of reaching individual level conclusions on the basis of aggregate statistics. Estimates of effect, particularly correlation coefficients, are typically larger with aggregate measures than with individual level variables. Thus, if we measure individual mental health attitudes, compute community averages, and correlate them with type of mental health treatment received by the community, that correlation is typically larger than if we randomly assigned individuals and then correlated individual attitudes with type of treatment received by the individuals. The reason for this difference is the fact that there exists a great deal of between-individual, but within treatment condition, variation that is omitted from the analysis in the aggregate case but is not in the individual case.

### Decisions to increase conclusion validity

Even though many of the design decisions that we have already discussed have implications for an experiment's conclusion validity, there are a number of design modifications that can be used for the exclusive purpose of enhancing statistical power. As mentioned in the previous chapter, conclusion validity is perhaps of more importance in applied social research than in basic research because of the fact that the interventions we evaluate are costly and massive. We do not want to say that they have no effect when in fact they do. Therefore, techniques to increase statistical power merit serious consideration.

The two basic techniques that can be used consist of:

1 The use of a *randomized blocks design;* and
2 The use of *analysis of covariance.*

Each of these techniques is discussed in turn.

*Randomized blocks design.* The randomized blocks experimental design was first used in agricultural experiments where researchers were interested in exploring the effects of various seed or fertilizer types on crop productivity. The experimental units were small areas of a field that were to be randomly assigned to the levels of an experimental factor. It became apparent to researchers that areas in fields differed greatly in their crop productivity, regardless of treatment conditions. The researchers decided that it made sense to group the areas in the field by their productivity and then randomly assign areas within productivity groups to treatment conditions. In the subsequent analysis of the experimental data, groups of areas were treated as a factor in the analysis of variance model.

This example identifies all the essential elements of the randomized blocks design. Experimental units, whether areas in a field, individuals, or aggregates, are grouped or "blocked" on some variable that is expected to be highly related to the outcome variable to be assessed. These blocks are formed with the intention of increasing the similarity of units within blocks and the dissimilarity of units between blocks. Random assignment of units to treatment conditions is then conducted within blocks. In essence, the design amounts to matching units on the blocking factor and then randomly assigning units to treatments.

The randomized blocks design increases statistical power for reasons similar to those that make the repeated measures design powerful. If the blocking variable is entered into the analysis of variance as a factor, and if it is highly related to the dependent measure, then the amount of residual error variance in the data against which the treatment effects are tested is substantially reduced. Just as in the repeated measures design each unit serves as its own control, so in the randomized blocks design, similar units within blocks are the basis for treatment comparisons.

More statistical power is gained in a blocked design as the blocking variable is more highly correlated with the outcome or dependent variable. In addition, as units within blocks become more and more homogeneous with respect to the outcome measure, the higher becomes the power of the design.

Besides increasing the conclusion validity of a study, the randomized blocks design may also reveal interesting interactions between treatment variables and the blocking variable. For instance, in the original agriculture example, a randomized blocks design may reveal that a particular fertilizer makes a difference in relatively unproductive areas of a field, but in the productive areas, the effect is trivial. Such outcomes represent the interaction between the treatment variable and the blocking variable. This interaction is, of course, tested within the analysis of variance (ANOVA). In many applied research problems, interactions between treatment conditions and characteristics of the experimental units, which may be used for blocking purposes, are likely to be particularly informative. For instance, education curricula may have different effects on

high-achieving versus low-achieving students, an income mainte-
nance plan may differentially affect job search behavior of the
recently and the chronically unemployed worker, and day-care
facilities may influence the developmental progress of precocious
children differently than more slowly developing children.

     *Analysis of covariance.* The second technique for increasing
statistical power in an experimental design is by measuring some
variable that is related to the outcome variable, prior to administering experimental treatments, and using such a measure as a
covariate in an analysis of covariance (ANCOVA). We shall
discuss the analysis of covariance in more detail later in this chapter
(and elsewhere in the book). Suffice it here to say that it is
analytically a very similar technique to the randomized blocks
analysis of variance, except that the blocking variable, which is the
covariate in ANCOVA, is treated as a continuous, interval variable
rather than as an experimental factor having discrete levels or
categories. In addition, as analysis of covariance is usually
conducted, the covariate by treatment interaction, which is equivalent to the blocking variable by treatment interaction, is assumed
not to exist.
     The use of a covariate in the analysis of treatment effects
increases the statistical power of that analysis for the same reason
that a blocking variable increases power in the randomized blocks
design. If the covariate is substantially correlated with the outcome
measure, then controlling for it reduces the residual error variance
against which treatment effects are tested.
     There are four potential difficulties in using analysis of covar-
iance to increase statistical power in randomized experiments. First,
we must be concerned about the relationship between the covariate
and the treatment. If the covariate is measured before treatment
delivery (better yet, before randomization of subjects to condition),
and if subjects are truly randomly assigned, then the covariate and
the treatment factor will on the average be uncorrelated. If,
however, the researcher mistakenly employs a covariate that has
been measured after treatment delivery, it may be that the treatment affects the covariate. If the covariate is affected by the
treatment, then controlling for it statistically through analysis of
covariance causes us to estimate treatment effects incorrectly. In
such a case, analysis of covariance controls for treatment effects
reflected in the covariate while testing treatment effects. *Using*

*analysis of covariance to increase power with a covariate that is caused by the treatment is thus inappropriate and leads to bias.*[3]

The lesson from this is that the experimenter should be sure to measure covariates well prior to treatment delivery, and even before treatment assignment decisions have been randomly made. In addition, to be sure that the covariate and treatment are uncorrelated, the experimenter may wish to set up the equivalent of blocks on the covariate, randomly assign within blocks, but then proceed to analyze outcomes via analysis of covariance. The advantages of this strategy over the traditional randomized blocks analysis of variance are detailed below.

The second potential difficulty in using ANCOVA is that the pretest–posttest relationship is assumed to be linear. If it is not, then the use of ANCOVA will not lead to any increase in power. Appropriate transformations may be useful in rendering the relationship linear (Mosteller & Tukey, 1977).

The third potential problem to using ANCOVA for increasing power in true experiments is the assumption implicit in ANCOVA that the covariate and treatment do not interact.[4] When they do, traditional analysis of covariance is inappropriate. In such cases, using a randomized blocks design, where such interactions are tested in the ANOVA, may be preferable. However, this problem is of minor consequence if the analysis of covariance is recast into multiple regression, as we shall show later in this chapter. When ANCOVA is reformulated in multiple regression, covariate by treatment interactions can be tested and interpreted.

The fourth problem concerns the possibility that the measurement of a pre-treatment variable may cause the post-treatment outcome to be different than it would be had no pretest been given. Further, it is possible that the delivery of a pretest may affect the posttest in some treatment conditions but not in others. The potential threat of a pretest by treatment interaction was discussed in the third chapter. A pretest effect and a pretest by treatment interaction are problematic only if pretests would not normally be administered in the treatment conditions to which the research results are to be generalized. In fact, many social programs that would be the

---

[3] This analysis is appropriate, however, when examining the mediation of treatment effects. See Chapter 10.

[4] Whether or not the covariate and treatment interact is, of course, a completely different question from the one of whether the covariate and the treatment are correlated. The reader should beware of confusing the two.

subject of evaluation include some sort of pre-treatment assessment or interview as a normal and expected component of the program. In such cases, pretest effects and interactions do not constitute the interpretive problem that they would otherwise.

If in fact the researcher feels that a pretest is essential and yet suspects that pretest effects and pretest by treatment interactions constitute potential problems for generalization, then he or she would be well advised to run some experimental units without giving the pretest. If some subjects are randomly assigned to a no-pretest condition, and this pretest factor is crossed with the experimental treatment factor, we have what is called a *Solomon four group design* (Campbell & Stanley, 1963). Within this design the pretest effect and interaction can be tested.

*Comparison of ANCOVA and randomized blocks.* Feldt (1958) has examined the relative power of ANCOVA and the randomized blocks design under the assumptions of linearity and no treatment by covariate interaction. If the pretest–posttest relationship is less than .4, he has shown that the randomized blocks design is more powerful than ANCOVA. This reverses when the correlation is greater than .6. The reason for this difference is that the randomized blocks design is less efficient because it discards degrees of freedom by not assuming linearity of the pretest–posttest relationship. Also, it ignores the pretest–posttest relationship within levels of the blocking factor. On the other hand, the randomized blocks design gains power because it constrains the blocking variable–treatment correlation to be exactly zero, assuming randomization within blocks. Although it is not generally recognized, it is possible to use ANCOVA within a randomized blocks design, using the blocking variable as the covariate. It seems to us that such a strategy would be more efficient than the traditional analysis of variance, even when the blocking variable–posttest correlation is relatively low, so long as the pretest–posttest relationship is linear.

ANCOVA has the advantage of allowing the use of a number of covariates, controlling for them all simultaneously in testing treatment effects. In a randomized blocks design, the use of a second blocking factor may create problems unless the two blocking factors are only weakly correlated in the population. If they are not, then the researcher will have trouble maintaining their orthogonality in the research design, a requirement for the use of analysis of variance. Thus, analysis of covariance is generally preferable if a number of pre-treatment measures are to be used to increase statistical power.

## Analysis of randomized experiments

### Analysis of variance

The standard analytic procedure for randomized experiments employing a factorial design is analysis of variance. In a design involving two crossed factors, it is assumed that

$$Y_{ijk} = \mu + \alpha_j + \beta_k + \alpha\beta_{jk} + e_{ijk}$$

That is, the analysis of variance assumes that individual observations ($Y_{ijk}$) are determined by the population mean ($\mu$) across all treatment conditions, plus an effect due to the first factor ($\alpha_j$), an effect due to the second ($\beta_k$), and the interaction between the two ($\alpha\beta_{jk}$). The sum of these effects across rows and columns is set to zero. In addition, there is some component of error ($e_{ijk}$) in every observation. It is assumed in this model that $e_{ijk}$ has an expectation, or mean, of zero, and it is normally and independently distributed. In addition, it is assumed that the variance in errors is the same in all cells of the factorial design, and that there are an equal number of observations in each cell. Under these assumptions, analysis of variance compares variation in the data associated with the treatments and their interaction to residual or error variation in the data. These comparisons yield $F$ statistics that are used to test the significance of the respective treatment effects.

The analysis of the randomized blocks design is a straightforward extension of this model. One of the experimental factors, say, $\alpha_j$, is assumed to be the blocking variable rather than an experimentally manipulated variable.[5]

---

[5] The only complexity in this blocking analysis is that the assumption of equal numbers of observations per cell may be violated. For instance, if subjects are already divided up into blocks such as classrooms, and we then randomly assign subjects within blocks to some set of treatment conditions, the number of subjects in each block by treatment cell will differ if the number of subjects in each block varies. Unequal numbers of subjects in cells pose problems only if they result in correlated experimental factors. Although the cell sizes may differ in blocked designs, they will be proportional. By this we mean that if, for example, the size of one block is half the size of another, the number of subjects in a given treatment from the first block will be half the number in the treatment from the second block. Proportional cell frequencies make the treatment uncorrelated with the blocking factor. However, the

In a repeated measures model, where the experimental unit is assessed under all experimental treatments, the model behind the data is assumed to be

$$Y_{ik} = \mu + \pi_i + \beta_k + e_{ik}$$

where $Y_{ik}$ represents the observation of subject $i$ under treatment level $k$; $\mu$ is the population mean of all responses in all treatment–subject combinations; $\pi_i$ is a constant associated with all responses of subject $i$ and represents variation between subjects (in the previous model this component is part of $e_{ijk}$); $\beta_k$ represents the effect of the different treatment conditions; and $e_{ik}$ is error associated with any $Y_{ik}$. Thus, we assume that each individual observation reflects a subject difference, a treatment effect, and error or residual variation. Treatment effects are said to be measured within subjects. Differences in treatment effects between subjects constitute the $e_{ik}$ or residual variation. This treatment by subject interaction is used to determine the significance of the treatment effect.

In addition to a set of treatments in which all subjects are assessed, we may have another experimental factor under which subjects are nested. An example of such a design is found in Table 4.3, discussed earlier, in which sequence is used as a between-subjects factor. Under this design, the model of observed outcomes is

$$Y_{ijk} = \mu + \alpha_j + \pi_i + \beta_k + \alpha\beta_{jk} + e_{ijk}$$

where $Y_{ijk}$ represents the observation of subject $i$, nested within level $j$, under treatment level $k$. The grand mean of all observations is $\mu$; $\alpha_j$ represents the effect of the between-subject factor; $\pi_i$ is a constant associated with all observations of subject $i$; and $\beta_k$ represents the effects of different treatment conditions. Under this model, there are two sources of variation between subjects, variation due to the factor under which subjects are nested, and variation due to subjects within levels of the factor. The significance of effects due to the between-subject factor is estimated by comparing the former source of variation with the latter. Variation in observations within subjects may be due to three different elements, treatment effects across all subjects ($\beta_k$), treatment effects that differ with the level of the between-subject factor ($\alpha\beta_{jk}$), and treatment effects that differ

blocking factor by treatment interaction is partially confounded with its components. Appropriate analysis of variance procedures for proportional cell sizes are described in Winer (1971, pp. 419–22).

by subjects within levels of $j$ ($e_{ijk}$). Analysis of variance provides significant tests for the treatment effect ($\beta_k$) and treatment by between-subject factor interaction ($\alpha\beta_{jk}$) by comparing each of these sources of variation with variation due to treatment effects differing between subjects, or the treatment by subjects within group interaction ($e_{ijk}$).

### Analysis of covariance

In experiments where covariates have been assessed prior to treatment assignment, analysis of covariance is routinely used to gain statistical power. In analysis of covariance, the statistical model is very similar to the analysis of variance models presented in the preceding section. We can think of analysis of covariance as an analysis of variance on dependent measures from which variation associated with the covariate has been subtracted out.

The analysis of covariance model for an experiment involving one covariate and two crossed factors under which subjects are nested is the following:

$$Y_{ijk} = \mu + b(X_{ijk} - \overline{X}) + \alpha_j + \beta_k + \alpha\beta_{jk} + e_{ijk}$$

where $Y_{ijk}$ and $\mu$ are defined as previously, $X_{ijk}$ is the covariate measured on individual $i$ in treatment condition $jk$, and its mean across all subjects is $\overline{X}$; $\alpha_j$, $\beta_k$, and $\alpha\beta_{jk}$ are the two treatment effects and their interaction, and $e_{ijk}$ is residual error about which we make the same assumptions as previously. The coefficient $b$ is the least-squares coefficient resulting from the regression of $Y_{ijk}$ on the covariate, controlling for treatment effects. In order to estimate the treatment effects in this model, we must assume that the covariate does not interact with treatments, that is, that $b$ does not vary across levels of the treatments. This assumption is referred to as the *homogeneity of regression assumption.*

With repeated measures designs, analysis of covariance can be used to reduce residual variation in testing both between and within subject experimental factors. In the design described by Table 4.2, where there is both a factor under which subjects are nested and one that is crossed with subjects, covariates can take one of two forms. There can either be one measure for each subject on the covariate, in which case controlling for the covariate only increases statistical power for testing the between-subject factor, or we may measure a covariate for each $Y_{ijk}$, thus measuring it for each subject as frequently as there are treatment conditions. In this latter case the use of the covariate reduces residual variation against which both between-subject and within-subject experimental factors are tested.[6]

### Analysis of pre–post change scores

It is frequently the case that instead of using a pre-treatment measure as a covariate as discussed in the previous section, differences between pre and post, or change scores, are used as the dependent measure in an analysis of variance. This is especially likely when the pretest measures the identical construct as the posttest, and when researchers want to present the "amount of change" in $Y$ caused by the treatment.

This change score analysis is closely related to the analysis of covariance. As we have already said, we can think of the analysis of covariance as the analysis of variance on a dependent measure that has been adjusted for the covariate. From the ANCOVA model, we see that the adjustment coefficient for the covariate is its partial regression coefficient, $b$. In the analysis of pre–post change scores, we also adjust the post-treatment outcome, $Y_{ijk}$, for the pretest, or covariate, but the adjustment coefficient equals one rather than $b$. In other words, we can think of analysis of covariance as an analysis of variance on the adjusted outcome score

$$Y_{ijk} - b(X_{ijk})$$

where $b$ is the partial regression coefficient of $X_{ijk}$, controlling for treatment effects.[7] In the analysis of change scores we conduct an analysis of variance on

$$Y_{ijk} - X_{ijk}$$

The only difference in these two adjusted outcomes is that in the second the adjustment coefficient equals one.

The conceptual difference between these two adjustment procedures is important for the reader to grasp, particularly in light of later chapters where pretest adjustment strategies are discussed at

---

[6] When the covariate does not vary within subjects, ANCOVA should not be performed within subjects. If it is performed, the degrees of freedom for error are underestimated. Most statistical packages ignore this problem.

[7] If this were done instead of an actual ANCOVA, the standard error of the treatment effect would be artificially smaller, because the treatment–covariate correlation is ignored. ANCOVA should be conducted in the usual manner.

greater length (Chapter 6). In the analysis of covariance, the adjustment weight, $b$, is derived such that the adjusted dependent measure is uncorrelated with the pretest that was used as the covariate. In the change score analysis, this will not be the case. Thus, the amount of change assessed for each subject, and subsequently analyzed, is correlated (negatively when $b < 1$, as is usually the case) with the subject's pretest. This fact illustrates the "regression to the mean" problem that was discussed in the last chapter. Extremely high scores have a greater probability of change downwards than upwards, and vice versa for extremely low scores. In Chapter 3, we labeled such regression to the mean a threat to internal validity. However, in randomized experiments where the probability of an extreme pretest scorer receiving any given treatment is the same as the probability for a less extreme scorer, regression to the mean does not threaten internal validity.

Although the use of change scores in randomized experiments does not harm internal validity, from the point of view of conclusion validity it is usually less efficient than using pretest scores as covariates. Because the adjusted outcome measure in analysis of covariance has removed all variation in $Y$ associated with $X$, there is no other linear adjustment of $Y$ on $X$ that can reduce residual variation in $Y$ to a greater extent. Or, to put it another way, because in the change score analysis variation in the adjusted outcome is associated with variation in the pretest, we have not reduced residual variance in the outcome as much as if the regression weight had been used. In fact, it is not unusual for the change score analysis to be even less powerful than an analysis of the unadjusted outcome variable, if the pretest–posttest correlation is less than .5. For these reasons, the analysis of covariance is generally preferable in randomized experiments to the analysis of change scores. There may be cases in which the two analyses yield nearly identical results. In such cases the change score analysis might be preferred because of its greater ease of interpretation.

### The use of multiple regression as a general analytic strategy

As others before us have noted (e.g., Cohen, 1968; Fennessey, 1968), the analyses of variance and covariance are specific instances of the more general linear model that is estimated using multiple regression analysis. Once this is realized, the different types of analyses may all be conducted using regression. In addition, the use of the general linear model for the analysis of randomized experiments permits the testing of certain effects that are assumed not to exist under the analysis of variance and covariance models, as we discuss in the following pages.

It is frequently assumed that analysis of variance and multiple regression are quite different techniques. The former is usually used to answer questions concerning differences in means between treatment conditions. The latter is traditionally used to assess covariation or correlation between two variables. In fact, however, beyond traditional assumptions concerning the measurement scale of the independent variables, the two sorts of questions are identical. The traditional analysis of variance question can be rephrased as the degree to which a continuous dependent measure covaries with a set of discrete, categorically measured independent variables. It is entirely appropriate to code categorical independent variables as predictors in a multiple regression equation. In fact, analysis of variance is the specific instance of the general linear model in which orthogonal independent variables are measured on categorical, noncontinuous scales of measurement. Multiple regression is the more general technique under which independent variables can be measured on either discrete or continuous scales and may or may not be correlated.

If treatment variables in experimental research are included as predictors in a multiple regression equation, they must be coded or assigned numerical values according to some convention. Frequently, so-called *dummy* coding is the convention used. Dummy coding means that we code a separate predictor in the equation for each level of an experimental factor, such that an experimental unit is assigned a score of one on the predictor if he or she receives that treatment, a zero if not. A somewhat simpler alternative is to use the *effects* coding convention.[8] Under such a convention, if an experimental factor has two levels, a predictor is created such that units in one level are assigned a score of $-1$ on the predictor and units in the other level are assigned a score of $+1$.

As an example, we might imagine a study evaluating psychotherapeutic treatments. There may be two experimental factors in the

---

[8] The results of an analysis using effects coding are preferred in this chapter because they yield parameters that are equivalent to those that result from analysis of variance. At other times, dummy coding may be preferable.

Table 4.4. *Example of effects coding for a* 2 × 2
*experimental design:* $Z_1 = +1$ *if individual therapy,*
$-1$ *if not;* $Z_2 = +1$ *if theoretical orientation* A; $-1$ *if not*

|  | Theoretical orientation | |
| --- | --- | --- |
| Therapeutic setting | A | B |
| Individual | $Z_1 = +1$ | $Z_1 = +1$ |
|  | $Z_2 = +1$ | $Z_2 = -1$ |
| Group | $Z_1 = -1$ | $Z_1 = -1$ |
|  | $Z_2 = +1$ | $Z_2 = -1$ |

study, each having two levels. The first might manipulate the
setting in which therapy is conducted: individual versus group. The
second factor might be two different theoretical orientations
espoused by the therapist. For the first factor, we might code one
variable, $Z_1$, under the effects coding convention, arbitrarily assigning a $+1$ to those in the individual setting and a $-1$ to those in the
group setting. Likewise, a second variable, $Z_2$, is created for the
second factor, arbitrarily assigning a $+1$ to those under theoretical
orientation A and a $-1$ to those under theoretical orientation B. As
can be seen from Table 4.4, each cell of the 2 × 2 experimental
design has been assigned a unique set of values on these two new
variables, $Z_1$ and $Z_2$.

If a multiple regression analysis is conducted on the outcome
measure, $Y$, in this experimental design, regressing it on the two
coded variables, $Z_1$ and $Z_2$, the resulting equation will have this
form:

$$Y = b_0 + b_1 Z_1 + b_2 Z_2 + e$$

From this equation, by substituting in the proper values for $Z_1$ and
$Z_2$, the values of $Y$ predicted for each cell of the experimental design
can be generated. Thus for instance, the predicted value of $Y$, $\hat{Y}$, for
subjects in the individual setting, orientation A condition is

$$\hat{Y} = b_0 + b_1(+1) + b_2(+1)$$

Table 4.5 presents these predicted outcomes for each treatment
condition. From this table, it can be seen that the difference in the
predicted values of $Y$ between the two levels of therapeutic setting is

Table 4.5. *Predicted outcomes from the linear additive model derived from the equation $Y = b_0 + b_1 Z_1 + b_2 Z_2 + e$, where $Z_1, Z_2$ are defined as in Table 4.4*

| Therapeutic setting | Theoretical orientation | |
|---|---|---|
| | A | B |
| Individual | $\hat{Y} = b_0 + b_1(+1) + b_2(+1)$ | $\hat{Y} = b_0 + b_1(+1) + b_2(-1)$ |
| | $= b_0 + b_1 + b_2$ | $= b_0 + b_1 - b_2$ |
| Group | $\hat{Y} = b_0 + b_1(-1) + b_2(+1)$ | $\hat{Y} = b_0 + b_1(-1) + b_2(-1)$ |
| | $= b_0 - b_1 + b_2$ | $= b_0 - b_1 - b_2$ |

$2b_1$. The difference in predicted values of $Y$ between the two levels of orientation is $2b_2$. It is clear, then, that these are the predicted or estimated effects of the two factors.

Although this model estimates treatment effects, it does not allow for their interaction. In other words, in Table 4.5 the effect of setting is $2b_1$, regardless of the level of theoretical orientation. By taking the product of our two predictors, and entering this product into the regression equation, we can allow for and test the interaction of the two treatment variables.

In the full interactive model, the regression equation has the form

$$Y = b_0 + b_1 Z_1 + b_2 Z_2 + b_3 Z_1 Z_2 + e$$

Under this model, the predicted values for the outcome in each cell of the design are presented in Table 4.6. These predicted values are identical to the cell means. From this table, it can be seen that the presence of the product term $(Z_1 Z_2)$ in the equation allows the effects of one factor to depend on the level of the other. Thus, the effect of setting under orientation A equals $2b_1 + 2b_3$. Under orientation B, the effect of setting is equivalent to $2b_1 - 2b_3$.

Each of the regression coefficients in these models has associated with it a standard error that can be used to define its confidence interval and hence to test the null hypothesis that the coefficient equals zero in the population. These tests are equivalent to the tests of treatment effects and their interaction if we were to conduct analysis of variance on the data.

We have thus shown how multiple regression can be used to

Table 4.6. *Predicted outcomes from the linear interactive model derived from the equation* $Y = b_0 + b_1 Z_1 + b_2 Z_2 + b_3 Z_1 Z_2 + e$, *where* $Z_1, Z_2$ *are defined as in Table 4.4*

| Therapeutic setting | Theoretical orientation | |
|---|---|---|
| | A | B |
| Individual | $\hat{Y} = b_0 + b_1(+1) + b_2(+1)$ $+ b_3(+1)$ $= b_0 + b_1 + b_2 + b_3$ | $\hat{Y} = b_0 + b_1(+1) + b_2(-1)$ $+ b_3(-1)$ $= b_0 + b_1 - b_2 - b_3$ |
| Group | $\hat{Y} = b_0 + b_1(-1) + b_2(+1)$ $+ b_3(-1)$ $= b_0 - b_1 + b_2 - b_3$ | $\hat{Y} = b_0 + b_1(-1) + b_2(-1)$ $+ b_3(+1)$ $= b_0 - b_1 - b_2 + b_3$ |

analyze the data from a factorial experimental design that is traditionally analyzed using analysis of variance. The inferential statistics resulting from the two techniques are identical. In the design just discussed, subjects are nested within levels of both experimental factors. It is also possible to analyze repeated measures designs using multiple regression, either by coding subjects as a set of predictor variables, and thus controlling for them when assessing treatment effects, or by removing variation in the dependent measure associated with subjects prior to conducting the regression analysis. (See Cohen & Cohen, 1975, chap. 10, for an elaboration of repeated measures designs in multiple regression.)

The major benefit to be gained from analyzing experimental data with multiple regression derives from the fact that predictors in a multiple regression equation may be measured on any measurement scale. Both continuous, interval-scale variables and categorical, nominal-scale variables may simultaneously serve as predictors. In addition, in multiple regression the analysis of variance assumption of equal cell $n$, or orthogonality of independent variables, is relaxed. Analysis of variance constitutes the special case of multiple regression in which independent variables are measured on categorical scales and in which independent variables are assumed to be uncorrelated.

With the relaxation of these two assumptions, analysis of covariance can be incorporated into the regression model. Analysis of covariance is incorporated by introducing both the continuously measured covariate, or covariates, and the treatment variables into the same multiple regression equation. Thus, suppose we had measured some pre-treatment measure, $X$, in the experimental design discussed in the preceding analysis of variance model. We could either conduct analysis of covariance, treating $X$ as a covariate, as it is usually conducted, or, alternatively and identically, we could analyze the data using the following regression equation:

$$Y = b_0 + b_1(X - \overline{X}) + b_2Z_1 + b_3Z_2 + b_4Z_1Z_2 + e$$

Inferential tests conducted on the treatment regression coefficients of this model are identical to those that would result from an analysis of covariance conducted on the same data.

The reason for preferring this regression over the analysis of covariance is that covariate by treatment interactions can be examined, tested, and interpreted in the regression, whereas in analysis of covariance they are assumed not to exist. If in our additive equation we had allowed for the possibility of treatment by covariate interactions by including appropriate product terms, the regression equation would be

$$Y = b_0 + b_1(X - \overline{X}) + b_2Z_1 + b_3Z_2 + b_4Z_1(X - \overline{X})$$
$$+ b_5Z_2(X - \overline{X}) + e$$

If the regression coefficient for one or both of the treatment by covariate interactions is statistically different from zero, we have violated the homogencity of regression assumption and hence should not conduct traditional analysis of covariance. There exists no valid reason at all, however, for not interpreting this regression equation and basing the analysis of the experimental design on it. Suppose, for instance, that the $b_4$ coefficient was significant, but not the $b_5$, so that the resulting equation was in fact

$$Y = b_0 + b_1(X - \overline{X}) + b_2Z_1 + b_3Z_2 + b_4Z_1(X - \overline{X}) + e$$

We could then compute separate equations for each of the four cells of our experimental design by substituting in the appropriate values for the $Z_1$ and $Z_2$ variables. These separate equations are presented in Table 4.7. In this model, $2b_3$ is the estimated effect of the orientation factor: Predicted outcomes in the columns of Table 4.7 differ by that amount. The effect of therapeutic setting cannot be so easily summarized. Predicted outcomes differ between the rows of Table 4.7 by both $2b_2$ and $2b_4(X - \overline{X})$. In words, the effect of

Table 4.7. *Evaluations of the regression equation* $Y = b_0 + b_1(X - \overline{X}) + b_2Z_1 + b_3Z_2 + b_4Z_1(X - \overline{X}) + e$ *in the experimental design of Table 4.4*

| Therapeutic setting | Theoretical orientation | |
|---|---|---|
| | A | B |
| Individual | $\hat{Y} = b_0 + b_1(X - \overline{X})$ $+ b_2(+1)$ $+ b_3(+1) + b_4(+1)$ $(X - \overline{X})$ $= b_0 + b_2 + b_3 + (b_1 + b_4)$ $(X - \overline{X})$ | $\hat{Y} = b_0 + b_1(X - \overline{X})$ $+ b_2(+1)$ $+ b_3(-1) + b_4(+1)$ $(X - \overline{X})$ $= b_0 + b_2 - b_3 + (b_1 + b_4)$ $(X - \overline{X})$ |
| Group | $\hat{Y} = b_0 + b_1(X - \overline{X}) + b_2(-1)$ $+ b_3(+1)$ $+ b_4(-1)(X - \overline{X})$ $= b_0 - b_2 + b_3 + (b_1 - b_4)$ $(X - \overline{X})$ | $\hat{Y} = b_0 + b_1(X - \overline{X})$ $+ b_2(-1)$ $+ b_3(-1) + b_4(-1)$ $(X - \overline{X})$ $= b_0 - b_2 - b_3 + (b_1 - b_4)$ $(X - \overline{X})$ |

setting depends on the level of the pretest, $X$. If $X = \overline{X}$, or if we are dealing with someone who scores at the pretest mean, then $2b_2$ estimates the effect of setting. If we are discussing someone who scores one unit above the mean on the pretest, the predicted effect of setting would be $2b_2 + 2b_4(1)$. Subjects who perform differently on the pretest are affected differently by the treatment.

To be more concrete, suppose that the values for the coefficients in the preceding equation are as follows, with $X$ and $Y$ assessed on 10-point scales:

$$Y = 4.0 + .4(X - \overline{X}) + 1.0Z_1 + .5Z_2 + .2(Z_1)(X - \overline{X}) + e$$

We could then graphically display the relationship between the pretest and posttest for each of the four treatment conditions, as in Figure 4.1. The two lines with the steeper slopes refer to the individual setting conditions. The flatter slopes are found in the group setting conditions. Taking the difference between predicted posttest scores by orientation, it can be seen that regardless of the value of the pretest and of the setting, orientation A achieves higher outcomes than orientation B. The magnitude of the setting effect, however, depends on the value of the pretest. For poor pretest

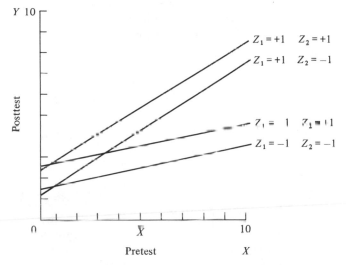

Figure 4.1. Relationship between pretest ($X$) and posttest ($Y$) for each treatment condition, based on $Y = 4.0 + .4(X - \overline{X}) + 1.0Z_1 + .5Z_2 + .2(Z_1)(X - \overline{X}) + e$.

scorers, four units below the mean, there is essentially no difference due to setting. For subjects way above the mean on the pretest, the setting effect is substantial. At the mean of the pretest, the setting effect is exactly 2.0 units.

Recasting analysis of covariance as a multiple regression model thus permits covariate by treatment interactions, interactions that may be quite informative for policy purposes. In the regression example just examined, we would conclude that the setting for psychotherapy makes a difference only for those who are relatively stable to begin with (assuming that high scores on both $X$ and $Y$ indicate psychological stability). If the analysis had not been conducted under a regression model, we would not have conducted analysis of covariance because of assumption violations. We would then have not fully understood the effect of setting.

Some treatment by covariate interactions may include three or more variables. In other words, the triple product $(Z_1)(Z_2)(X - \overline{X})$ may have a significant regression coefficient. The interpretation of such higher-order interactions is only slightly more complicated than the example we have presented. The correct interpretation amounts to saying that the magnitude of the treatment by treatment interactions depends on the level of the pretest. In *all* cases, the researcher is advised to graph or table predicted relationships between pre- and posttest for each experimental treatment, as we have done, to aid interpretation.

Further generalizations of the analysis of covariance can be specified once it is recast into multiple regression. For instance, it becomes possible to test for a curvilinear relationship between the covariate and outcome by entering the covariance squared as a predictor in the regression. Likewise, higher-order polynomials can be specified as well as their interactions with the treatment variables.

## *The analysis of multiple outcomes*

It is frequently the case that applied researchers are interested in the effects of treatments on numerous outcomes or dependent measures. Thus, for instance, evaluators of school curricula may be interested in their effects on learning, motivation, and attitudes; evaluators of welfare programs may seek to assess effects on motivation to find work, family relationships, and economic well-being; and those who evaluate a mental health facility may be interested in a variety of mental health indicators. In all these cases the researcher analyzes multiple dependent measures. There are four different ways in which such multiple outcomes might be analyzed. Each of these is discussed below.

First, and most typically, the outcomes are analyzed one at a time. That is, separate analyses of variance or multiple regressions are computed on each of the outcome measures. There are two major problems to this procedure. First, multiple significance tests can result in Type I conclusion errors unless the $\alpha$ level is properly adjusted. Second, the procedure may pose interpretive problems if the outcomes are intercorrelated. Instead of conducting separate tests, we may really be doing the same analysis over and over again. Suppose that our mental health treatment evaluator assessed outcomes such as symptoms of depression, drug use, and family quarrels in evaluating whether a mental health treatment made a difference. Further, suppose that depressives typically were the same people who used drugs and quarreled, regardless of treatment condition. If separate analyses were conducted on all three outcomes, and treatment effects were found, the researcher might conclude that this treatment should be instituted to alleviate depression, drug use, and family fighting wherever these occur, either separately or in combination. In fact, the effect of the treatment may just be on one of the three directly and on the other two only indirectly. For instance, the treatment may have affected the degree of family fighting which then caused a decrease in depression, which then caused a decrease in drug usage. Clearly, then, we would not expect the treatment to affect drug usage for other subjects who are not taking drugs because of family fighting.

Rather than conducting separate analyses, we might attempt to combine outcomes, based on their intercorrelations, and then analyze the combination. Such a strategy constitutes the second way in which multiple outcomes may be analyzed. Under this strategy, outcomes are grouped together because they are related to each other. Factor analysis can be used to identify clusters of outcomes that are intercorrelated and that might properly be thought of as a single outcome rather than several. Under one particular model of factor analysis, principal components, a linear combination of the dependent variables is defined as

$$F_1 = b_1 Y_1 + b_2 Y_2 + b_3 Y_3$$

(where $F_1$ is the factor, $Y_1$ to $Y_3$ are the three outcome measures, and $b_1$ to $b_3$ are weights), such that as much of the variance in the outcomes is associated with the factor as possible. This factor, or equivalently the linear combination of outcome measures, would then be used as the dependent variable. More than one factor may be defined from a set of outcomes. These are usually constrained to be uncorrelated, however, so that separate analyses on them are independent.

Other types of factor analysis can also be used instead of a principal components analysis. A recent major innovation makes the estimation of the factor and the testing of treatment effects on that factor a simultaneous procedure (Jöreskog & Sörbom, 1978). We discuss this at more length in Chapter 9.

The third way in which multiple outcomes might be analyzed simultaneously is through techniques such as multivariate analysis of variance and canonical correlation. Multivariate analysis of variance is very similar to the second method we have discussed, in that a weighted combination of the outcomes is analyzed. The difference lies in the way in which the weights are derived. In the second method, using principal components factor analysis, the weights are derived so that the weighted linear combination, or factor, explains as much of the variance in the original outcomes as possible. In multivariate analysis of variance and canonical correlation, the weights are derived so that the independent variables or predictors, in combination, are as highly correlated as possible with the weighted combination of outcomes. Just as in factor analysis, there are other linear combinations of the outcomes that are orthogonal to the first. Here too we might define a second set of weights, such that the second linear combination of outcomes is uncorrelated with the first, but is as highly correlated with the weighted combination of treatment variables as possible.

The fourth way of analyzing multiple outcomes is by using repeated measures models in analysis of variance and multiple regression. Earlier in this chapter, when we discussed such models, it was in the context of repeated exposures of the same subject to different treatment levels, with the same outcome measured repeatedly. Thus, treatment is the experimental factor with which subjects are crossed. It is possible, however, to define the within-subjects factor as type of outcomes, while nesting subjects within treatment conditions. If the outcome variables are measured in the same metric, treatment effects that are found in such a repeated measures ANOVA estimate the effect of treatment on the average of the outcome variables. In essence, this analysis weights the outcomes equally. A treatment by outcome interaction tests whether the treatment effects are larger on some outcomes than on others. Such tests of interaction however are biased if the homogeneity of covariance assumption is violated.

The last three procedures that have been identified, factor analysis, multivariate analysis of variance, and repeated measures ANOVA, analyze a weighted linear combination of the outcome variables. If the researcher believes that the outcomes tap a few well-defined underlying constructs, then the factor analytic solution is to be preferred because it allows us to analyze an estimate of the construct. The multivariate analysis of variance approach is a more exploratory one, to be used when the researcher does not have a firm idea concerning the constructs represented by the outcome variables. Interpreting the weighted combination of outcome variables in multivariate analysis of variance may therefore be difficult.

## Problems in the conduct of randomized experiments

Although randomized experiments are the research design of choice if the goal is to maximize internal validity, they are not easily conducted. Many ambiguities may arise during the course of experiments that can have profound effects on the construct, internal, and conclusion validities of the research. In the following paragraphs we review some of these problems and their implications. We have organized these problems under two headings: problems concerning the integrity of the treatment- control distinction, and problems concerning the independence of observations. Most of these problems are issues in quasi-experiments as well. We discuss them here only because researchers are prone to think that the interpretation of experimental results is unambiguous

### *Integrity of the treatment variable*

Throughout much of this chapter, and indeed throughout most of this book, the treatment variable is conceptualized as a simple dichotomously coded distinction. Those who receive the treatment are assumed to have equivalent scores on the treatment construct. They are all assigned the same score on the treatment variable. Likewise, those in the comparison group are all assigned the same score on the treatment variable. Thus, there is no within-group variance. In fact, however, if we were to assess exactly the treatment received by each subject within groups rather than assigning them all the same score, we probably would find considerable within-group variation. Within the group of treated subjects, there is likely to be variation in how the treatment was received, the length of exposure to the treatment, the person or persons delivering the treatment, and so forth. Thus the treatment received by the treatment group is multifaceted rather than a single construct Likewise, within the comparison group, subjects may receive other than the intended "nontreatment" because of administrative inattention or because of a desire to compensate them informally for the fact that they were not given a possibly desirable treatment. Thus, within both the treatment and comparison groups, there is likely to be variation in the treatment construct that is not normally included in the measured treatment variable.

The presence of unassessed variation in the treatment construct gives rise to problems of construct and conclusion validities. By measuring the treatment variable as a simple dichotomous variable, we measure the true level of treatment received with error. We fail to assess the true treatment variable adequately and hence the construct validity of our treatment variable is lowered. In addition, it is likely that the within-group variation in the treatment construct would reveal a multidimensional construct if it were assessed. That is, within treatment groups as well as between them, subjects differ in the treatments they receive in many ways. We normally assume that the treatment is a single construct, whereas in reality it is likely to be much more complex.

In addition to problems of construct validity, within-group variation in the treatment construct has implications for conclusion validity. In Chapter 9 we show how errors of measurement in the treatment variable lead us to underestimate the magnitude of the treatment effect. As this effect is attenuated, we are less likely to find that it is statistically significant.

Related to the problem of within-group variation in the treatment construct is a problem we referred to in Chapter 3 as the treatment by mortality threat to internal validity. In essence, this threat means that some subjects within the treatment group may drop out because of the treatment they receive. For instance, if the treatment were an alcohol rehabilitation program, when subjects felt they were free of alcohol they might drop out of the treatment. Hence, "successful" subjects may differentially drop out. Likewise, in some studies, subjects may be more likely to drop out of the control group, particularly if the treatment is compensatory. It is frequently quite difficult to keep subjects in the research design, and yet it is imperative to do just that if we are to believe that the assignment to treatment conditions continues to be randomly based.

In addition to threatening internal validity, differential mortality may also affect conclusion and construct validities. Suppose that some subjects dropped out of the treatment or the control group but that we were able to gather posttest measures from them even though the treatments they received were terminated. To maintain the experimental design, their posttest scores should be included in the analysis. However, to the extent that they dropped out of the treatment or comparison groups, they did not receive the treatment intended for them. Thus, there is likely to be unintended within-group variation in the treatment construct, causing the problems of treatment construct validity and conclusion validity discussed above.

### Independence of observations

One of the most difficult problems faced in applied research is maintaining the independence of units or subjects in the research. All of the commonly employed statistical inference procedures make the assumption that observations are independent. Violations of this assumption have effects on the precision or conclusion validity of the research.

Most typically, subjects within treatment conditions may interact in such a way that there is less variation within treatments than might be expected if observations were truly independent. Suppose, for instance, that children were randomly assigned to classrooms. In one classroom a new curriculum to be evaluated is used. The other classroom is the control condition. Within classrooms, the students interact and learn from each other. As they do so, their outcome scores are likely to be more homogeneous than if they had not interacted. The effect of this attenuation of within-group variation is to increase the chance of Type I conclusion errors.

Although nonindependence of observations is usually thought to induce Type I conclusion errors, in fact there are a variety of ways in which the independence assumption may be violated, and these violations may cause either Type I or Type II conclusion errors. In Chapter 8, problems caused by nonindependence of observations are discussed further. There we show the conditions under which nonindependence can cause either Type I or Type II conclusion errors.

### Conclusion

Randomized experiments in applied social research have much to recommend them. By the use of a random assignment rule, the researcher overcomes many threats to internal validity, because it is known that the assignment variable is uncorrelated with the outcome on the average. Although experimental data are typically analyzed using analysis of variance, we have shown that this analysis and the analysis of covariance are subsumed under multiple regression. Hence, randomized experimental data, like data from all of the other designs in this book, can be analyzed through the same basic analysis model that was presented in Chapter 2. Because the assignment variable is known to be uncorrelated with the outcome, it is unnecessary to control for it in order to eliminate bias in the estimate of treatment effects. This is the major difference between the analysis of randomized experiments and the analysis of the quasi-experiments that are discussed in later chapters.

Although randomized experiments are the design of choice if internal validity is to be maximized, they can be difficult to conduct. Assuring randomized assignment is often an arduous task. Making sure that all subjects stay in the design may be quite difficult. Perhaps most important, the control that is necessary for randomized experiments may be difficult to achieve in applied settings. It may be quite hard to justify a random assignment variable to a program staff that sees differential need for the treatment. Even if justified, such a rule may be difficult to carry out. In addition, maintaining the necessary control may have deleterious effects on both conclusion and construct validities, as we pointed out in the last chapter. Thus, although randomized experiments are to be preferred from the point of view of internal validity, other designs may be more useful in settings where efficiency or the other research validities are crucial.

# 5

# The regression discontinuity design

The magic of the experiment works because treatment groups that are formed using a random assignment rule should in principle score just about the same on the dependent variable in the absence of treatment effects. Thus, with a large number of subjects, the mean for the treatment and comparison subjects should be virtually the same. If the means are different, then a treatment effect is indicated. The principle of the regression discontinuity design is that groups which are different by a *known amount* should score the same after a *rational adjustment* strategy if again there is no treatment effect. This design stands as a bridge between the randomized experiment and the quasi-experimental designs discussed in the next three chapters. It is like the randomized experiment in that the assignment rule is explicitly known. It is like a quasi-experiment in that random assignment is not employed. The groups are thus not equivalent, and so some form of adjustment on the basis of prior information is necessary.

The defining characteristic of the regression discontinuity design is that the assignment rule is known. The researcher knows exactly on what basis persons are assigned to groups. The typical assignment rule in this design is as follows: Those scoring above or equal to a certain value on some pre treatment measure will receive the treatment, and those who score below the value will not receive the treatment. For instance, receipt of a National Merit Scholarship is awarded in the following way: All those scoring above a given value receive a scholarship, whereas those scoring below that value do not receive a scholarship. We shall refer to the value on the pre-treatment measure that separates the two groups as the *cutting point*. A cutting point on a test has been used to admit students to higher learning in a number of countries. Cutting points are being increasingly applied in order to determine eligibility for government subsidies. For instance, federal money for Medicaid in the United States depends on a person's income. For Medicaid as well as other social programs, it is those who score below the cutting point who are treated. A treatment that is awarded to low scorers is usually a compensatory one, because variables are normally scaled in such a way that more of the variable means having more of some social good. The treatment, therefore, is given to those who have less. To ease presentation, we assume throughout that the assignment is *not* compensatory; that is, those *above* the cutting point receive the treatment and those below are untreated. All of what we say, however, is equally applicable to a compensatory assignment plan.

In the regression discontinuity design, the assignment rule is exactly known rather than approximately known. This design does *not* include cases in which the researcher has only hunches about what the assignment variable is. For instance, an evaluation of a weight-reduction program may include a measure of the desire to lose weight. We might think that this motivational variable is the assignment variable, but it would be a mistake to employ the procedures we describe in this chapter to estimate treatment effects. First, even if motivation were the assignment variable, then the true motivation of the subjects would cause assignment rather than the researcher's measure of motivation. Second, there would surely be other causes of assignment besides motivation. To act as if motivation were the only source of assignment is to ignore the complexity of the matter. Other designs should be employed (see Chapters 6 and 8). Uncontrolled assignment is not the topic of this chapter.

The reader should be warned that a post hoc or pseudoregression discontinuity design is not appropriate. By a pseudoregression discontinuity design we mean a design where the researcher, after initially *uncontrolled* assignment to treatments, throws out all those untreated subjects scoring above an arbitrarily fixed cutting point and all those treatment subjects scoring below that value. Such a "design" should not be analyzed by the procedures discussed in this chapter, because the assignment variable is not known.

At a minimum, there are three variables that must be considered in the regression discontinuity design. First, there is the known assignment variable, $Z$. We shall denote the value that is the cutting point as $Z_0$. For reasons to be discussed later, the assignment variable should be measured on an interval scale and should have at least three levels. Frequently, this assignment variable is a pretreatment measure of the outcome variable, that is, a pretest. However, any variable that is measured prior to treatment adminis-

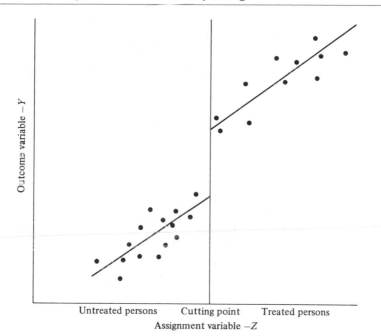

Figure 5.1. A scatter diagram from a regression discontinuity design.

tration may be used. For instance, income level could be used for assignment to a health clinic. The assignment variable is typically a measure of deservingness. Those who score higher on it are thought to be more deserving of the treatment. The second variable is a dichotomous treatment variable, $X$, which equals one for those who are treated and zero for those who do not receive the treatment. Because the assignment variable determines treatment condition, it is necessarily related to the treatment variable; however, the relationship is not perfect. The third variable to be considered is the outcome variable, $Y$, a variable on which we expect treatment effects. As will be discussed, the form of the outcome's *relationship* to the assignment variable must be specified in advance.

The basic descriptive result of the classical regression discontinuity design is the simple scatter diagram between assignment and outcome variables. Suppose that the assignment variable is a personnel test, the outcome is job performance, and the treatment is a raise. A vertical line is drawn through the cutting point, $Z_0$, as in Figure 5.1. Next, *parallel* regression lines are separately fitted to the data for those scoring below $Z_0$ and those above $Z_0$. One simply regresses job performance on the personnel test for each of the two groups and pools or averages the slope. (The assumptions of linearity and common slopes or parallelism will be relaxed in the second part of this chapter.) Finally, one extrapolates both lines to the point $Z_0$. The difference in $Y$ between the lines at this point is the measure of the treatment effect.

A more direct method of extrapolating the regression lines for treated and untreated subjects to the cutting point is available through the estimation of a single regression equation:

$$Y = b_0 + b_1 Z + b_2 X + e \tag{5.1}$$

which is fitted to all the data points, from both treated and untreated subjects.[1] Thus, the outcome variable is regressed on the assignment variable and the treatment variable. This regression equation yields a predicted value of $Y$ for persons at $Z_0$, in both treated and untreated conditions. If we set $X$ equal to zero in this equation, therefore looking at untreated subjects, their predicted $Y$ at $Z_0$ is

$$b_0 + b_1 Z_0$$

For the treated subjects, setting $X$ equal to one, the predicted $Y$ at $Z_0$ is

$$b_0 + b_1 Z_0 + b_2$$

The difference between these two extrapolations is $b_2$, the coefficient for $X$, which is the effect of treatment.

Given parallel slopes, the estimate of the treatment effect, $b_2$, can also be viewed as the difference between the $Y$ intercepts of the comparison and the treatment groups. The intercept for the comparison group is simply $b_0$ and $b_0 + b_2$ for the treated group. The test that $b_2 = 0$ evaluates whether one or two regression lines are needed. If $b_2$ is not needed, then only a single line need be fitted. If $b_2$ is needed, two lines with the same slope but different intercepts are fitted. The difference between these two intercepts is the measure of treatment effect and, therefore, the test that $b_2$ equals zero evaluates whether or not there is a treatment effect.

The idea behind the regression discontinuity design is the "tie-breaking experiment" (see Campbell & Stanley, 1963, p. 63).

---

[1] To increase the interpretability of the intercept, it is advisable to use $Z - Z_0$ and not $Z$. If $Z - Z_0$ is used, then the intercept refers to the predicted value for the controls at the cutting point.

Table 5.1. *Nonlinear functional form:* $Y = 2Z + .5Z^2$

| Person | Z | Y |
|---|---|---|
| Untreated | | |
| 1 | .5 | 1.125 |
| 2 | 1.0 | 2.500 |
| 3 | 1.5 | 4.125 |
| Treated | | |
| 4 | 2.0 | 6.000 |
| 5 | 3.0 | 10.500 |
| 6 | 4.0 | 16.000 |

Imagine a large number of persons scoring at the cutting point $Z_0$. Suppose that half the persons are randomly assigned to the treatment group and the other half to the comparison group. We would have then a randomized experiment, albeit of limited generalizability because we have only observed subjects at $Z_0$. To broaden the generalization we would expect those scoring just above $Z_0$ to have about the same score on $Y$ as those scoring just below $Z_0$, assuming no treatment effects. For those scoring some distance above and below $Z_0$, we would not expect them to score the same on the outcome measure in the absence of treatment effects. Therefore, some adjustment procedure is necessary to detect treatment effects. The most natural adjustment is a linear one.

The form of the adjustment, for example, linear, is not a matter of simple convenience, but depends on the assumed relationship between the assignment variable and the outcome variable; that is, it should reflect the true underlying relationship between $Z$ and $Y$. If the true relationship is linear, then the adjustment should be linear. If the true relationship is more complex (e.g., quadratic), the adjustment strategy should be equally complex. For the six scores in Table 5.1, the data were generated by setting $Y = 2Z + .5Z^2$. In other words, the outcome variable is a perfect quadratic function of the assignment variable. Setting the cutting point at 1.75 and fitting a *linear* regression line, we obtain the result

$$Y = -2.02 + 4.6Z - .95X + e$$

A spurious treatment effect of $-.95$ is indicated because we failed to fit the correct functional form between $Z$ and $Y$. This example then illustrates that to employ the regression discontinuity design validly, the researcher must know that $Z$ relates to $Y$ linearly and to the same degree for both treated and untreated subjects.

Our approach to the regression discontinuity, as with other designs, is to estimate a single regression equation. We do not recommend analyzing the observations separately above and below the cutting point. Such double extrapolation procedures are typically inefficient, unparsimonious, and awkward.

Before we turn our attention to the complexities of this design, we shall briefly consider two points of historical importance. First, the estimation procedures that were considered by Thistlethwaite and Campbell (1960) are less efficient than the regression procedure we have discussed, although they arrive at similar conclusions. Second, if we fit separate regression lines for the two groups, one might think that in the absence of treatment effects the two regression lines would not meet at $Z_0$. Because of regression toward the mean, the lines would tilt so that the "top" line would be above the "bottom" line. This view, stated by Campbell (1969), is in fact wrong, because the lines do intersect when there are no treatment effects.

## Complexities of design and analysis

The regression discontinuity design is simple and elegant. However, if we are practical we must realize that various complexities preclude a simple analysis. First, there may be more than just the three variables we have mentioned: treatment, assignment variable, and outcome variable. We must then consider multiple outcome variables, covariates, multiple assignment variables, and multiple treatment variables. Second, the specification of linear, parallel lines for treated and control subjects may not be true. Third, more complicated assignment rules are possible. Fourth, various factors affect the power or conclusion validity of the design.

### *Multiple variables*

Classically, the discussion of the regression discontinuity design considers only three variables: the assignment variable, the outcome variable, and a dichotomous treatment variable. It is difficult to imagine that a researcher would implement the design with only these three variables. In practice, there are usually many more. First, there are typically a set of covariates. These variables do not affect assignment but may be correlated with the assignment variable. Examples of common covariates are age, sex, and ethnicity. Second, the outcome variable is not usually a single variable. Rather, there are a whole host of outcome variables. Third, the treatment variable need not be a simple dichotomy. Fourth, the assignment variable itself may be a multivariate composite.

*Covariates.* Most researchers routinely gather data on a set of covariates. For instance, it is standard practice in educational research to measure age, sex, ethnicity, parental socioeconomic status, grade in school, and the like. These variables are called covariates. In the context of the regression discontinuity design, a covariate (1) must not be the assignment variable, and (2) must not be caused by the outcome variable. Although each covariate is not the assignment variable, it may well be correlated with it. For instance, a score on a reading test may be used as the assignment variable. We would expect that age, a potential covariate, would be highly correlated with the test, although age itself is not the assignment variable. To ensure that the covariate is not caused by the outcome variable, either (1) the covariate should be measured before or simultaneously with the assignment variable;[2] or (2) if measured after assignment, it should be an unchanging variable like sex or ethnicity.

The purpose of including covariates is to increase the conclusion validity of the research. For a randomized experiment, any covariate should, on the average, be uncorrelated with the treatment. For the regression discontinuity design, the covariate may be correlated with the treatment, but its partial correlation with the treatment, controlling for the assignment variable, should on the average be zero. Without covariates the design produces unbiased (internally valid) results; with covariates the results are more efficient (higher conclusion validity).

The presence of multiple covariates creates no special problems for the regression discontinuity analysis. They can simply be added to the regression equation. For instance, Seaver and Quarton (1973) investigated the effect of being on the dean's list. Grade-point average for one semester determined who was put on the dean's list, and therefore it was the assignment variable. The outcome variable

---

[2] If a variable is assumed to cause the outcome variable but is measured after the treatment has been administered, *in some very special circumstances,* as discussed in Chapter 10, the variable can be used as a covariate.

was grade-point average the next semester. Although they did not, Seaver and Quarton (1973) could have controlled for sex, age, year in college, and the like.

*Multiple dependent variables.* Ordinarily there is not one but a series of outcome variables. For instance, in the Thistlethwaite and Campbell (1960) investigation of the effect of being a National Merit finalist, a number of outcome variables were investigated. The typical strategy for investigating such cases is to examine each variable one at a time. Such a strategy may adversely affect conclusion validity, as explained in Chapter 4. We briefly outline four different and potentially more powerful alternatives.

The first is the repeated measures analysis of variance, which was discussed in Chapter 4. This procedure in effect simply takes the mean of the outcome variables and treats it as the only outcome. Such a procedure is advisable only when the variables have the same unit of measurement.

The second way to analyze multiple outcomes is to use a multivariate analysis of covariance. The covariates must include the assignment variable and, in addition, other covariates can be included to increase power. The treatment is the independent variable in the multivariate analysis, and the dependent variable in the analysis is a weighted sum of the set of outcome variables, where the weights are chosen empirically to maximize the variance explained by the treatment. Such a strategy is advisable when the researcher is uncertain about how the treatment affects the constellation of dependent variables, which is to say, the construct validity of the outcomes is uncertain.

The third strategy is to factor analyze the outcome measures. If a meaningful solution arises, then the regression discontinuity analysis can proceed on the smaller number of derived factor scores. Either the factor scores can be analyzed one at a time, or a multivariate analysis can be employed. Factor analysis is advisable if the measures tap a relatively small number of constructs, and if the researcher has hypotheses concerning how the treatment differentially affects these constructs.

The fourth strategy is closely related to the third. It involves setting up a structural model in which the outcome variables are not single measures or even factor scores but unmeasured constructs themselves. Assume, for instance, that we are examining the effect of an enrichment program for gifted children. This program might cause a change in two constructs, cognitive skill and affect. Each of

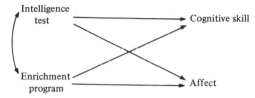

Figure 5.2. A structural model of treatment effects.

these is measured by three indicators ($C_1$, $C_2$, $C_3$ and $A_1$, $A_2$, $A_3$). The children are assigned to the treatment on the basis of an intelligence test. The effect of the treatment, controlling for the assignment variable, on the outcome constructs is depicted in Figure 5.2. The structural modeling approach, introduced in Chapter 9, estimates these effects in the following way. First, a confirmatory factor analysis of the outcome variables is conducted, forcing the two-factor solution in Table 5.2, where zero denotes a loading that is forced to be zero and x denotes a loading that is free to take on any value. The test of this factor structure establishes the construct validity of the outcome variables. Then, using the *correlations* of the cognitive and affective factors with the treatment and assignment variable, the treatment effect is estimated using multiple regression. Actually, the two steps of factor analysis and multiple regression are done simultaneously. This strategy is advisable only if the researcher has a theoretical model specifying which variable loads on which factor and a moderate to large sample size.

*Multiple treatment variables.* When we think of experiments, we usually think of two groups: a treatment group and a comparison group. In reality, as we saw in Chapter 4, most experiments contain many more groups. In the first place, the effects of more than one variable are usually investigated simultaneously. Standard practice for such experiments is to combine the levels of two or more independent variables factorially. In the second place, multiple levels of a single treatment variable may be used. In applied settings the researcher is usually not satisfied in measuring only two levels of the treatment variable, because with only two levels the generalization to other levels of the independent variable is restricted.

For the regression discontinuity design the effects of both multiple independent variables and multilevel independent variables can be estimated by multiple regression using the procedures described

Table 5.2. *Two-factor model of outcomes*

| Variable | Construct[a] | |
| --- | --- | --- |
| | Cognitive skill | Affect |
| $C_1$ | x | 0 |
| $C_2$ | x | 0 |
| $C_3$ | x | 0 |
| $A_1$ | 0 | x |
| $A_2$ | 0 | x |
| $A_3$ | 0 | x |

[a]Zero indicates a loading fixed at zero, and x denotes a free loading.

in Chapter 4. There is one special complication that does occur for the regression discontinuity design. If there are three or more treatment groups, a single cutting point is not possible. We shall return to this problem in the section on assignment rules.

*Multivariate assignment rules.* The assignment variable need not be a single variable. It may be some function of a set of variables, such as a linear composite. For instance, admission to some law schools is determined by 200 times the grade-point average plus LSAT score. If such a variable is to serve as an assignment variable, then every person's score must be created by the same rule. As always, the assignment variable enters the regression equation.[3]

### Functional form specification

The analysis of the regression discontinuity design rests on the adequacy of the adjustment strategy. One must specify the functional form of the relationship between the assignment variable and the dependent variable. Below we consider two sources of incorrect specification.

*Nonlinear function form.* As was illustrated in Table 5.1, if the relationship between the assignment variable ($Z$) and the

---

[3] If a linear composite is used to form an assignment variable, it is advisable to use as covariates all but one variable (which one does not matter) of those used to form the composite. If all the variables are used, then perfect multicollinearity results.

outcome variable ($Y$) within levels of the treatment ($X$) is non-linear, the researcher might reach an incorrect conclusion concerning treatment effects if the relationship was assumed to be linear. However, if the researcher knew the relationship between $Z$ and $Y$ to be quadratic, he or she could specify a quadratic term and estimate treatment effects with the following regression equation:

$$Y = b_0 + b_1 Z + b_2 Z^2 + b_3 X + e$$

If the functional form between $Z$ and $Y$ cannot be specified in advance, one might attempt to derive it empirically by polynomial regression [including terms such as $Z^3$, $Z^4$, and so on (Cohen & Cohen, 1975)]. That is, the researcher fits various regression equations to the data, using various powers of $Z$ as independent variables, in order to assess the degree of polynomial relation between $Z$ and $Y$. The problem is that the exact degree of polynomial can rarely be specified in advance, and there are different risks between either underfitting or overfitting the polynomial. If the polynomial is underfitted, that is, if $Z$ and $Y$ are related by a higher-order polynomial than is estimated in the regression equation, then the estimate of treatment effects may be biased. If the polynomial is overfitted, that is, if higher-order powers of $Z$ are included in the regression equation, there is a decrease in conclusion validity (greater tendency toward Type II errors) without any bias in the estimate of treatment effects. In other words, finding the correct polynomial relation between $Z$ and $Y$ involves a potential trade-off between internal and conclusion validity. If too low a polynomial is fitted, internal validity may be low as the treatment effect estimate may be biased. If too high a polynomial is fitted, conclusion validity is reduced. As was stated in Chapter 3, we take no a priori position on trade-offs between research validities, and hence on the relative merits of over- and underfitting in this case. In some contexts, internal validity is of the essence and overfitting is preferable. In other contexts, conclusion validity is the top priority and so underfitting is preferable. However, given moderate to large sample sizes, we see little danger in overfitting.

If the relationship between the assignment variable and the outcome is nonlinear, it may be possible to transform either variable and in the process "straighten out" the functional relationship (Mosteller & Tukey, 1977).

*Nonparallel regressions.* It may be that the regression of $Y$

on $Z$ differs in the treatment groups. This condition, called *non-parallel regressions,* means that the treatment and the assignment variable interact. For instance, if the slope for the treated subjects were steeper than the slope for the untreated subjects, we would say that those who scored higher on the assignment variable benefited more from the treatment. We saw in Chapter 4 that the procedure for estimating interactions in multiple regression is to enter the product of the variables into the equation. If the assignment variable and treatment interacted, we would specify an equation of the following form:

$$Y = b_0 + b_1 Z + b_2 X + b_3 ZX + e \qquad (5.2)$$

In this equation the treatment effect changes with the value of the assignment variable. For instance, if $b_2 = 1$ and $b_3 = .2$, then the treatment effect would be $1 + .2Z$. Hence, at the following different values of $Z$ we would obtain different estimates of the treatment effect:

$$
\begin{array}{lll}
Z = \ \ 1: & 1 + (.2)(1) & = 1.2 \\
Z = \ \ 5: & 1 + (.2)(5) & = 2.0 \\
Z = 10: & 1 + (.2)(10) & = 3.0
\end{array}
$$

If the relationship between $Z$ and $Y$ is nonlinear, the nonlinear interaction terms (e.g., $XZ^2$, $XZ^3$) must be included. In a later section we discuss procedures for testing and interpreting interactions in multiple regression.

In practice, it is difficult to distinguish a nonparallel regression from a nonlinear relationship between the assignment variable and the outcome. For the regression discontinuity design, the explanations of nonlinearity and interaction are virtually confounded. Consider the graphs in Figure 5.3. The slope for the treated subjects is steeper than for the untreated subjects for both graphs. However, the nonlinearity of Figure 5.3a is difficult to distinguish from the nonparallel regression in Figure 5.3b, given the typically noisy data and small to moderate sample sizes we have in the social sciences.[4] The choice of which explanation to prefer depends on the plausibility of each given the nature of particular variables under study.

In addition to treatment by assignment variable interactions, there may also be treatment by covariate interactions. These should

---

[4] The power to detect nonlinear trends depends on the range of the predictor variable. Because nonlinearity is measured within levels of $X$, the amount of nonlinearity is measured separately below and above the cutting point. Thus the range is considerably narrowed.

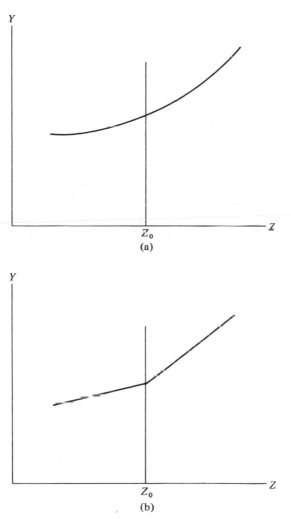

Figure 5 3  (a) Nonlinearity and (b) interaction.

be estimated by the appropriate product terms in the regression equation.

### Complex assignment rules

*Probabilistic assignment.* We have so far considered only a deterministic rule. All those scoring above the cutting point receive the treatment and all those who score below do not. The rule could be probabilistic. For instance, among those who score above $Z_0$, 80% receive the treatment and 20% are untreated, whereas among those scoring below the cutting point, 80% are untreated and 20% are treated. Unlike the typical regression discontinuity design, one can here compare treatment effects within those above and those below the cutting point, and so the design is actually a randomized experiment or, more exactly, a variation on a randomized blocks design as discussed in Chapter 4.

This probabilistic rule is actually a mixture of two different assignment rules. The variable $Z$ is an assignment variable, because persons scoring above $Z_0$ are more likely to receive the treatment than those who score below $Z_0$. The assignment rule is also in part random. Thus the assignment rule contains both known and random aspects. In such cases one must control for the known assignment variable either by linear adjustment or by blocking (Rubin, 1977).

Assignment can also be based on a known variable and an unknown variable. Consider a program to help gifted children. Eligibility to the program is determined by having an IQ above 150. For reasons that are not clear, however, some persons with IQs greater than 150 are not in the program whereas others with IQs less than 150 are in the program. An IQ of 150 is said to be a "fuzzy" cutting point (Cook & Campbell, 1979). Thus assignment to the program depends on more than just the child's IQ. Relatively little work has been done on this problem of a mixture of known and unknown assignment variables. We can, however, offer a few suggestions. First, in all analyses one should control for the known assignment variable. Second, if the percentage of misclassifications is small (say, less than 5%), one might exclude the misclassified cases and proceed as if the design were a regression discontinuity design. Third, one should never take a variable that is only presumed to be an assignment variable and use it to derive a posteriori the assignment rule. The presence of unknown assignment rules necessitates the procedures discussed in Chapters 6 and 8.

*Multiple cutting points.* The regression discontinuity design is not limited to either a dichotomous treatment variable or a single cutting point on the assignment variable. Consider a day-care center that has three programs. For various reasons age must be used as the assignment variable. We might imagine the following plan:

| Program | Assignment variable score |
|---------|---------------------------|
| A | 2-year-olds |
| B | 3-year-olds |
| C | 4-year-olds |

Another way we might have multiple cutting points is to combine both probabilistic and deterministic assignment rules. Given two treatments, A and B, we might employ the following rule:

| Treatment level | Assignment variable score |
|-----------------|---------------------------|
| 100% A | Below 25 |
| 50% A; 50% B | 26–50 |
| 100% B | Above 50 |

For this assignment plan, a randomized experiment is conducted across the middle range of the assignment variable (26–50). The extremes on the assignment variable show the typical regression discontinuity pattern. This plan might be used when extremely needy subjects must receive the treatment, and those less needy do not deserve the treatment. Those in the middle, whose status is uncertain, would be assigned randomly. The design is useful if it is unethical to withhold treatments from the very needy and to give a scarce treatment to those with little need.

Finally, consider the following assignment plan:

| Treatment level | Assignment variable score |
|-----------------|---------------------------|
| A | Below 30 |
| B | 30–45 |
| A | Above 45 |

The purpose of this assignment plan is to make the treatment–assignment variable relationship curvilinear. The simple correlation between the two should be low. This low correlation increases the power of the test of treatment effects, as is discussed in a later section.


*Special cases.* Earlier it was stated that the assignment variable must be measured on an interval scale. We consider here some limiting cases of assignment variables. First, suppose that the assignment variable were a dichotomy. For example, all the males receive the treatment and the females serve as comparison subjects.

In such a case there is a total confounding between the assignment variable (sex) and the treatment. If our regression strategy were employed, it would break down because of perfect multicollinearity. Thus, a dichotomy cannot serve as a deterministic assignment rule.

Consider another example in which subjects above (or below) the cutting point all score the same on the assignment variable. For instance, a scholarship is given only to those who obtain a perfect score on a test. The analysis is still possible, because the slope (either linear or nonlinear) can be estimated from those who score below the cutting point. We cannot estimate the slope for those above the cutting point, but given the assumption of parallel regressions we can still proceed. The power of such a design would tend to be limited, and it would be impossible to test for nonparallel slopes.

The minimum number of levels of the assignment variable is three for the regression discontinuity design. This minimum was employed in a quasi-experimental evaluation of the Salk vaccine for polio (Meier, 1972). The vaccine was given to second graders while first and third graders served as controls. The design has a known assignment rule (i.e., grade) and a specified functional relationship (i.e., linear) between grade and the probability of contracting polio. Moreover, the strength of that linear relationship can be measured using the first and third graders. The prediction is that for the case of no effect, the second grade should fall halfway between the first and third graders. The problem with the design is that because there are only two levels of the assignment variable for the untreated subjects, the linearity assumption cannot be tested. When the results of this study were compared with a randomized experiment, the linearity assumption was only approximately true and the effectiveness of the vaccine was seriously underestimated in the regression discontinuity design.[5]

### Conclusion validity

Although the inferences drawn from a regression discontinuity design are almost as valid as those from a randomized experiment, there are costs. In particular, the conclusion validity in a regression discontinuity design is lower than in an experiment. If the assignment variable is normally distributed and the cutting point is at its

---

[5] Other, more serious problems occurred with this quasi-experimental study (see Gilbert, Light, & Mosteller, 1975).

mean, the regression discontinuity design requires many more subjects than a randomized experiment to achieve equal power (Goldberger, 1972). As the cutting point becomes extreme, power is further decreased. This lowered power is due to the built-in collinearity between the assignment variable and the treatment.

The type of assignment rule plays an important role in determining power. As we have already said, the more uneven the sizes of the treatment groups, the lower the power. Although this is also the case for randomized experiments, it is even more so for the regression discontinuity design. The reduced power is a function of the correlation between the treatment and the assignment variable. Assignment rules that reduce this correlation increase power. For instance, the assignment rule that we discussed previously, in which the two extreme groups serve as comparison groups and the middle group is treated, reduces this correlation. In fact, the worst rule (given a linear relationship between $Z$ and $Y$) in terms of conclusion validity is one with a single cutting point.

If the assignment variable does not relate to the outcome measure, it might be dropped from the regression equation. This would lead to an increase in power, with the risk of introducing some bias.

One advantage of the design over other quasi-experimental designs is that the partial correlation of the treatment with the covariates controlling for the assignment variable is zero. The use of covariates when they share no unique variance with the treatments, just as in randomized experiments, is optimal for increasing statistical power.

### Complex regression equations

Given interactions and covariates, the simple regression equation becomes much more complex. We must consider how to set up, sequentially test, and interpret such equations.

Let us consider in some detail an example illustrating how the multiple regression equation is set up and sequentially tested when interactions and a covariate are present. A researcher wishes to evaluate the effectiveness of an intensive drug rehabilitation program. Persons are assigned to the program on the basis of a pre-treatment measure of drug consumption. The cutting point on this variable is 4.0. The outcome variable is drug consumption measured 6 months after the program has ended. The researcher wishes to estimate the effect of treatment $(X)$, a covariate, sex $(S)$, pre-treatment consumption $(Z)$, and their interactions on post-treatment consumption $(Y)$.

The interactions $XS$, $XZ$, $SZ$, and $XSZ$ can be computed by forming product terms as was described in the previous chapter. Testing proceeds in a hierarchical fashion. For the first equation one regresses $Y$ on $X$, $S$, $Z$, $XS$, $XZ$, $SZ$, and $XSZ$. One tests *only* the highest-order interaction, in this case $XSZ$, and if it is significant, one interprets the results of that equation. (Interpretation is discussed later in this section.)

If the highest-order interaction is not significant, one drops it from the regression equation, and for the second step in the hierarchy one regresses the outcome variable on the remaining effects. For our example one would regress $Y$ on $X$, $S$, $Z$, $XS$, $XZ$, and $SZ$. At this step one tests *only* the set of highest-order interactions remaining in the equation: $XS$, $XZ$, and $SZ$ for our example. If they are all significant, one stops and interprets the equation.

If one or more of the interactions tested in the second step is not significant, one drops it or them from the equation and estimates a third equation. So if $XS$ and $XZ$ are significant, but $SZ$ is not, one would regress $Y$ on $X$, $S$, $Z$, $XS$, and $XZ$. One then tests from the third equation the main effects $(X, S,$ and $Z)$ of those terms that are *not* included as components in any interaction in this equation. So, for example, if only $XS$ is included in the third equation, one would test only $Z$; or if no interaction was included, one would test $X$, $S$, and $Z$; or if $XS$ and $XZ$ were included, one would test no main effects. If all of the *tested* main effects are significant, one stops and interprets the equation.

If some of the tested main effects in the third equation are nonsignificant, one deletes them and estimates a fourth equation. At this point this final equation is interpreted.

One always moves down to the next order of interaction and drops terms tested in the previous step that are not significant. One then tests terms at that order of interaction whose components are not included in the higher-order interactions that remain in the equation. If all the terms tested at that step are significant, one stops and interprets. If not, one moves down to the next order of interaction and repeats the procedure. This procedure can be accomplished only by a series of multiple regression runs, each based on the previous run, hence the name *hierarchical regression*.

Table 5.3. *Regression equation for Y under alternative coding schemes*

|  | Coding of assignment variable | |
|---|---|---|
| Coding of *X* and *S* | *Z* | *Z'* |
| Dummy | $4.0 + .5Z + .5X + 2.0S - 1.0XS - .25XZ + e$ | $6.0 + .5Z' - .5X + 2.0S - 1.0XS - .25XZ' + e$ |
| Effects | $5.0 + .375Z + 0.00X + .75S - .25XS - .125XZ + e$ | $6.5 + .375Z' - .5X + .75S - .25XS - .125XZ' + e$ |

It cannot be stressed strongly enough that *hierarchical regression is not stepwise regression.*

The result of these hierarchical regressions is a trimmed regression equation. The coding of the variables affects the coefficients in equations. The coding does not, however, affect whether or not a given variable remains in the final trimmed equation. So, for the example, no matter how we coded $X$, $S$, or $Z$, the terms that are dropped do not change.

Although the terms in the trimmed equation are invariant with respect to coding schemes, the coefficients, including the intercept, are not. Table 5.3 shows under alternative coding schemes a hypothetical trimmed regression equation. Two different coding schemes, described in the previous chapter, were used for $X$ and $S$. The first is *dummy coding.* Females and treated subjects were given a value of one on $S$ and $X$, respectively, and males and untreated subjects a value of zero. The second type of coding used was *effects coding:* Females and treated subjects were given a $+1$, whereas males and untreated subjects were given a $-1$. The assignment variable is also coded in two ways, first in its raw metric or $Z$ and second as deviations around the cutting point: $Z' = Z - 4.0$.

As can be seen in Table 5.3, the coding scheme of the variables does affect the coefficients of the regression equation. They change sign, become larger and smaller, and go to zero. Even though these changes are dramatic, we should realize that the four equations in Table 5.3 are in fact the same equation. They all have the same $R^2$, yield the same predicted values of $Y$, and each can be derived mathematically from the other. The predicted values of all four equations are given in Table 5.4. Because they are fundamentally

Table 5.4. *Predicted values generated by the regression equations of Table 5.3*

|  | Z = 4.0 | |
|  | Untreated | Treated |
|---|---|---|
| Male | 6.0 | 5.5 |
| Female | 8.0 | 6.5 |

|  | Z = 8.0 | |
|  | Untreated | Treated |
|---|---|---|
| Male | 8.0 | 6.5 |
| Female | 10.0 | 7.5 |

the same equation, the choice between the various coding schemes rests on meaningfulness and ease of interpretation, a topic to which we now turn.

We strongly urge that for continuous variables like $Z$, researchers subtract off "a typical value," especially when such variables are entered into product terms. When the variable is an assignment variable, then the logical "typical value" is the cutting point. For other variables one might choose the sample mean, median, or mode. Although it is not necessary to subtract off a typical value (Cohen, 1978), it definitely increases the meaningfulness of various coefficients. Consider, for example, a program in a nursing home in which admission is solely a function of age, say, 70. If one were to evaluate the effects of the nursing home and enter the age by treatment product term and not subtract off a typical value, the coefficient for treatment estimates the treatment effect for newborns! Obviously such an extrapolation to babies in a study of elderly people is meaningless. Using age minus 70 would give an estimate of the effect for those aged 70. This would seem more sensible.

We do not take a position on the relative merits of dummy versus effects coding. Rather we urge researchers to understand how each should be interpreted. Returning to Table 5.3, we see that the effect of sex using dummy coding refers to the sex difference for untreated subjects (see Table 5.4), whereas using effects coding the coefficient for sex is one-half of the average difference between males and females. The coefficient for the $SX$ interaction measures under dummy coding the additional impact of the treatment for females. Under effects coding the interaction coefficient is one-half of the difference between the treatment effect for males and the treatment effect for females.

To aid in the interpretation of the coefficients, one can graph the results as was done in Chapter 4. One can also set up a table of predicted values as was done in Table 5.4. The values in the table were obtained by substituting values for the predictors in the equations of Table 5.3. For instance, the predicted score for male and treated subjects whose score on $Z$ is 4.0 is

$$5.5 = 4.0 + .5(4.0) + .5(1.0) + 2.0(0.0) - 1.0(0.0) - .25(4.0)$$

given dummy coding and $Z$ in the raw metric.

### Conclusion

The regression discontinuity design, a design that has a known assignment rule, yields internally valid results when the researcher can specify the functional relationship between the assignment variable and the outcome variable. Bias-free results emerge because we can control for the assignment variable in estimating treatment effects.

The regression discontinuity design has received careful technical attention, but it has been underutilized in applied social research. Although it has been used in archival studies, the design has rarely been chosen to evaluate new programs. There are two reasons for this underutilization. First, if decision makers can be convinced of the necessity of a universally applied assignment rule, they can often be convinced of the need for random assignment. Once an assignment rule is defined explicitly, it can seem arbitrary and in some cases unfair. Hence, it often happens that in cases where regression discontinuity designs are feasible, so too are randomized experiments, and the latter are undertaken. The second reason for the underutilization of the design is the requirement of universal application of the rule. Even though legislation may impose cutoffs for eligibility, these may be waived for political, administrative, or ethical reasons. Thus the rule may not be applied universally.

Nevertheless, the design is a useful alternative for the applied social researcher. Dawes (1979) highly recommends the use of cutoffs for admission to schools and for hiring. He claims that such rules are both fairer and are more efficient than any other admission procedure. If such rules become more common, the design may be used much more in the future.

# 6

# The nonequivalent control group design

If the researcher cannot control assignment to the treatment and comparison groups, then subjects in the two groups can be expected to differ. Therefore, even in the absence of treatment effects, the comparison and treatment groups may not score the same on outcome measures. In order both to assess how nonequivalent the groups are and to allow for possible adjustment to make the groups equivalent, the subjects are pretested. The *nonequivalent control group design* is defined by a pretest and an unknown assignment rule. The design has been used to evaluate the first year of *Sesame Street* (Ball & Bogatz, 1970), manpower training programs (Hardin & Borus, 1971), and a variety of other programs. The nonequivalent control group design, the archetypal quasi-experimental design, is often the most internally valid design that many researchers can implement in applied settings. Very often the only alternative to it is a post-only correlational study, discussed in Chapter 9.

There are a variety of ways to form the two groups in the nonequivalent control group design. The first and most common procedure is to use groups that were formed naturally prior to the research. Campbell and Stanley (1963) originally viewed the design as one in which two intact groups were assigned randomly to the treatment and the comparison conditions. More typically, one group is slated to receive a treatment and a second classroom, school, hospital, or city is used for comparison. Usually an effort is made to ensure that the comparison group is roughly equivalent to the treated group, for example, same grade, same socioeconomic status, same area, and so on. Such attempts to match on relevant variables do not change the fact that we still have a nonequivalent control group design. They do, however, strengthen the design.

Another way of forming the treatment and comparison groups is to have a clearly definable pool of possible program participants. From that pool a subset either volunteer for the program or are chosen by the staff. The remainder of the subjects or a subset are not treated. Quite clearly those who are not treated differ from the treated in some unknown way.

A final way is to examine only the treated subjects, but to compare those subjects who received large amounts of the treatment with those who received small amounts. Such an approach becomes necessary when the comparison group ends up receiving the treatment, as happened to the comparison group for the evaluation of *Sesame Street* (Ball & Bogatz, 1970). It is also useful when the treated group receives differing amounts of treatment.

An essential feature of the design is a pretest and a posttest. The same construct is measured on the same subjects at two points in time. If we give the same name to both the pretest and posttest, we believe them to be measures of the same construct. What do we mean when we say that we have measured the *same* construct at two time points? Consider evidence that would suggest we have not. Infant "intelligence" tests typically correlate with sensory motor skills, whereas childhood intelligence measures typically correlate with cognitive skills. This has caused some researchers to doubt that they measure the same construct. Construct validation (see Chapter 3) requires two measures to show the same pattern of covariation with other measures. Such a pattern would imply that the constellation of causes for the pretest is the same as the constellation for the posttest.

The essential difficulty in the nonequivalent control group design is that the assignment rule is neither known nor random. To analyze the design the researcher must begin with this realization: The assignment variable is unknown and most likely unmeasured. Reasonable estimates of the treatment effect are obtainable only if assumptions can be made about the unknown and unmeasured assignment variable. There is then a necessary element of risk because assumptions must be made about an unknown variable.

For some studies that employ the nonequivalent control group design, it may seem as if we know the assignment variable. For instance, in studying the effects of a mass media campaign, Maccoby and Farquhar (1975) assigned one northern California city to be the comparison group and a second to be the treated group. Because the assignment rule is apparently the city, it seems as if we need control only for city in our analysis to estimate treatment effects. However, city is totally confounded with treatment. Technically, because of perfect multicollinearity, the effects of city and treatment cannot be estimated simultaneously. The assignment variable is apparently known and measured, but we are unable to control for it. We can consider, however, the variable city to be merely a proxy for the reasons that sort people into the different cities. For example, these variables would include occupational group, ethnicity, age, and the like. The reason for doing this is that they are not likely to be perfectly correlated with treatment.

Some might argue that the study with two cities is really a randomized experiment with $N = 2$ if cities were randomly assigned or a quasi-experiment with $N = 2$ if they were not. The basis of this argument is the rule we gave in Chapter 4 that the unit of analysis should be the unit of assignment. However, to follow such a rule in this case sacrifices conclusion validity for the sake of internal validity. With only two cases there is no estimate of error, making significance tests impossible.

We may sometimes suspect that the assignment variable has been measured. We have what might be called a presumed assignment variable. In other cases, we might suspect that assignment is virtually random. In both cases the pretest can be regressed on the treatment and any presumed assignment variables. If these variables include the actual assignment variable, or if the assignment were random, the treatment variable should have a zero coefficient in this regression. Recall that once the assignment variable's effects are controlled, the residual variation in the treatment is, by definition, random. Thus, in the previously described regression equation, the treatment should share no variance with the pretest after the assignment variable is controlled. In practice this strategy has some drawbacks. First, one might be tempted to pick a presumed assignment variable from a pool of variables with the intent of identifying the assignment rule empirically. That is, one would select as the assignment rule those variables which, when included in the regression, caused the treatment effect on the pretest to be zero. Such an empirically based strategy leads to capitalization on chance and biased results. Second, it is not clear by what criterion one decides that the treatment has a zero coefficient. Suppose that the test of the effect of treatment on the pretest is a beta coefficient of .10 and yields a $t$-test of 1.00. The .10 coefficient is hardly trivial, and yet it is not statistically significant. There may well be other variables causing assignment that remain unmeasured, or some that were measured may contain error, and there is then a reasonable chance that bias would result.[1]

Typically, the background variables that a researcher assesses do not include the assignment variable nor is the assignment rule random, and so he or she cannot establish the assignment rule empirically. We are then back to the problem that the assignment variable is unknown and nonrandom. We do have a pre-treatment measure, however, and perhaps there is some way to use this measure to control for the effects of the assignment variable. Even though we do have a measure of pre-treatment differences, it is not clear how we can use the pretest to project over time how large the posttest difference between groups would be, given no treatment effects. We can argue that the "gap" between groups would remain the same, widen over time, or move closer together. Let us consider each argument.

An approach of one naive investigator to adjusting for pre-treatment differences is to expect no change over time. If the treated children are one-half a grade equivalent behind before treatment, the program would be judged a success if the gap can be narrowed.

"Not so," says a second investigator. Because of regression toward the mean, the scores of the two groups should converge over time even in the absence of treatment effects. Thus we should expect the gap to attenuate even in the absence of treatment effects.

"Quite the contrary," says a third investigator. We all know that in school, children who start out behind fall further and further behind. Thus, the gap should increase over time.

Thus, one can make strong arguments that the gap will remain constant, diminish, or even increase. Which argument is correct? The answer, we shall see, depends on how the assignment variable relates to the pretest and posttest.

---

[1] There is yet another reason why this strategy may fail: an unreliable pretest. For instance, consider a program that trains persons to operate a complex piece of machinery. If a pretest were administered and no subject had any prior experience with the machinery, pretest performance would probably be random and have zero reliability. For such a case, neither the treatment nor any other variable would correlate with the pretest. Thus a zero coefficient for the treatment in predicting the pretest mistakenly indicates random assignment. We must then make certain that our pretest measure is reliable.

### Analysis strategies

Two general types of analysis strategies compete for use in the nonequivalent control group design: regression adjustment and change score analysis. Let us designate the outcome variable as $Y_2$ and the pretest as $Y_1$. The treatment variable, $X$, is dummy coded such that $X = 1$ for the treated subjects and $X = 0$ for the untreated subjects. The general equation is

$$Y_2 = b_0 + b_1 Y_1 + b_2 X + e \tag{6.1}$$

where $e$ represents residual variation in $Y_2$. The two analysis strategies differ in the value of the coefficient for the pretest, $b_1$. The regression adjustment sets $b_1$ to be the partial regression coefficient of the posttest on the pretest controlling for treatment. Raw change score analysis simply fixes $b_1$ at one. If $b_1$ is set to one, then the equation becomes

$$Y_2 - Y_1 = b_0 + b_2 X + e$$

Which procedure is correct? Many textbooks recommend the regression approach, but many researchers still use the change score approach. As we shall see, the choice should depend on how the assignment variable is presumed to relate to the pretest and posttest.

If we solve from Equation 6.1 for the means of the treatment ($E$) and comparison ($C$) groups, we have

$$\overline{Y}_{2E} = b_0 + b_1 \overline{Y}_{1E} + b_2$$
$$\overline{Y}_{2C} = b_0 + b_1 \overline{Y}_{1C}$$

The estimate of the treatment effect in terms of the pretest and posttest means is then

$$b_2 = (\overline{Y}_{2E} - \overline{Y}_{2C}) - b_1(\overline{Y}_{1E} - \overline{Y}_{1C}) \tag{6.2}$$

Thus the treatment effect equals the posttest difference between the treatment groups subtracting out or adjusting for the corresponding pretest difference times $b_1$. When there are covariates in the regression equation, the means in Equation 6.2 must be adjusted for the effects of the covariates.

Throughout the remainder of this chapter we refer to *pooled* standard deviations, *pooled* correlations, and *pooled* reliabilities. Because such pooled values are needed for various formulas, we must define them here. By pooled we mean that the standard deviation, correlation, or reliability is computed within each treatment group (and within each covariate) and then averaged or pooled across treatment groups (and covariates). The general procedure for computing the pooled standard deviation of, for instance, the pretest is to regress it on the treatment variables and the covariates. The variance of the residuals from such a regression (or the *mean square error* of the pretest) is the pooled within-treatment and covariate variance. The pooled correlation of the pretest and posttest can be obtained by taking the residuals of the pretest and posttest, controlling for treatment and covariates, and correlating them. When statistics are pooled in this fashion, $k$ degrees of freedom are lost, where $k$ is the number of treatment variables and covariates. We denote such pooled within-group standard deviations, correlations, and reliabilities by the subscript $w$.

In the remainder of this chapter we discuss conditions under which each of the two adjustment strategies, regression and change score, is appropriate. It will be shown that the choice depends on the nature of the assignment rule. A different approach, a value-added approach, is discussed in Chapter 8.

### Regression adjustment

There are two analysis strategies that are formally equivalent to regression adjustment, where regression adjustment is defined as the regression of the posttest on the treatment and the pretest. The estimate of treatment effects by analysis of covariance (ANCOVA) is identical to this multiple regression approach, as we saw in Chapter 4. As we saw there, however, the regression approach is more flexible. The second analysis strategy that is equivalent to multiple regression is to regress change, $Y_2 - Y_1$, on the treatment and the pretest. Again, the coefficient for the treatment is the same as its coefficient in regression adjustment, and the coefficient for the pretest equals the coefficient for the pretest in a regression adjustment minus one.[2]

---

[2] An analysis known as residualized change score analysis can be equivalent to regression adjustment. A residualized change score is obtained by regressing the posttest on the pretest, and computing the residual from such a regression. All subsequent analyses are

Most textbook discussions of multiple regression and analysis of covariance fail to emphasize the two different purposes of regression adjustment. The first may be called the precision purpose. The precision in the estimation of treatment effects or, equivalently, the conclusion validity tends to be enhanced by including the pretest as a covariate. The second purpose is adjustment. When the pretest is included in the analysis, the estimate of the treatment effect typically differs from that obtained when it is not included. The adjusted treatment effect is $(\overline{Y}_{2E} - \overline{Y}_{2C}) - b_1(\overline{Y}_{1E} - \overline{Y}_{1C})$, where $b_1$ is the regression coefficient of $Y_2$ on $Y_1$ controlling for treatment (see Equation 6.2). In the unlikely event of no pretest difference between the means of the groups, there is no adjustment. The purpose of this adjustment is to produce more internally valid estimates. Whenever multiple regression is applied, it serves both purposes: precision *and* adjustment. It is informative to examine these purposes for the randomized experiment, the regression discontinuity design, and the nonequivalent control group design.

The main purpose for including a pre-treatment measure as a covariate in a randomized experiment is to reduce the error term and thereby to produce a more precise estimate of treatment effects. Incidentally, the size of the treatment effect is also adjusted. The magnitude of the adjustment depends on the size of the difference between treatment groups on the pre-treatment measure. Given randomization, this difference should be relatively small. However, some difference on the pretest is likely and there is some adjustment. Both the adjusted and unadjusted treatment effects are internally valid, because the assignment rule is random.

For the regression discontinuity design, it is the adjustment purpose that necessitates controlling for the pretreatment measure; because the pretest *is* the assignment variable, it *must* be controlled. Precision may be affected in the process, but the purpose is adjustment.

For the nonequivalent control group design, the effect on internal validity of adjusting for the pretest is not so clear. For purposes of conclusion validity, it is true that entering the pre-treatment measure into the regression equation maximally explains the post-

---

then performed on this residual score. This is equivalent to what we call regression adjustment if, first, all other variables (treatment and covariates) are similarly residualized (i.e., have the pretest effect subtracted out), and, second, the degrees of freedom for error are reduced by one. Typically, neither of these adjustments is made, resulting in both bias and reduced power.

test; that is, a regression-weighted pretest produces a larger $R^2$ for the posttest than any other weighting strategy. It would seem that a weighting that maximally explained the posttest would be optimal. However, such a weighting yields an unbiased estimate of treatment effects only in very special circumstances. Typically, using regression adjustment leaves bias in the estimate of the treatment effect, and the bias may even be greater than an unadjusted analysis of the posttest alone (Reichardt, 1979).

### Mediational model

The implicit model for regression adjustment is the causal model contained in Figure 6.1. For instance, suppose that the pretest is a measure of reading skill in the evaluation of a remedial reading program. A teacher decides whether each student receives the treatment or not. The teacher's decision is likely to be affected by the pretest, and it is also plausible that the teacher's beliefs about the student affects the pretest (Rosenthal & Jacobson, 1968). Thus the assignment variable causes and is caused by the pretest. The assignment variable by definition determines treatment. Both the treatment and the pretest affect the posttest. However, we assume in this causal model that the effect of the assignment variable on the posttest is totally mediated via the pretest and via the treatment if there is a treatment effect. (See Chapter 10 for a discussion of the concept of mediation.) Thus there is no *direct* effect of the assignment variable on the posttest variable and hence no path between the two in Figure 6.1. For such an idealized model, regression is the appropriate adjustment strategy, because all the variance that the assignment variable shares with the posttest is controlled by including the pretest and the treatment in the regression equation.[3]

For our remedial reading example, if the teacher's perception of the students' ability is the assignment variable, we must assume that this variable does not directly cause the posttest. Rather its effects on the posttest are totally mediated by the pretest and by the treatment if there are treatment effects. This seems like an implausible assumption if the teacher continues to teach the child. However, if the child is removed from the classroom and given a new remedial teacher, the mediational model becomes more plausible.

---

[3] Technically, we need assume only that the assignment variable is uncorrelated with the residual to the posttest, once the pretest is controlled.

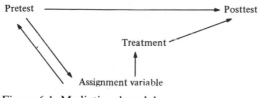

Figure 6.1. Mediational model.

*Reliability correction.* The mediational model virtually never holds, because what mediates the assignment variable's effect is the *true* pretest, not the *measured* pretest. The measured pretest contains the true pretest plus measurement error. It is unlikely that these errors in the pretest are related to the assignment variable. Errors of measurement represent, in part, chance phenomena that determine performance on a test. Even something as reliable as weighing oneself may yield two different readings if one varies the scale, or shifts one's feet, changes one's clothes, or changes what one ate for dinner. Even more than the measurement of physical data, social science measurement is subject to the vagaries of test content (is the test taker asked something that he or she just happens to know), subject motivation (is the test taker mentally up or down for the test), test administrator's skill (does the test administrator give the test taker exactly the allotted amount of time), and pure luck (does the test taker guess correctly). Virtually everything in life has its chance aspect, whether it is winning a football game, obtaining an A in a course, or even living and dying. We should not be surprised that social science measures are chance driven.

This is not to say that a test score is totally determined by chance. Someone who scores higher on a test than someone else probably outperformed the other person. Tests tell us about relative performance, but only imperfectly. Failure to recognize that tests are fallible indicators of true performance very often leads us astray.

If we assume that every test score is not a perfect measure of performance, then we can speak of variation in the test score that is error and variation that is true performance. The pretest, $Y_1$, is assumed to be a function of true performance, $T$, and chance performance, $E$. In practice, researchers do not measure $T$ or $E$, only $Y_1$, but it aids us conceptually if we can partition the variance of the pretest into these two theoretical and unmeasured components.

In many cases it is plausible that the assignment variable is correlated with the pretest true score but not with errors of measurement. For instance, in our example of a remedial reading program, the teacher does not directly observe the true score $T$, but presumably his or her perceptions of need are determined in part by $T$ and not at all by $E$. If the assignment variable is associated with $T$ and not with $E$, then controlling for $Y_1$ does not adjust successfully for the effect of $T$. In our remedial reading example, if the assignment variable, teacher's perception of ability, is caused by or causes true reading skill, we need to control for that true reading skill. It seems most reasonable that the chance or random aspects of the reading test score are unrelated to the assignment variable. In such a case we must control for the true reading ability and not the measured pretest score.

If $E$ is associated with the assignment variable – for instance, if the actual pretest score is used to determine assignment – then we should control for the actual pretest as in the regression discontinuity design. In the rest of this chapter errors in the pretest are assumed not to determine assignment. When the true pretest mediates the effect of the assignment variable, then the true pretest should be the basis for the adjustment. Essentially we want to treat the posttest as the outcome variable in a regression equation and the true pretest and the treatment as the independent variables. But the true pretest, $T$, is an unmeasured, hypothetical variable and cannot be entered into a computer program. If we regress the posttest on the treatment and the measured pretest, the coefficient for the pretest underestimates what would be the coefficient for the true pretest. Thus we are underweighting pretest differences. Because the regression coefficient for the pretest is too small, we do not subtract out enough from the posttest difference in means (see Equation 6.2). Thus if the pretest favors the treated group, we overestimate treatment effects because we subtract too small an amount. If the pretest favors the untreated group, we add too small an amount and hence underestimate treatment effects. This is an example of regression adjustment being unfair to programs in which the comparison groups are superior, which are sometimes called compensatory programs (Campbell & Erlebacher, 1970).

The amount of underweighting in this case depends solely on the amount of error in the pretest, as is discussed in Chapter 9. A quantitative measure of the amount of error in the pretest is the reliability coefficient. If we knew the pooled reliability of the pretest within treatment conditions, we could obtain internally valid estimates of the treatment effects, given the mediational model in Figure 6.1. This is accomplished by weighting the pretest by its reliability; that is, we create an estimated pretest true score, $Y_1^A$. We denote $\rho_w$ as the reliability of the pretest pooled within treatment groups. We create $Y_1^A$ by subtracting out the treatment mean, multiplying by $\rho_w$, and adding in the treatment pretest mean. So, for the treated group the estimated pretest true score is

$$\rho_w(Y_1 - \overline{Y}_{1E}) + \overline{Y}_{1E}$$

and for the untreated group $Y_1^A$ is

$$\rho_w(Y_1 - \overline{Y}_{1C}) + \overline{Y}_{1C}$$

We now regress $Y_2$ on $X$ and $Y_1^A$, and the coefficient for treatment is unbiased given certain assumptions. This procedure is called *reliability correction*.

The assumptions behind this analysis are as follows:

1　The assignment variable's effects on the posttest are mediated by the true pretest.
2　The value chosen for $\rho_w$ is accurate.
3　The errors in the pretest are uncorrelated with the posttest.
4　The relationship between the true pretest and posttest is linear.

If these conditions are met, the treatment coefficient is unbiased.[4]

The first of these conditions can be met only through theory and previous research findings. The second condition, knowing $\rho_w$, is a stumbling block. In practice we can only estimate $\rho_w$, not know it. Reichardt (1979) has pointed out that it may not be so easy to estimate a value of $\rho_w$: Normally, an estimate of reliability based on a parallel form or a retest is not available. At best we may have an internal consistency estimate. Such a reliability is usually inflated because of time-specific errors common across items. Published estimates of reliability should be applied cautiously. When they are available, we should use as the measure of reliability

$$\frac{s_a^2 - (1 - r_{YY})s_b^2}{s_a^2}$$

---

[4] There is the additional assumption of equal reliabilities across the treatment groups (Campbell & Boruch, 1975).

where $s_b^2$ is the variance of the test for the published reliability, $s_a^2$ is the pretest variance pooled within treatments and covariates, and $r_{YY}$ is the published reliability.[5] Usually one would choose a range of estimates for $\rho_w$, perhaps taking the internal consistency estimate as the upper bound and the pretest–posttest correlation as the lower bound. For instance, for the remedial reading example we may have no internal consistency estimate for the particular sample tested. If the published reliability is .9 with a $s_b^2$ of 10 and the pooled within-treatment and covariates variance is 5, then the estimated reliability would be

$$\frac{5 - (1.0 - .9)10}{5} = .8$$

This would be taken as the upper bound. The lower bound would be the pretest–posttest correlation partialling out the treatment and covariates.

The third assumption, uncorrelated errors of measurement over time, is probably unreasonable (Cronbach & Furby, 1970). Errors of measurement in the pretest are likely to be correlated with errors of measurement in the posttest. Although violation of this assumption cannot be handled by reliability correction, at a later point in this chapter we discuss a structural modeling solution to this problem.

The viability of regression adjustment rests on still yet another assumption; that is, the pretest relates to the posttest in a linear fashion. Violation of this assumption biases estimates of treatment effects (Reichardt, 1979), as we illustrated in the previous chapter. The researcher should consider transformations to increase the likelihood that the assumption is met.

### Summary

In sum, regression adjustment without a reliability correction is rarely a defensible strategy. If it can be assumed that the true pretest mediates the effect of the assignment variable, then a reliability correction procedure can be employed. This is a very stringent assumption and may be difficult to satisfy. Three major problems exist with this procedure. First, a measure of reliability

---

[5] This procedure equates the variance due to errors of measurement in the sample used for the published reliability with the variance in the sample at hand.

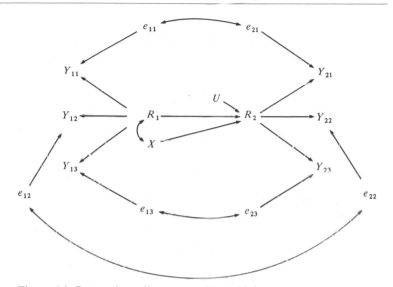

Figure 6 2. Regression adjustment with multiple indicators.

must be obtained. Second, measurement errors must be uncorrelated over time. And third, the pretest–posttest relationship must be linear. We must assume for this procedure that the assignment variable does not directly affect the posttest.

### Multivariate extensions

The treatment need not be a simple dichotomy, and there may be covariates such as sex, age, and ethnicity. Treatment variables that code the multiple treatments can be created by procedures we discussed in Chapter 4. They and the covariates can be simply added to the regression equation, as well as treatment by covariate interactions.

The reliability correction procedures must be modified when we have either a multivariate treatment or covariates. This modification can be accomplished by the following two-step procedure. First, we regress the pretest on the set of treatment variables and covariates. Let us designate the resultant predicted pretest as $\hat{Y}_1$. Let $Y_1^A$ equal $\rho_w(Y_1 - \hat{Y}_1) + \hat{Y}_1$, where $\rho_w$ is the pretest reliability within treatments and covariates. We now regress the posttest on the treatment variables, covariates, and $Y_1^A$.

If there are multiple measures of the pretest, one can use

structural modeling to estimate treatment effects. Although the details of this method are given in Chapter 9, we can outline the procedure here. As an example, let us assume that we have three measures of reading skill: $Y_1$, $Y_2$, and $Y_3$. We need to have a second subscript to denote the pretest measures ($Y_{11}$, $Y_{12}$, $Y_{13}$) and posttest measures ($Y_{21}$, $Y_{22}$, and $Y_{23}$). The structural model for these six variables and the treatment, $X$, is presented in Figure 6.2. The two latent variables in the model are pretest reading skill ($R_1$) and posttest skill ($R_2$). When there are three indicators of each construct at each time point, as there are in this example, correlated measurement error between $e_{11}$ and $e_{21}$, $e_{12}$ and $e_{22}$, and $e_{13}$ and $e_{23}$ can be estimated. This analysis still assumes that the true pretest mediates the effect of the assignment variable on the posttest.

There are three major advantages to this structural modeling approach, as discussed by Sörbom (1978). First, reliability can be estimated from the data instead of inferred from other sources. Second, correlated measurement errors over time can be included in this model. And third, the pretest–posttest slope can be tested for parallelism between groups.

### Change score analysis

Regression adjustment is valid when the true pretest mediates the effect of the assignment variable on the posttest. What if the assignment variable causes the posttest independently of the pretest? We could take an entirely different tack. Let us assume that the pre- and posttest are both caused by the assignment variable. We also assume that the effect of the assignment variable is the same on both the pre- and posttest. We shall see that these assumptions allow us to employ some form of change score analysis.

In the following we shall first present a simple, idealized rationale for change score analysis. We shall then discuss the type of assignment rules for which the assumptions of change score analysis are relatively more plausible. Transformations of the pretest and posttest that enable us better to approximate these assumptions will then be discussed. Finally, we shall consider the traditional arguments against the use of change scores.

Before we begin, we should note that a change score analysis is equivalent to the results of a repeated measures analysis of variance. The treatment by time (pretest versus posttest) interaction from a repeated measures analysis of variance is identical in size and statistical significance to the treatment main effect of the change score analysis.

Regression adjustment presumes that the pretest mediates the assignment variable–posttest relationship. Change score analysis presumes that the assignment variable directly affects both the pretest and the posttest and that those effects are of equal magnitude. This assumption of equal effects is called the assumption of stationarity of causal effects or, more simply, *stationarity*. The model for change score analysis is presented in Figure 6.3. In this figure, the assignment variable causes both the pretest and posttest, and those causal effects are equal (i.e., $a = a$). The causes of the pre- and posttest, other than the assignment variable and the treatment, may be correlated over time. There are three major differences between the change score model and the regression model. First, the mediational assumption is not made in the change model. The assignment variable affects both the pre- and posttest. Second, the pretest does not cause the posttest in the change model.[6] Third, the assignment variable causes the pretest and is not caused by it in the change model.

The crucial assumption here is that the effect of the assignment variable on the pretest is equal to the effect of the assignment variable on the posttest, that is, stationarity. To see how change score analysis is effective, let us presume that we could measure the assignment variable $Z$. Then the equation for the posttest is

$$Y_2 = b_0 + b_1 X + b_2 Z + e_2$$

and for the pretest the equation is

$$Y_1 = b_3 + b_4 Z + e_1$$

The change score is then the difference between these two equations:

$$Y_2 - Y_1 = (b_0 - b_3) + b_1 X + (b_2 - b_4)Z + (e_2 - e_1)$$

Stationarity of the causal effects of $Z$ on $Y$ over time means that $b_2 = b_4$, which reduces the change equation to

$$Y_2 - Y_1 = (b_0 - b_3) + b_1 X + (e_2 - e_1) \tag{6.3}$$

---

[6] Variables, which are uncaused by their prior value, are also involved in the time-series models discussed in the next chapter.

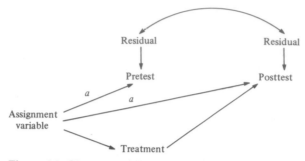

Figure 6.3. Change model.

Because the assignment variable is not in the equation, internally valid estimates of treatment effects are possible even if $Z$ is unmeasured. Just as we did with regression adjustment, we have made some strong assumptions that require more careful examination.

The assumption of stationarity implies something more readily understandable: constant growth rates. Consider persons who score low on the assignment variable. We can define for these persons a growth rate, that is, their average score on the posttest minus their average score on the pretest controlling for covariates and treatment effects. We can similarly define the growth rate for those who score high on the assignment variable. Stationarity implies that these two growth rates are equal. More exactly, the rate of growth is uncorrelated with the assignment variable. Campbell and Stanley (1963) refer to this assumption as the absence of an interaction between selection (the assignment variable) and maturation (growth rate). Thus stationarity, constant growth rates, and the absence of a selection by maturation interaction are essentially the same thing. Returning to our remedial reading example, it may be that the teacher's assessment of ability is largely a function of the child's age. Thus, the younger children are presumed to have less reading skill than the older children. In order to use change score analysis, it must be assumed that children's growth rates in reading skill are independent of age, perhaps an unlikely assumption.

### Stable assignment variables

What type of assignment variables is consistent with the change score model? First and foremost, the assignment variable must not be caused by the pretest. If it were, *ceteris paribus,* we would expect that the pretest would share more variance with the assignment variable than the posttest would. This would be a violation of stationarity. It would then seem likely that assignment variables such as motivation, perception, and knowledge that may be influenced by the pretest do not allow for a change score analysis.

Generally, assignment variables that change over time are poor candidates for a change score analysis. This is for two reasons. First, a changing variable could be caused by the pretest, whereas an unchanging variable could not by definition be caused by any variable in the model. Recall that if the pretest causes the assignment variable, stationarity is implausible. Second, covariation between variables is greatest when they are measured concurrently, *ceteris paribus.* We would then expect that a changing assignment variable would tend to correlate more highly with the pretest than with the posttest. Thus, because changing variables make poor candidates, by default stable variables are more plausible. Examples of stable variables are demographic and background variables such as ethnicity, sex, year of birth, and variables that are relatively stable during the course of the quasi-experiment, such as socioeconomic status and marital status. For stable variables like those we have just mentioned, it seems somewhat reasonable to expect that, in the absence of treatment effects, the pretest difference would remain at the posttest.

How likely is it that the assignment variable is unchanging in the nonequivalent control group design? A typical plan for the design is to use another classroom, school, or city as the control group. It would seem reasonable that the source of differences between classrooms, schools, or cities might be stable variables. However, this would not always be the case. For instance, if children were assigned to classrooms on the basis of a test score, we would expect the test score to change over time, making the assignment variable a changing variable. In the main, however, we would expect the use of a second intact group to be symptomatic of an unchanging assignment variable.

In summary, stable assignment variables are better candidates for a change score analysis than changing variables. Of course, researchers do not know if the assignment variable is a stable one. With intact groups, stable assignment variables are somewhat more likely. Even if the assignment variable is stable, however, change score analysis still may not yield unbiased estimates of treatment effects: The crucial assumption of constant growth rates or stationarity must hold.

## Transformations to promote stationarity

For the assumption of stationarity to be plausible, the pretest and posttest must be measured in the same metric, that is, the same units of measurement. If one is to measure a change in height, one would not use centimeters for the pretest and inches for the posttest. Unfortunately, it is too easy to make just this mistake. For instance, a pretest with a ten-item test and a posttest with twenty items make a "change score" that largely reflects the increase in the number of items. That is, if someone got 20% correct on both tests, his or her "change" score would be 2, whereas if someone got 40%, the change score would be 4. Quite clearly, percentage correct would be a better measure than number correct.

Test makers claim that they have made different forms of the same test in the same metric. They also claim that they have tests for different age groups that are in the same metric. The best-known example is the intelligence test. Tests used for 5-year-olds are somehow thought to be in the same units as tests for college students. Such claims should not be taken at face value. For instance, Barker and Pelavin (1975) have shown that "alternate forms" of the same test that are supposed to have the same mean or variance do not in fact. This implies different metrics.

In sum, the pre- and the posttest must be measured in the same metric. For every variable, however, alternative metrics can be used. In one metric, growth rates of the outcome variable may be correlated with the assignment variable, but in another metric this may not be the case. Therefore, transformations that alter the metric of the pre- and posttest may increase the likelihood of stationarity. In other words, the constant-growth-rate assumption may refer not to the raw metric but to some transformed metric.

How might such transformations be successful? Recall that the violation of constant growth rates implies an interaction between the assignment variable and time. One particular example of such an interaction is shown in Figure 6.4. What characterizes the interaction is that those who score low on the assignment variable grow at a slower rate than those who score high on the assignment variable. The rate of growth is correlated with the level of the assignment variable. Such a pattern has been characterized as fan

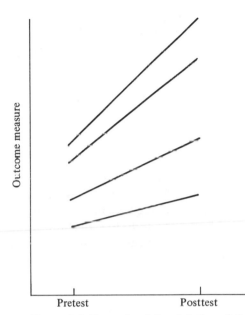

Figure 6.4. Example of the violation of the constant-growth assumption; the different growth curves refer to different levels of the assignment variable.

spread (Campbell, 1967) and a bilinear interaction (Anderson, 1974). Given the pattern of interaction in Figure 6.4, it is possible in theory to transform the pretest and posttest to remove the differential growth rates.

The researcher must consider the possibility of transforming the pretest and posttest to increase the plausibility of the constant-growth assumption. In practice, we do not know the assignment variable, and so we do not know what transformation to employ. One yardstick that researchers can use to evaluate a transformation is equality of variances of the pretest and posttest. Transformations that make the within-group variance equal across time would tend to promote, but not guarantee, stationarity. Thus equal variance is a good sign, but not proof, of stationary growth rates.

One can force equal variance by measuring the pre- and posttests in standard deviation units; this is known as a standard score or a $Z$ score. The effect of a $Z$-score transformation is to equate the variances of the pretest and posttest. Other transformations may also have this effect. For instance, if the outcome variable is a count, a square-root transformation often results in nearly equal variances in the pretest and posttest. Similarly effective would be a logarithmic transformation for quantities (e.g., dollars) and the reciprocal for latencies. Mosteller and Tukey (1977) provide a number of conceptual and empirical guides for transformation. The simplest way to ensure equal variances is through standardization. Although this approach is the most direct, other transformational procedures may often be normally better grounded in theory and research and may therefore be preferable.

Using a $Z$-score transformation of the pretest and posttest has been called standardized change score analysis. The use of the overall posttest variance for its standardization, however, is inappropriate, because the presence of a treatment effect alters the variance of the posttest. Therefore, we would like to standardize the pretest and posttest using the pooled-within variances. This can be done by using the following measure of change:

$$Y_2 - \frac{s_{Y_2(w)}}{s_{Y_1(w)}} Y_1$$

where the standard deviations are pooled with treatments and covariates. The pretest has been transformed so that its pooled within variance is the same as that of the posttest. This change score is now regressed on the set of treatment variables and covariates.

Because the variances of the pretest and posttest reflect error variance as well as true variance, a better transformation would be one that equates the pre- and posttest *true score variance*. The following measure of change does this:

$$Y_2 - \frac{s_{Y_2(w)} \sqrt{r_{Y_2 Y_2(w)}}}{s_{Y_1(w)} \sqrt{r_{Y_1 Y_1(w)}}} Y_1$$

where $r_{Y_2 Y_2(w)}$ and $r_{Y_1 Y_1(w)}$ are the reliabilities of the posttest and pretest, respectively, again computed within treatment variables and covariates. A difficulty with this approach, as with the reliability correction procedure discussed for regression adjustment, is the problem of obtaining reliability measures.[7]

In sum, transformations to achieve stationarity should be consid-

---

[7]  We have not discussed the Campbell-Erlebacher (1970) suggestion for a *common-factor* correction. Their intent is similar to the reliability correction strategy discussed in the regression adjustment section of this chapter. However, instead of using the reliability

ered by the researcher, because stationarity may hold in another metric than the raw one. Identifying the appropriate transformation is difficult. However, transformations that equalize variance over time may accomplish this purpose.

### Criticisms of change scores

We now turn our attention to criticisms of a change score approach. One criticism is that change scores are highly unreliable. Another is that regression toward the mean is a problem. It has also been argued that change score analysis a priori sets the regression weight for the pretest at one instead of a posteriori estimating it. Finally, Reichardt (1979) has argued that change scores can be distorted by floor and ceiling effects. Let us consider each criticism in detail.

The issue of unreliability can be stated very simply. Change scores are notoriously unreliable. What we need, however, is an adjustment strategy that is most internally valid, not the most reliable dependent variable. Even if reliability should be a criterion for a selection of an adjustment strategy, change scores are more reliable than residualized change scores (see note 2).

A second criticism of the change score approach is that a change score is subject to regression toward the mean. Assuming equal variance for the pre- and posttest, persons with high change scores would tend to be below the mean of the pretest, whereas those with low change scores would be above the mean of the pretest. Thus, it has been argued that change scores reflect regression toward the mean, a statistical artifact. Change score analysis in the nonequivalent control group design is criticized because change is correlated with the pretest. The pretest is not the assignment variable, however; rather, some unknown variable is. It is this variable and not the pretest that needs to be controlled to yield valid estimates of the treatment effects. Given equal effects of the assignment variable on $Y_1$ and $Y_2$, the assignment variable's coefficient in the equation for a change score (Equation 6.3) is zero. Therefore, regression does not result in bias so long as the assumption of stationarity is met.

A criticism has also been made that change score analysis is only a naive attempt to perform regression-weighted adjustment, setting the regression coefficient arbitrarily at one. This point of view

coefficient to adjust the pretest, they suggest using the pretest–posttest correlation, although their intention was to produce a change score adjustment that is very similar to the standardized change approach.

presumes that regression-weighted adjustment is the valid approach and change score is only an approximation. We hope we have dispelled this notion.

Finally, it has been argued that change scores will be distorted by a floor effect in the pretest and a ceiling effect in the posttest. For instance, a ceiling effect in the posttest implies that change scores reflect mostly the pretest score. That is, low scorers at the pretest change more than high scorers. The presence of floor and ceiling effects certainly does distort change measures, but it also distorts the regression coefficient for the pretest's effect on the posttest. Thus, floor and ceiling effects are fundamental problems with measures, and they create problems with any method of analysis. Change score analysis is not an exception.[8]

### Summary

Like regression adjustment, change score analysis makes some very strong assumptions about how the assignment variable operates. In particular, it must be assumed that the effect of the assignment variable is stationary over time. Such an assumption cannot be demonstrated conclusively, but it is more plausible when there is evidence that the assignment variable is stable. In addition, certain transformations may make the assumption more tenable.

Standardized change score analysis has done relatively well when compared to alternative analysis strategies in various simulations. Director (1974) compared various statistical methods in their ability to detect no effect when it was known a priori that there was no effect in the data. Data were used from a situation in which it was known that the treatment had not been implemented. Standardized change score analysis outperformed the other techniques. Also, Monte Carlo simulations by Bryk (1977) have shown that although no statistical method is consistently unbiased, standardized change score analysis is no worse than the others and may be a bit better in some circumstances. These results do not argue for the universal adoption of a change analysis, but they do suggest that at times it is appropriate.

---

[8] There is even one clear advantage that change score analysis possesses that regression adjustment does not. Regression adjustment using a pretest is possible only when the design is longitudinal. It is possible to have a nonequivalent control group design in which persons are assigned randomly to either pretested or posttested. By examining the time (pretest vs. posttest) by treatment interaction, one can assess treatment effects. Such an analysis is very much like a change score analysis.

### Multivariate extensions

The presence of multiple treatment variables and covariates can be incorporated into the change model. The basic dependent variable is a measure of change, either raw or transformed. If there are multiple indicators of the pre- and posttest, one can employ a structural modeling approach. For both raw and standardized change, the model would be similar to that in Figure 6.2 with the following exceptions. Treatment should "cause" the unmeasured pretest, and the unmeasured pretest should not cause the unmeasured posttest. Rather, their errors or disturbances are correlated. Second, the paths from the unmeasured pre- and posttests to their indicators should be equal across time. If equal variances in the unmeasured pre- and posttests are desired, their disturbance variances should be equal. Treatment effects are indicated by unequal coefficients from the treatment to the unmeasured pre- and post-tests. The covariance, not the correlation, matrix should be analyzed.

Kenny and Cohen (1980) have developed a procedure to test the constant-growth-rate assumption. Because the assignment variable is unknown and most likely unmeasured, we cannot use it to test for constant growth. Kenny and Cohen suggest using demographic and background variables to assess the assumption. For example, one could look at males and females and determine if they grew at the same rate. Kenny and Cohen have also developed a procedure to measure the violation of the constant-growth assumption and a method to transform the pretest to reestablish constant growth. For instance, if those scoring high on the pretest were growing faster than those scoring low, the pretest would be multiplied by a number greater than one. Thus constant growth is established empirically. The viability of their procedure hinges on the assumption that the known demographic variables relate to the pretest and posttest in the same way as the unknown assignment variable does.

## Complications

### Assignment after the pretest

It often occurs that researchers use as "pretest" measurements taken some time before assignment. This is often the case in the evaluation of educational innovations. Researchers use a test taken

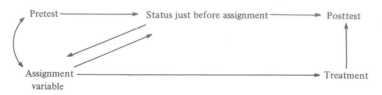

Figure 6.5. Regression-based model of assignment after the pretest.

in the fall as a pretest even though the program is begun in January. Such a design plan violates the basic assumption of regression adjustment analysis. The model would have to be modified, as in Figure 6.5. The variable "Status just before assignment" is what the pretest would have been had it been measured at the time of assignment. The fundamental rule of regression adjustment has been violated: The effects of the assignment variable on the posttest are not totally mediated by the pretest but rather flow through the "status" variable.

Such a design plan also necessitates altering the model behind change score analysis. The model is in Figure 6.6. For the change model to hold, the assignment variable must relate equally to the pre- and posttest ($a = a$). This is the same assumption we have made all along.

### Nested designs

It occasionally happens that there is more than one intact group in the treatment and comparison groups, and these groups are then said to be *nested within treatments*. Imagine a study involving four halfway houses. Two of them serve as the treated group and the other two serve as the untreated. Given the small number of houses, the unit of analysis cannot be the halfway house, but rather it is the person within the halfway house. Because there are four halfway houses, there are three possible independent comparisons among them. The first comparison is to contrast the treated and untreated halfway houses. The other two comparisons refer to a comparison first within the treatment group and then within the comparison group. The coding using three dummy variables, $Z_1$, $Z_2$, $Z_3$, for four halfway houses $A$, $B$, $C$, and $D$, is illustrated in Table 6.1. If the first comparison is significant and so is either the second or the third, there are two possible explanations. First, there is a treatment effect, but it varies among houses. For instance, if $Z_2$ is significant as well as $Z_1$, one of the treated halfway houses changed more than

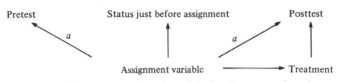

Figure 6.6. Change score-based model of assignment after the pretest.

the other. Perhaps in the one that changed more, the treatment was better implemented. If $Z_3$ is significant, then the houses in the comparison group differ. It is possible that one of the comparison group houses received some treatment. The second interpretation is that the assumptions behind the analysis, whatever it is, are incorrect. For instance, within the treatment condition the houses may be growing at different rates: This constitutes a violation of a change score analysis. Thus, if the researcher is fairly confident that variation in the treatment effect is unlikely, the tests of $Z_2$ and $Z_3$ can be used to evaluate the viability of the statistical analysis.

### Conclusion validity

Regression adjustment and change score analysis differ not only in how they estimate the treatment effect, but also in their conclusion validity. When the pretest difference between the comparison and treatment groups is small, regression adjustment is substantially more powerful than change score analysis. If the regression coefficient for the pretest is close to one, this advantage of regression adjustment disappears. As the pretest difference grows, regression adjustment loses power because the treatment–pretest correlation produces multicollinearity. It is even possible for change score analysis to have greater power.

The inclusion of covariates besides the pretest in this design also results in an uncertain outcome on conclusion validity. Power is increased by lowering the error variance. It is decreased to the extent that the covariates are correlated with the treatment. We should realize that in this design the main reason for including covariates is to enhance internal validity and not conclusion validity.

### Conclusion and comparison of strategies

Failure to know the assignment variable results in uncertainty in the accuracy of conclusions drawn from the nonequivalent control

Table 6.1. *Nested design*

| | Halfway house | | | |
| | Treated | | Untreated | |
| | A | B | C | D |
|---|---|---|---|---|
| $Z_1$ | 1 | 1 | 0 | 0 |
| $Z_2$ | 1 | −1 | 0 | 0 |
| $Z_3$ | 0 | 0 | 1 | −1 |

group design. However, because we have a pretest measure of the outcome variable, we can partially assess the degree to which assignment is nonrandom. Moreover, by making certain strong assumptions about the causal effects of the assignment variable over time, we can use the pretest information to adjust the posttest for the confounding effects of the assignment variable. Through these assumptions, the inclusion of the pretest in the analysis approximates the inclusion of the unknown assignment variable.

Different statistical procedures make different assumptions about the effect of the assignment variable over time. Regression adjustment presumes that the causal·effect of the assignment variable is mediated through the pretest. That is, the assignment variable does not directly cause the posttest. If this assumption holds, it is most likely to be accurate for the *true* pretest rather than the measured pretest. This requires a reliability correction procedure.

Change score analysis presumes that the causal effects of the assignment variable are stationary over time. This assumption implies that the growth rates are constant for persons at different levels of the assignment variable. Such constant growth rates may, under certain circumstances, be more plausible when the pretest and posttest are transformed.

Of course, neither of these models ever holds perfectly. Both are always inexact approximations of reality. Thus, an exactly unbiased estimate of the treatment effect is more a matter of luck than anything else. At issue is what is the *direction of the bias* when the assumptions are not met.

In the regression adjustment strategy, the assignment variable is assumed not to affect the posttest directly. If this assumption is violated, the estimate of the treatment effect is biased. To aid us in understanding the direction of bias, we must define the direction of the scale of the outcome and assignment variables. We define the scale of the outcome variable in such a way that having a higher score on it indicates that a person has more of some social good, for example, more income, more intelligence, more health. The assignment variable is defined to correlate positively with the pretest. Thus, those high on the assignment variable have more of the social good at the pretest.

When the assignment variable affects the posttest directly, the direction of bias in regression adjustment depends on two factors. First, it depends on whether the mean pretest difference between conditions favors the treated or untreated subjects. This difference can be *estimated* by computing the mean (covariate adjusted) difference of the treated and untreated subjects on the pretest. The second factor that the direction of bias depends on is the sign of the effect of the assignment variable on the posttest that was mistakenly assumed to be zero in the regression adjustment strategy. Recall that both the assignment variable and the posttest have been scaled in such a way that more means "better off."

If the pretest difference favors the untreated subjects, and if the assignment variable's direct effect on the posttest is positive, then the estimate of the treatment effect is too small. If the pretest difference favors the untreated subjects, and if the assignment variable's direct effect on the posttest is negative, then our estimate of the treatment effect is too large.

If the pretest difference favors the treated subjects, and if the effect of the assignment variable on the posttest is positive, then we overestimate the treatment's effect. If the effect of the assignment variable on the posttest is negative when the pretest difference favors the treated subjects, the treatment effect is underestimated.

Because we have scaled the assignment variable to correlate positively with the pretest, it seems likely that the assignment variable's direct effect on the posttest will be positive. Thus, with a pretest difference that favors the untreated subjects, the most likely direction of bias is toward *underestimating* the treatment effect. With a pretest difference that favors the treated subjects, the most likely direction of bias is toward *overestimating* the treatment effect.

Even if the direct effect of the assignment variable on the posttest is zero, bias results when the reliability of the pretest is incorrectly estimated in the regression adjustment strategy. If the pretest difference favors the untreated subjects, too high a reliability estimate causes underestimation of the treatment effect and too low an estimate causes overestimation of the treatment effect. If the pretest difference favors the treated subjects, too high a reliability estimate causes overestimation of the treatment effect and too low an estimate causes underestimation of the treatment effect.

The above discussion refers to regression adjustment. Change score analysis typically weights the pretest information more heavily than regression adjustment. This is so because the partial regression coefficient for the pretest is usually less than one even after correcting for unreliability. Because the weight for the pretest in change score analysis is one, the pretest differences are generally weighted more heavily in change score analysis than in regression adjustment. Change score analysis *usually* results in larger estimates of treatment effects when the pretest difference favors the untreated subjects and smaller estimates when the pretest difference favors the treated subjects. It can be shown that a change score analysis after a variance-stabilizing transformation results in a greater weighting of the pretest than raw change when the variances increase over time, and lighter weighting when the variances decrease. Because variances tend to increase over time, the variance-stabilizing transformations generally result in a greater weighting of the pretest than when change scores are used without transformations.

The direction of bias in change score analysis depends on how the constant-growth-rate assumption is violated. It can be violated in one of two ways. Either those who score high on the assignment variable grow at a faster rate than those who score low (divergent growth), or those higher grow at a slower rate than those who score low (convergent growth). Divergent growth might be called fan-spread and convergent growth fan-close. For convergent growth and a pretest difference that favors the untreated subjects, treatment effects are overestimated. For convergent growth and a pretest difference that favors the untreated subjects, treatment effects are overestimated. For convergent growth and a pretest difference that favors the treated subjects, effects are underestimated. For divergent growth the pattern is reversed. If the pretest difference favors the untreated subjects, program effects are underestimated; and if it favors the treated subjects, program effects are overestimated.

Thus, for both regression adjustment and change score analysis the researcher can at least begin to speculate about the direction of bias of each technique. There is, however, no guarantee that the bias will be in the expected direction. Moreover, there is no guarantee that the bias in the regression and change analysis will be in opposite directions and that the truth will lie somewhere in the middle. So even if both regression adjustment and change analysis yield a positive estimate of the treatment effect, the true treatment effect may be negative. Although consistent results of the two procedures is comforting, it is not the proof of a lack of bias (cf. Byrk & Weisberg, 1977).

It is important to recognize that neither change analysis nor regression adjustment is a single method of analysis. Change analysis can be done on raw scores, standardized scores, or transformed scores. Similarly, regression adjustment can be "simple" regression or regression with reliability correction using a range of possible reliability values. Moreover, each can be adapted into a structural modeling framework.

It may seem that one can choose the analysis procedure to give any desired estimate of the treatment effect. Actually, the range of possible treatment effect estimates is much narrower than one might think. If the pre- and posttest variances are nearly equal, the range of treatment effect estimates is only about half the difference in the pretest means between the treated and untreated groups. Thus researchers cannot choose the analysis procedure to give exactly the desired estimate of the treatment effect.

Assessing treatment effects in the nonequivalent control group design is an extremely difficult process. Straightforward solutions to the problems posed in the analysis are frequently not possible. However, if the reader is dismayed about the inference possibilities of the nonequivalent control group design, he or she should realize that the presence of a pretest is an immeasureable aid. Inference problems are really much more severe without a pretest, as we shall see when the post-only correlational design is discussed in Chapter 9.

# 7

# The interrupted time-series design

Every day thousands of new innovations begin. New laws are passed, new programs start, and organizations change their structure or procedures. The effect of these changes can be measured and tested through a time-series design. By having observations for many time periods before the innovation, we can measure trends, cycles, and the amount of instability in the data. We can then use the observations taken before the innovation as a baseline to measure and test for treatment effects.

We consider one simple example throughout this chapter. Imagine a governmental agency that has encouraged driving safety for the past decade. The government wishes to know how the campaign has affected automobile fatalities. Data on fatalities per 10,000 persons are available for the past 20 years, the last 10 of which included the safety campaign. The artificial data for this example are presented in the first two columns of Table 7.1, where $Y_t$ refers to the number of fatalities. The subscript $t$ refers to time point or year for this example. The data are also graphed in Figure 7.1. The data structure is called a *time series* because there is a single data point for each point in time. The design is called an *interrupted* time series because there is a clear dividing line (as is drawn in Figure 7.1) at the beginning of the intervention. Time is interrupted by the intervention.

The design has been used to evaluate a crackdown on speeding (Ross & Campbell, 1968), the effect of mandatory sentencing on violent crime (Deutsch & Alt, 1977), as well as other interventions. Many time series are similar to our hypothetical example: Both the unit (e.g., subject) and time are highly aggregated; that is, they are averages or totals across many observations. The unit is a nation, a state, or a school system, and the time unit is a year, a month, or a week. Thus unit refers to many persons and time to many days. For

Table 7.1. *Automobile safety example*

| Year | $Y_t$ | $Y_{t+1}$ | $T_t$ | $X_t$ | $\hat{Y}_t$ | $e_t$ | $e_{t+1}$ | $Y_t^*$ | $T_t^*$ | $X_t^*$ | $u_t$ |
|------|-------|-----------|-------|-------|-------------|-------|-----------|---------|---------|---------|-------|
| 1955 | 4.1 | 4.4 | 1  | 0 | 4.0 | .1  | .2  | —    | —    | —   | —     |
| 1956 | 4.4 | 4.7 | 2  | 0 | 4.2 | .2  | .3  | 2.76 | 1.6  | 0   | .180  |
| 1957 | 4.7 | 4.3 | 3  | 0 | 4.4 | .3  | −.3 | 2.94 | 2.2  | 0   | .242  |
| 1958 | 4.3 | 4.6 | 4  | 0 | 4.6 | −.3 | −.2 | 2.42 | 2.8  | 0   | −.396 |
| 1959 | 4.6 | 4.6 | 5  | 0 | 4.8 | −.2 | −.4 | 2.88 | 3.4  | 0   | −.054 |
| 1960 | 4.6 | 5.2 | 6  | 0 | 5.0 | −.4 | .0  | 2.76 | 4.0  | 0   | −.292 |
| 1961 | 5.2 | 5.2 | 7  | 0 | 5.2 | .0  | −.2 | 3.36 | 4.6  | 0   | .190  |
| 1962 | 5.2 | 5.8 | 8  | 0 | 5.4 | −.2 | .2  | 3.12 | 5.2  | 0   | −.168 |
| 1963 | 5.8 | 6.1 | 9  | 0 | 5.6 | .2  | .3  | 3.72 | 5.8  | 0   | .314  |
| 1964 | 6.1 | 5.7 | 10 | 0 | 5.8 | .3  | .6  | 3.78 | 6.4  | 0   | .256  |
| 1965 | 5.7 | 5.5 | 11 | 1 | 5.1 | .6  | .2  | 3.26 | 7.0  | 0   | .407  |
| 1966 | 5.5 | 5.1 | 12 | 1 | 5.3 | .2  | −.4 | 3.22 | 7.6  | 1.0 | −.066 |
| 1967 | 5.1 | 5.4 | 13 | 1 | 5.5 | −.4 | −.3 | 2.90 | 8.2  | .6  | −.504 |
| 1968 | 5.4 | 5.3 | 14 | 1 | 5.7 | −.3 | −.6 | 3.36 | 8.8  | .6  | −.162 |
| 1969 | 5.3 | 6.0 | 15 | 1 | 5.9 | −.6 | −.1 | 3.14 | 9.4  | .6  | −.500 |
| 1970 | 6.0 | 6.5 | 16 | 1 | 6.1 | −.1 | .2  | 3.88 | 10.0 | .6  | .122  |
| 1971 | 6.5 | 6.7 | 17 | 1 | 6.3 | .2  | ?   | 4.10 | 10.6 | .6  | .224  |
| 1972 | 6.7 | 6.7 | 18 | 1 | 6.5 | .2  | .0  | 4.10 | 11.2 | .6  | .107  |
| 1973 | 6.7 | 7.1 | 19 | 1 | 6.7 | .0  | .2  | 4.02 | 11.8 | .6  | −.091 |
| 1974 | 7.1 | —   | 20 | 1 | 6.9 | .2  | —   | 4.42 | 12.4 | .6  | .191  |

instance, a now-classic time series cited earlier involves the monthly automobile fatalities in the state of Connecticut over a period of 5 years. A time series need not be so highly aggregated. It may be made at a much finer level of measurement. As an example, the measurements might be the intensity of the speech of a single individual measured second by second (Warner, 1979).

The unit that is assigned to treatment conditions is a point in time, not a person or a group of people as in designs discussed in previous chapters. The $N$ different time points are each assigned to either the treatment or the comparison group. It may seem that time is always the rule by which time points are assigned to conditions, but a moment's reflection will reveal that this is not the case. The rule that assigns time points to treatments, just as the rule that assigns persons to treatments in other designs, can be random, known, or unknown. Let us consider each in turn.

A random rule requires that each time point have a known probability of being assigned to a given treatment condition. Such a

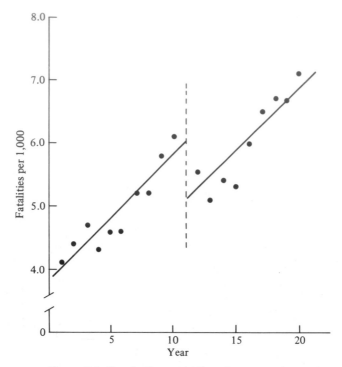

Figure 7.1. Graph of automobile safety example.

rule implies that the program is turned on or off randomly at different time points. For instance, at each time point a coin is flipped. If it is heads the program is delivered, and if it is tails it is not delivered. A random assignment rule across time is not very practical for the following reasons. First, programs are usually massive and difficult to turn on or off at a moment's notice. For instance, it seems inconceivable that a government would undertake a safety campaign and would remove and reinstate it randomly year after year. Second, most interventions have effects that persist over time even if the treatment is taken away. Thus, comparison observations measured after the treatment is removed may exhibit persisting treatment effects. Purely random assignment rules may be possible for single-person experiments with short-duration effects as in behavior modification studies, but for large-scale interventions a random rule is rather impractical.

The assignment variable may not be random, but it may be

known. For instance, the researcher in a token economy experiment might take 10 weeks of baseline measurements and then introduce the treatment for the next 10 weeks. The known assignment variable is time. A second example illustrates a known assignment variable that is not time. A doctor instructs a parent to take the child's temperature in the morning. If it is over 102°, a medicine is administered. The assignment variable is the child's temperature. More typically, if there is a known assignment variable, it is time. If time is a known assignment rule, then the point at which the treatment begins is determined *before* the data are collected and examined.

If time is the known assignment rule, we might wonder if there are any similarities between this design and the regression discontinuity design that also has a known assignment rule. Comparing Figures 5.1 and 7.1, we see a number of similarities. In both cases the variable on the $X$ axis is the assignment variable and the one on the $Y$ axis is the outcome variable. Also, both designs have a strict cutting point. For the regression discontinuity design, no one below a certain value receives the treatment, and for the time-series design, treatments are not delivered before a certain point in time. Many of the problems of analysis and interpretation for the regression discontinuity design also apply to the interrupted time-series design.

The most typical pattern of assignment for the interrupted time-series design is an unknown assignment rule. Administrative and governmental agencies at some time point decide to mount a new program. The reasons for such a venture are often so complex as to defy simple analysis. Consider the decision in 1973 to discontinue the military draft in the United States. This decision was brought about by a host of conflicting trends, and once the discontinuation was decided upon it was difficult to reverse. Some of the variables responsible for this decision might be measured, but we can never be certain that we have measured all of the relevant ones.

If the assignment variable is unknown, to obtain unbiased estimates we must assume that it does not cause the outcome variable. Alternatively and more realistically, we are forced to assume that the unknown assignment rule covaries with time, and that the assignment variable is unrelated to the outcome when time is controlled. Thus, we must assume that time acts as a proxy variable for the unknown assignment variable. To the extent that the assignment variable is related to the outcome even when time is controlled or, equivalently, to the extent that time is a poor proxy for the assignment variable, then the estimate of treatment effects may be biased even if time is controlled. The problem here of controlling for an unknown assignment rule is very similar to the problems discussed in the preceding chapter in the analysis of the nonequivalent control group design. In this case, however, time is used as a proxy for the unknown assignment variable, whereas in the nonequivalent control group design, pretest scores are used. If time is a poor proxy for the assignment variable, treatment effects may be either overestimated or underestimated depending on the direction of the relationship between the outcome and the unknown assignment variable controlling for time.

If we know that time is the assignment variable or if we can assume that it is a good proxy for the unknown assignment variable, we can borrow a model for analyzing the time-series design from the regression discontinuity design:

$$Y_t = b_0 + b_1 T_t + b_2 X_t + e_t \qquad (7.1)$$

where $Y$ is the outcome variable, $T$ is time (e.g., year 1, 20, 33), $X$ is a dummy variable for treatment (0 = untreated, 1 = treated), $e$ is a residual error, and $t$ refers to time point. We set $t$ and $T$ to one for the first observation, at two for the second, and at $N$ for the last observation. Using this convention, the intercept $b_0$ estimates what the observation would be if there were a data point taken the year before the first measurement. If the chronological year were used for $T$, then the intercept is the predicted value for the year before Christ was born! Equation 7.1 implicitly assumes that time is an adequate proxy for the assignment variable and that time's relationship with the outcome variable is linear. Both of these assumptions may not hold.

For our highway safety example in Table 7.1, we can estimate the parameters of Equation 7.1 by multiple regression:

$$Y_t = 3.8 + .2T_t - .9X_t + e_t \qquad (7.2)$$

The intercept value refers to the estimated value for the year 1954. The positive coefficient for time indicates that the rate of fatalities is increasing over time; the negative coefficient for the treatment indicates a decline in the rate of 9 deaths per 100,000. This is a relative decline, because the absolute number of deaths is increasing over time. The $t$-test for time is 8.030 and $-3.133$ for treatment.

There is a difficulty with the preceding analysis that creates a problem for significance testing. It is called *serial dependency*. Using a multiple regression, one must assume that the errors (the $e_t$'s) are independent. (The errors are the differences between the observed $Y_t$ and the $Y_t$ predicted by the regression equation.) In time-series designs, this assumption is improbable because the same unit is repeatedly observed. An examination of Figure 7.1 shows that the observations that are greater than their predicted values are adjacent and the observations that are less than their predicted value are also adjacent. This is the usual pattern for time-series data, and it has the following consequence: The estimates of the standard errors for all coefficients, including the treatment effect, are biased, making their *t*-tests also biased (Hibbs, 1974). Fortunately, the coefficients themselves are unbiased.

The problem of serial dependency is not something with which most applied social researchers are familiar. Before we plunge into a detailed discussion of it, a simple metaphor might increase our understanding. Serial dependency is a *disease* that infects time-series data. Before we can analyze our data by multiple regression, we must first run some tests. Once we have identified that our data are infected, we must perform a series of more detailed tests to diagnose accurately the exact form of the disease. There are two strains of the disease: autoregressive serial dependency and moving-average serial dependency. Interpreting these diagnostic tests is much like reading a set of x-rays, but instead of x-rays we have autocorrelograms. Once we have identified the disease we can operate on our data to remove the serial dependency. This is done by transforming the variables. The type of operation or transformation is determined by the strain of serial dependency. After the operation we can analyze the data by multiple regression. We should perform one last follow-up test to check whether we have removed all of the serial dependency.

Because some readers may be familiar with the literature on the analysis of interrupted time-series data, we shall briefly describe our perspective. There are two fairly independent traditions in the analysis of interrupted time-series data. The dominant tradition is the *forecasting approach* of Box and Jenkins (1970). This elegant but complicated approach is oriented primarily toward identifying a model of serial dependency. Glass, Willson, and Gottman (1975) and McCleary and Hay (1980) are primarily responsible for the diffusion of this approach to applied social researchers. The second approach, which is very similar to the procedures we have discussed

in previous chapters, is the econometric method. Various econometrics textbooks describe this method. Our approach, like that of
Gottman (1981), is to combine both the forecasting and econometric approaches.

The remainder of this chapter is divided into three sections. In the
first we pursue the problem of serial dependency. In the second
section we investigate the estimation of treatment effects given
serial dependency. In the third we consider complications in the
design.

## The problem of serial dependency

The major stumbling block of time-series analysis is the problem of
serial dependency. Serial dependency means that adjacent observations are more similar than observations that are not adjacent. It
violates the assumption of independence. We shall discuss first the
measurement of serial dependency, next models of serial dependency, then the issue of stationarity, and finally the direction of bias
when serial dependency is ignored.

### *Measurement of serial dependency*

Numerous measures of serial dependency have been proposed.
Economists usually employ the Durbin-Watson measure.[1] This
measure, while useful, is not as general as another measure of serial
dependency called *autocorrelation*. The measure of the lag one
autocorrelation or $r_1$ is defined as

$$r_1 = \frac{\sum\limits_{t=1}^{N-1} (Y_t - \overline{Y})(Y_{t+1} - \overline{Y})}{\sum\limits_{t=1}^{N} (Y_t - \overline{Y})^2}$$

where $\overline{Y}$ is the mean of the $Y$ observations. It is called the lag one
autocorrelation because observations that are being correlated are
separated by a lag of one unit of time. To compute the lag one
correlation, one simply staggers the observations as in the third
column of Table 7.1 and correlates these values with the unstag-
gered observations. The lag one autocorrelation is based on $N - 1$

[1] The Durbin-Watson statistic approximately equals $2(1 - r_1)$, where $r_1$ is the lag one
autocorrelation, which is defined later in this chapter.

observations, as can be seen in Table 7.1. One observation is lost through staggering. We should note that the autocorrelation is not, strictly speaking, a Pearson product-moment correlation, and so it requires specialized computer programs to compute it.[2] For the data in Table 7.1, the lag one autocorrelation is .750.

The autocorrelation can be estimated for different lags. The general formula of the lag $k$ autocorrelation or $r_k$ is

$$\frac{\sum_{t=1}^{N-k} (Y_t - \overline{Y})(Y_{t+k} - \overline{Y})}{\sum_{t=1}^{N} (Y_t - \overline{Y})^2}$$

Again the observations are staggered by $k$ steps, and $k$ observations are lost. Generally autocorrelations are computed up to $N/4$ lags.

For the models that we consider in this chapter, the autocorrelation is computed on the residuals and not the raw observations. Thus, for Equation 7.1, one computes for each time point

$$e_t = Y_t - b_0 - b_1 T_t - b_2 X_t$$

and then computes the autocorrelations on these residuals. (The values of $e_t$ are in column 7 of Table 7.1.) The formula for the autocorrelations of residuals is quite simple, because the mean of residuals is zero:

$$\frac{\sum_{t=1}^{N-k} e_t e_{t+k}}{\sum_{t=1}^{N} e_t^2}$$

The autocorrelations of the residuals for the first five lags are as follows:

$$r_1 = .431$$
$$r_2 = .057$$
$$r_3 = -.477$$
$$r_4 = -.546$$
$$r_5 = -.483$$

[2] An autocorrelation is not a true correlation, because the denominator is based on $N$ cases whereas the numerator is based on $N - 1$, creating an attenuation bias.

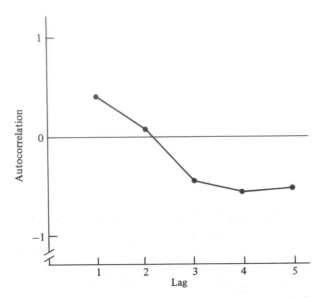

Figure 7.2. Autocorrelogram of residuals in Table 7.1.

Recall that the subscript of $r_k$ refers to lag length. In Figure 7.2 these autocorrelations are graphed in what is called an *autocorrelogram*.

It is possible to define the partial autocorrelations. The lag one partial autocorrelation ($r_{11}$) is identical to the lag one autocorrelation, because there is no intervening lag. The lag two partial autocorrelation or $r_{22}$ is the correlation between $e_t$ and $e_{t+2}$, partialling out $e_{t+1}$. Its formula is

$$\frac{r_2 - r_1^2}{1 - r_1^2} \tag{7.3}$$

In similar fashion, higher-order partials can be defined (cf. Glass et al., 1975). For instance, the partial autocorrelation between $e_t$ and $e_{t+3}$ controlling for $e_{t+1}$ and $e_{t+2}$ is denoted as $r_{33}$. To compute these partial autocorrelations one can input the simple autocorrelations into a computer package that computes partial correlations.

Autocorrelations are said to *dampen off* if, as the lag increases, the absolute value of the autocorrelation approaches zero at a deaccelerating rate. For instance, the series $.6^t$ ($t = 0, 1, 2, 3, 4, \ldots$) dampens off as follows:

1.0, .6, .36, .216, .1296, .07776

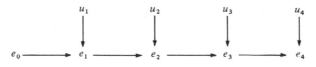

Figure 7.3. An autoregressive model of serial dependency.

because the rate of change is .4, .24, .144, .0864, and .05184. The series asymptotes at zero.

### Models of serial dependency

If there is serial dependence in the data, the researcher must adjust out that dependency. If he or she fails to do so, the tests of significance of the treatment effect are biased. To be successful in such adjustment, the type or model of serial dependency must be known. We shall consider the two classical models: autoregressive and moving-average. These are the two different "strains" of the "disease" of serial dependency. Moreover, we shall consider what are called second-order models of each type and a model that is a mixture of each.

Both autoregressive and moving-average models require that the data be *stationary*. The assumption of stationarity requires that the mean and variance of the time series be constant over time. The constant mean assumption implies no cycles or trends in the data, and the constant-variance assumption is similar to the homogeneity-of-variance assumption of multiple regression. These assumptions can be tested in part by splitting the pre-treatment time series in half and checking for stability of the mean and variance. We return to the issue of stationarity in a later section of the chapter.

Models of serial dependency have built into them a random or so-called white noise process. We shall denote the random variable or white noise process as $u$, all of whose autocorrelations are assumed to be zero. The models differ in the way that autocorrelation is introduced. We first consider the first-order autoregressive model and then consider the first-order moving-average model.

For the first-order autoregressive model, each error or residual, $e_t$, is assumed to be a function of only the previous error or residual. The equation is

$$e_t = ae_{t-1} + u_t$$

where $a$ is the autoregressive coefficient. The model is depicted in

Figure 7.4. A moving-average model of serial dependency.

Figure 7.3. It is called autoregressive because each error is regressed on a previous value of itself. A little bit of algebraic manipulation demonstrates that $a$ equals the autocorrelation of $e_t$ with $e_{t-1}$, that is, the lag one autocorrelation. A first-order autoregressive process also predicts the lag two correlation to be $a^2$ and, in general, the lag $k$ autocorrelation to be $a^k$. Thus, under the first-order autoregressive model, the autocorrelations should dampen off at a deaccelerating rate. For instance, if $a$ is .8, the autocorrelations are .800, .640, .512, .410, .328, .262, .168. Note that if $a$ is negative, which happens occasionally, then the autocorrelations alternate between positive and negative values, but they still dampen off over time.

Besides the dampening off of the autocorrelations for a first-order autoregressive process, there is a second and even more useful fact. All partial correlations of lag two or greater are zero. To see this for $r_{22}'$, we substitute into Equation 7.3 the values for $r_1 = a$ and $r_2 = a^2$,

$$\frac{a^2 - a^2}{1 - a^2}$$

which equals zero. In a similar fashion, $r_{33}$, $r_{44}$, and so forth can be shown to equal zero. The fact that the partial autocorrelations are zero makes intuitive sense. An autoregressive model implies that tomorrow's performance is due to today's. The link between yesterday and tomorrow is only through today. Once today is controlled, there is no relationship between tomorrow and yesterday.

The moving-average model looks superficially like an autoregressive model, but it has quite different implications for the autocorrelations. In equation form,[3] the model is

$$e_t = bu_{t-1} + u_t$$

where $b$ is the moving-average coefficient. The model is depicted in

[3] More commonly, the equation for the moving-average process is written as $e_t = u_t - bu_{t-1}$.

Table 7.2. *Five models of serial dependency*

| First-order autoregressive | $e_t = ae_{t-1} + u_t$ |
|---|---|
| Second-order autoregressive | $e_t = a_1 e_{t-1} + a_2 e_{t-2} + u_t$ |
| First-order moving-average | $e_t = bu_{t-1} + u_t$ |
| Second-order moving-average | $e_t = b_1 u_{t-1} + b_2 u_{t-2} + u_t$ |
| First-order autoregressive and moving-average | $e_t = ae_{t-1} + bu_{t-1} + u_t$ |

Figure 7.4. The lag one autocorrelation can be shown to be $b/(1 + b^2)$, whereas all other autocorrelations are zero. The estimate of $b$ is

$$\frac{1 - \sqrt{1 - 4r_1^2}}{2r_1}$$

The name "moving average" comes from the following fact.[4] If $b = 1.0$, then

$$e_t = u_{t-1} + u_t$$

Thus the value $e_t$ is an average (technically a sum) of $u_{t-1}$ and $u_t$.

If the autocorrelations are small, it may be virtually impossible to distinguish an autoregressive model from a moving-average model. Consider the case in which $a = .3$ and $b = \frac{1}{3}$. The resulting autocorrelations for both models are

|  | Lag | | | | |
|---|---|---|---|---|---|
|  | 1 | 2 | 3 | 4 | 5 |
| Autoregressive | .3 | .09 | .03 | .01 | .00 |
| Moving-average | .3 | .00 | .00 | .00 | .00 |

Given sampling error, these two patterns usually cannot be distinguished. We recommend treating such ambiguous patterns of autocorrelations as autoregressive, because such a process is gener-

---

[4] A moving average *transformation* is used to smooth a time series. Smoothing is an attempt to display trends in a time series more clearly. For instance, a stock's daily price might exhibit an increasing trend over time that is obscured by daily fluctuations. The time series is smoothed by computing a moving average of the average of each day and the previous day or each day and the previous 6 days. Any trend will now be more discernible. When smoothing the investigator computes a moving average to find trends, whereas our concern is trying to find the moving-average *process* that generates the serial dependency.

ally (though not always) more plausible as well as easier to adjust for.

Both the moving-average and autoregressive models can be extended. The autoregressive model that we have presented is called a first-order model, because the current residual is caused only by the previous value. A second-order model would have the current value caused by the two previous values as in Table 7.2. A $k$th-order model would have the previous $k$ values causing the present value.

Recall that for the first-order autoregressive process, the value of $r_{22}$ (the partial correlation of $e_t$ with $e_{t+2}$ controlling for $e_{t+1}$) and all higher-order partials should be zero. Similarly, for a second-order autoregressive process, $r_{33}$ and all higher-order partial autocorrelations are zero. Partial autocorrelations are especially diagnostic of the order of the autoregressive process, because all partial autocorrelations greater than the order of the autoregressive process should be zero. The simple autocorrelations should dampen off after $k$ lags, where $k$ is the order of the process.

For a second-order moving-average model, an error $e_t$ is assumed to be caused by $u_t$ and the previous two values of $u_t$ as shown in Table 7.2. The autocorrelations of the second-order moving average are

$$r_1 = \frac{b_1(1 + b_2)}{1 + b_1^2 + b_2^2} \tag{7.4}$$

$$r_2 = \frac{b_2}{1 + b_1^2 + b_2^2} \tag{7.5}$$

All other autocorrelations are zero. There is no simple solution for the values of $b_1$ and $b_2$ as a function of $r_1$ and $r_2$. One must then use trial values of $b_1$ and $b_2$ to determine the values that satisfy Equations 7.4 and 7.5.

A mixed autoregressive and moving-average model is also possible. Table 7.2 gives the equation for a first-order autoregressive, first-order moving-average model. For such a mixed model, none of the autocorrelations nor the partial autocorrelations is zero. Both functions dampen off. Fortunately, this complicated mixture of processes is rare. In fact, Gottman and Glass (1978) report finding none in their survey of 116 time series.

Table 7.3 summarizes the manner in which the autocorrelations and partial autocorrelations behave for the five different models we have presented. When we compare the autoregressive and moving-

Table 7.3. *Autocorrelograms and partial autocorrelograms for five models of serial dependency*

| Model | Autocorrelogram | Partial autocorrelogram |
|---|---|---|
| First-order autoregressive | Dampens off after lag one | Zero after lag one |
| Second-order autoregressive | Dampens off after lag two | Zero after lag two |
| First-order moving-average | Zero after lag one | Dampens off after lag one |
| Second-order moving-average | Zero after lag two | Dampens off after lag two |
| First-order autoregressive and moving-average | Dampens off after lag one | Dampens off after lag one |

average models, we note that they are, in a sense, the inverse of each other. For models of the same order, the autocorrelations of an autoregressive process behave like the partial autocorrelations of the corresponding moving-average process. Similarly, the partial autocorrelations of the autoregressive process behave like the auto-correlations of the corresponding moving-average process. A reason for this mirroring is that a first order moving-average process can be shown to be an infinite-order autoregressive process, and a first-order autoregressive process is an infinite-order moving-average process.

We must realize that Table 7.3 contains the idealized pattern of the correlations for the five models. In practice the picture is much more confused. Sampling error distorts the correlations. Values that are supposed to equal zero never exactly equal zero. We mentioned this problem earlier when we showed how first-order autoregressive and moving-average models can be virtually indistinguishable. The sampling-error problem is exacerbated if the time series contains no more than, say, thirty time points. Thirty is ordinarily a small sample, but in diagnosing serial dependency it is an extraordinarily small sample. Such diagnosing is often called an art instead of a science. With small sample sizes the art becomes largely guess-work.

There are significance tests that can aid us in our evaluation of serial dependency. The approximate standard error for a partial autocorrelation is $1/\sqrt{N}$. For the partial autocorrelation of residuals, we recommend substituting $N - m$ for $N$, where $m$ is the number of terms included in the regression equation from which the residuals are computed.

When all autocorrelations greater than lag $q$ are assumed to be zero, then the standard error for the lag $p$ autocorrelation $(p > q)$ is

$$\sqrt{\frac{1 + 2 \sum_{i=1}^{q} r_i^2}{N}} \tag{7.6}$$

One normally tests whether an autocorrelation of lag $k$ equals zero by setting $q$ at $k - 1$. To evaluate whether all correlations of lags $q$ through $p$ $(p > q)$ are zero, the following is approximately distributed as $\chi^2$:

$$N \sum_{i=q}^{p} r_i^2 \tag{7.7}$$

with $p - q + 1$ degrees of freedom. Again, for both Equations 7.6 and 7.7, when autocorrelations of residuals are computed, we recommend substituting $N - m$ (where $m$ is the number of predictor variables in the regression equation), as was done for test of the partial autocorrelations.

To evaluate autoregressive models, one should examine the partial autocorrelations. If only $r_{11}$ is significant, then the model is first-order. If $r_{22}$ is significant but the higher-order partials are not, then the model is second-order. For moving-average models, one tests autocorrelations rather than the partial autocorrelations. If the model is first-order, the autocorrelations can be tested individually using Formula 7.6 and setting $q$ equal to one. The autocorrelations can be tested as a group by using Formula 7.7 and setting $q$ equal to one and $p$ equal to $N/4$. If the process is second-order, $q$ in Formulas 7.6 and 7.7 is set to two.

### Issues in stationarity

If the time series is stationary, then the autocorrelations should dampen off over time. And so, the autocorrelations for long lags should be near zero, within the limits of sampling error. Suppose that there is a linear trend in the data as there is for the data in Figure 7.1. A time series with a linear trend is nonstationary, because the mean is increasing or decreasing over time. In the absence of any serial dependency, a linear trend produces a straight, descending autocorrelation function with no dampening. The strong linear trend in Figure 7.1 makes $r_1$ for the example .750 as opposed to .420 for the residuals from which the linear trend of time has been removed. Therefore, we want to examine the autocorrelations of data from which trends have been removed.

The presence of cycles also distorts the autocorrelational function. If there is a yearly cycle, as there would be for automobile accidents, given monthly data, there are typically high autocorrelations for lag $12k$, where $k$ is a positive integer. This is because certain months of the year will tend to have the highest rate of fatalities and other months will have the lowest.

Trends and cycles thus create spurious autocorrelations and their presence masks the true autocorrelational structure. The data must be adjusted to remove the nonstationary effects of trends and cycles. There are two alternative strategies to achieve this purpose: differencing and adding terms to the regression equation.

*Differencing.* This strategy has become the preferred approach of the Box-Jenkins method. A difference is just what the name suggests: A new variable is created by subtracting the most recent value from the present value. We take the *difference* between the present value and the previous value of data. To see how differencing can work, consider a linear trend model in which

$$Y_t = aT_t + e_t$$

where $T$ is time. The difference can be written as

$$
\begin{aligned}
Y_t - Y_{t-1} &= aT_t + e_t - aT_{t-1} - e_{t-1} \\
&= a(T_{t-1} + 1) + e_t - aT_{t-1} - e_{t-1} \\
&= a + e_t - e_{t-1}
\end{aligned}
$$

This result illustrates both the advantage and the disadvantage of differencing. The advantage is that the trend has vanished, because $T$ is removed from the equation for the difference; the disadvantage is that autocorrelation has been introduced, because both $e_t$ and $e_{t-1}$ are in the equation. The differenced time series is now a moving average. So, although differencing can remove a trend, it can also introduce serial dependency.

The difference between two observations is called the first difference. It is possible to perform a second difference, that is, a difference of differences:

$$(Y_t - Y_{t-1}) - (Y_{t-1} - Y_{t-2})$$

It can be illustrated that a second difference corrects for a quadratic trend. Consider the series $i^2$, where $i$ is the set of positive integers:

$$1, 4, 9, 25, 36, 49, \ldots$$

The first differences are

$$3, 5, 7, 9, 11, 13, \ldots$$

and the second differences are

$$2, 2, 2, 2, 2, \ldots$$

In general, a $k$th difference removes a $k$th-order trend. For instance, if the trend is cubic, the third difference removes it.

The logic for cycles is similar. If the data are monthly mean temperatures, we would certainly expect them to exhibit a cycle of 12 months. This should be evident in the autocorrelogram. If it peaks at lags that are multiples of 12, a yearly cycle would be indicated. To control for a yearly cycle by differencing, we take the difference between $Y_t$ and $Y_{t-12}$. Thus for the February 1983 data point we subtract the February 1982 data point. For certain data there may be two cycles. For instance, for hourly data there may be both a daily and a weekly cycle. We then subtract the measure for one day earlier and one week earlier to remove both cycles.[5]

The Box-Jenkins approach to time series denotes each model as a particular *autoregressive* (AR), *integrated* (I), *moving-average* (MA) or ARIMA model. Each ARIMA model has three characteristics: the order of the autoregressive process $(p)$, the order of the differencing $(d)$, and the order of the moving average $(q)$. Each model can then be characterized by the following convention: ARIMA $(p, d, q)$. For instance, an ARIMA $(1, 0, 0)$ model is a first-order autoregressive model. An ARIMA $(0, 2, 1)$ model is a second-order difference, first-order moving-average model. An

---

[5] More complicated models of cycles are discussed in McCain and McCleary (1979).

ARIMA (1, 0, 1) model is the mixed first-order autoregressive, moving-average model.

*Adding terms.* A simpler, though perhaps less elegant, procedure for removing trends and cycles is to add to the regression equation (Equation 7.1) terms that adjust for them. If a linear trend is suspected, one simply includes time or $T$ as a predictor in the regression equation. If it is suspected that nonlinear trends are present, powers of $T$ can be added. For cycles, a set of dummy variables must be created. For instance, for a yearly cycle a set of eleven variables representing months would be created. By entering them into the regression equation, the yearly cycle would be removed.

We prefer adding terms to the regression equation over differencing because we believe that differencing often introduces autocorrelation instead of removing it. Besides, if terms are added to the regression equation, their effects can be measured, interpreted, and tested. Others have taken a different point of view (McCleary & Hay, 1980).

### Direction of bias

As should be clear by now, serial dependency is a very complex problem. We might wonder if this problem is worth all the bother. It might be that the bias in the standard error introduced by serial dependency is positive. This would deflate the $t$-tests and make them conservative. We may be willing to live with a conservative test and ignore the bias.

The direction of bias depends largely on two factors. The first is the sign (positive or negative) of the autocorrelation of the errors. The second depends on the pattern of the treatment over time. The treatment is of course a variable, and one can compute an autocorrelation for it also. This treatment autocorrelation can be either positive or negative. The interrupted (i.e., using the first set of observations as untreated and the remaining as treated) design has a positive autocorrelation. A plan in which the treatment and comparison conditions alternate has a negative lag-one autocorrelation. The direction of the bias resulting from serial dependency depends on the product of the signs of the autocorrelation of the residuals and the autocorrelation of the treatment variable. If both

Table 7.4. *Estimates of autocorrelational parameters*

| Model | Coefficient estimate | Range |
|---|---|---|
| First-order autoregressive | $a = r_1$ | $|a| < 1$ |
| Second-order autoregressive | $a_1 = \dfrac{r_1 - r_1 r_2}{1 - r_1^2} \qquad a_2 = \dfrac{r_2 - r_1^2}{1 - r_1^2}$ | $a_1 + a_2 < 1$ <br> $a_2 - a_1 < 1$ <br> $|a_2| < 1$ |
| First-order moving-average | $b = \dfrac{1 - \sqrt{1 - 4r_1^2}}{2r_1}$ <br> Solve for $b_1$ and $b_2$ | $|b| < 1$ |
| Second-order moving-average | $r_1 = \dfrac{b_1 + b_1 b_2}{1 + b_1^2 + b_2^2} \qquad r_2 = \dfrac{b_2}{1 + b_1^2 - b_2^2}$ | $-b_1 - b_2 <$ <br> $1$ <br> $b_1 - b_2 < 1$ <br> $|b_2| < 1$ |
| First-order autoregressive and moving-average | $a = \dfrac{r_2}{r_1} \qquad b = \dfrac{k_2 - \sqrt{k_2^2 - 4k_1^2}}{2k_1}$ <br> where <br> $k_1 = \dfrac{r_1^2 - r_2}{r_1} \qquad k_2 = 1 + \dfrac{r_2^2}{r_1^2} - 2r_2$ | $|a| < 1$ <br> $|b| < 1$ |

are positive or negative, the *t*-test is usually too liberal. If one is negative and the other positive, the *t*-test is usually too conservative (Hibbs, 1974).

In the typical interrupted time-series design, both autocorrelations are positive, resulting in too liberal tests. In fact, the classic interrupted time-series intervention pattern yields a very substantial autocorrelation of the treatment variable. When the lag-one autocorrelation of the errors is .5, which is a common value, then the standard error is deflated by a factor of about .6 (Hibbs, 1974), and the *t*-test values are on the average 75% larger than what they should be.

We should note that if a random assignment rule is employed, there is no bias in the estimate of the standard error. Because the treatment is administered randomly over time, the autocorrelation for the treatment variable is zero, in principle, and the standard error is unbiased. However, as we stated earlier, a random assignment rule is rarely employed.

### Estimation

Once the researcher has established the model of serial dependency, the important task of estimating treatment effects can begin. To review, one 'cannot use ordinary multiple regression to estimate treatment effects because of the problem of serial dependency. Once a model of serial dependency is identified, however, the data can be transformed and the problem of serial dependency can be removed surgically. In order to perform the transformations, one must know the autoregressive or moving-average coefficients, that is, the $a$'s and $b$'s of Table 7.2. Table 7.4 summarizes how they can be estimated. This table also contains the permissible range of possible values. If the solution for a coefficient falls outside the range, the model is almost certainly wrong.

Gottman and Glass (1978) state that fifty observations are necessary to identify a model of serial dependency. If there are fewer than fifty observations, the coefficients as given in Table 7.4 are highly unstable and unreliable. One is in the same position as in Chapter 6, where the pretest reliability has to be estimated. One ought to choose a *range* of possible values.

To measure treatment effects, we need to "operate" on the data. The estimation of treatment effects in the interrupted time-series design has the following four steps:

1. The autocorrelation structure and its parameters are identified.
2. The outcome and predictor variables are transformed to make the error structure uncorrelated.
3. Using the transformed variables, the effects of treatment, trends, cycles, and covariates are estimated by multiple regression.
4. After computing the residuals of the transformed outcome variable, one checks to see if they are uncorrelated to ensure that the serial dependency has been removed.

Let us consider each step in detail. Step 1: One first fits the desired model with treatment effects, trends, cycles, and covariates. Using the residuals, one computes the autocorrelations and partial autocorrelations. We diagnose the autocorrelational structure by

Table 7.5. *Transformations to remove serial dependency:* $Z_t$ *stands for a predictor or outcome variable and* $Z_t{}^*$ *is the transformed value*

| | |
|---|---|
| First-order autoregressive | $Z_t{}^* = Z_t - aZ_{t-1}$ |
| Second-order autoregressive | $Z_t{}^* = Z_t - a_1 Z_{t-1} - a_2 Z_{t-2}$ |
| First-order moving-average[a] | $Z_t{}^* = Z_t - bZ_{t-1}{}^*$ |
| Second-order moving-average[a,b] | $Z_t{}^* = Z_t - b_1 Z_{t-1}{}^* - b_2 Z_{t-2}{}^*$ |
| First-order autoregressive and moving-average[a] | $Z_t{}^* = Z_t - aZ_{t-1} - bZ_{t-1}{}^*$ |

[a] Set $Z_1{}^*$ at $Z_1$.
[b] Set $Z_2{}^* = Z_2 - b_1 Z_1$.

the procedure we previously described under the section on models of serial dependency. If the autocorrelogram indicates the presence of trends or cycles, then the regression equation has to be reestimated to remove their effects. One would then recompute the residuals and rediagnose the model of serial dependence.

Step 2: If the autocorrelational structure is not random and serial dependency is indicated, then the data must be transformed. Given a particular model of serial dependency, a particular transformation of the data produces an uncorrelated error structure. The details of these transformations are given in Table 7.5. In Table 7.5 we have denoted the variable to be transformed as $Z_t$. We chose $Z_t$ to stand for each of the predictor variables including treatments and covariates as well as for the outcome variable. Because previous values are required, a problem arises for transforming the first observation of the series for first-order models and the first two observations for second-order models. Our recommendation is to drop these values from the analysis. Other complicated procedures have also been suggested (e.g., Glass et al., 1975).

Assume, for instance, that it is determined that the structure is a first-order autoregressive process:

$$Y_t = b_0 + b_1 T_t + b_2 X_t + e_t$$

where

$$e_t = ae_{t-1} + u_t$$

and $e$ has a mean of zero. If the value of $a$ is known, we could compute

$$Y_t - aY_{t-1} = b_0 + b_1 T_t + b_2 X_t + e_t$$
$$- a(b_0 + b_1 T_{t-1} + b_2 X_{t-1} + e_{t-1})$$
$$= b_0(1 - a) + b_1(T_t - aT_{t-1})$$
$$+ b_2(X_t - aX_{t-1}) + u_t$$

Because the $e$ variable has been removed from the equation and the only residual is $u$, there is no remaining serial dependency. If we regressed $Y_t^*$ ($= Y_t - aY_{t-1}$) on $T_t^*$ ($= T_t - aT_{t-1}$) and $X_t^*$ ($= X_t - aX_{t-1}$), we obtain a coefficient of $b_1^*$ for $T^*$ and $b_2^*$ for $X_t^*$ and an intercept of $b_0^*$. The value of $b_1^*$ is an effect of time, $b_2^*$ is an estimate of treatment effect, and $b_0^*$ is an estimate of the intercept[6] multiplied by $1 - a$.

A problem is that the transformation removes serial dependency only when the value of $a$ is known. In practice, $a$ must be estimated. As shown in Table 7.4, in the first-order autoregressive model, $a$ can be estimated by the lag one autocorrelation. Alternatively, one can use a series of values for $a$. For instance, we could try out all values from $-.95$ to $.95$ in steps of $.05$. We would settle on the value that produced the smallest value of $\Sigma u^2$, where $u$ is the residual from the transformed regression equation. This procedure, called a *grid search*, is employed by various specialized computer programs (Glass et al., 1975). If one employs this grid-search method, one must take care to determine that the range of possible values of the coefficients is within the ranges given in Table 7.4. [Besides a grid-search procedure one can also employ a more direct but more complicated algorithm (McCleary & Hay, 1980).] In Table 7.1 we have the transformed values of $Y^*$, $X^*$, and $T^*$ in columns 9, 10, and 11, assuming that $a = .4$. Note that the first observation is lost, because there is no $Y_0$, $X_0$, or $T_0$ to use for the transformation.

The transformation for the second-order autoregressive process is only slightly more complicated. As is shown in Table 7.5, one takes each variable (treatment, time, outcome variables, and covariates) and from each observation one subtracts off the previous two values weighted by the appropriate autoregressive coefficients:

$$Z_t^* = Z_t - a_1 Z_{t-1} - a_2 Z_{t-2}$$

---

[6] As explained later, the intercept "variable" of this transformed analysis should not be a set of ones, but rather it too should be transformed. The appropriate value for the transformed intercept is $1 - a$.

One can use the estimates of $a_1$ and $a_2$ in Table 7.4 or employ the grid-search method.

The transformation for the first-order moving-average model is slightly different. Each transformed observation equals the untransformed observation minus the previous *transformed* observation times the moving-average parameter as in Table 7.5. One important complication does arise for the intercept. Although not commonly recognized, the intercept can be considered a variable, all of whose values are ones. The intercept variable should, therefore, also be transformed. After transformation its values may not be constant. So, for example, in a first-order moving-average model, if $b$ equals .8, then the value of the intercept would be

$$
\begin{array}{lll}
1 - (.8)(1.0) & = .2 & t = 2 \\
1 - (.8)(\ .2) & = .84 & t = 3 \\
1 - (.8)(\ .84) & = .328 & t = 4 \\
1 - (.8)(\ .328) & = .7376 & t = 5
\end{array}
$$

Note that the value oscillates back and forth. This new transformed intercept must be used in the regression equation, not the usual intercept. This requires a multiple regression program that allows the user not to fit the intercept or, alternatively, to set it to zero. So if $T$ and $X$ are predictor variables in the equation, $T$, $X$, $Y$, and a "variable" all of whose values are one must be transformed. These four transformed variables and no intercept are used in the transformed regression equation. This problem does not occur for first-order autoregressive models, because the intercept "variable" remains a constant of $1 - a$.

Step 3: Once the variables and the intercept have been transformed, the researcher can input them into a multiple regression program. If serial dependency has been eliminated, then the $t$-tests are unbiased. For our example, using the values in Table 7.1, we regress $Y^*$ on $T^*$ and $X^*$ and we obtain the following equation:

$$
Y^* = 2.27 + .20T^* - .79X^* + u
$$

We should first note that the coefficients for $T^*$ and $X^*$ are different from the coefficients for $T$ and $X$ when $Y$ was regressed on them (Equation 7.2). The $t$-test for the treatment variable of the transformed equation is 2.405, which is 30% smaller than the $t$-test value obtained from the regression equation that ignored serial dependency.

Step 4: The autocorrelations between the transformed residuals can now be computed. (The transformed residuals, $u_t$, are in column 12 of Table 7.1.) One can test if the autocorrelations of these residuals are zero. If the $\chi^2$ test of Equation 7.7 is employed, the degrees of freedom of that test must be lessened by the number of autoregressive and moving-average coefficients estimated. If the transformed residuals exhibit no serial dependency, then the transformation has been successful. If they do, then the model of serial dependency needs to be rediagnosed.

For our example the autocorrelations of the transformed residuals are

$$r_1 = .116$$
$$r_2 = .099$$
$$r_3 = -.488$$
$$r_4 = -.300$$
$$r_5 = -.345$$

Using Equation 7.7 to evaluate if these five correlations are zero, we obtain $\chi^2 (4) = 7.99$.

### Complexities

As has been our custom, we have first discussed the basic, minimal design. We now consider the complications introduced by multiple variables, multiple units, and factors that influence power.

#### Multiple variables

We have assumed that the treatment variable is dichotomous and that its effect is immediate and constant. Also assumed is that there is a single outcome. Moreover, no covariates have been included. All of these limitations need not exist.

*Covariates.* As with all the designs we have considered in this book, it is useful to include covariates in the analysis.[7] In time-series designs there is the built-in covariate of time. We urge

---

[7] One should not use $Y_{t-1}$ as a covariate. The use of lagged values of the outcome variable (econometricians refer to them as lagged endogenous variables) creates the following problem. The effect of $Y_{t-1}$ on $Y_t$ is misestimated because the error for $Y_{t-1}$ ($e_{t-1}$) is correlated with $e_t$. Such a correlation is present because of serial dependency. Measures can be taken to remedy this problem, but they are beyond the scope of this book.

the inclusion of time as a covariate to control for linear trends in the outcome variable. The inclusion of time as a covariate both removes trends, promoting stationarity, and controls for the linear effects of the assignment variable. We also recommend fitting powers of time to handle nonlinear trends. Many times these nonlinear trends can be removed by transformation of the dependent variable (Mosteller & Tukey, 1977).

All covariates should be included in the Step 1 regression. They should then be transformed in Step 2 and these transformed values should be included in the Step 3 regression. If nonsignificant covariates are dropped from the Step 1 regression, the step should be repeated with the dropped variables not included in the regression equation.

*Dependent variables.* Very often there will be multiple outcome measures. For instance, the effect of an anticrime campaign could be measured on crimes, arrests, convictions, and public attitudes. These dependent variables could be analyzed separately if different effects are expected, or they can be combined in some fashion if their effects are presumed to be in the same direction. Glass et al. (1975) present a strategy that is analogous to canonical correlation for time-series data.[8]

It is sometimes advisable to consider disaggregating a time series by breaking it up into multiple time series. In essence this takes a single outcome measure and creates multiple measures. Such disaggregation may provide a more clear-cut test of treatment effects. For instance, Ross, Campbell, and Glass (1970) found that the breathanalyzer test for drunkenness reduced accidents in the late night hours but not during weekday commuting hours.

*Treatment.* We have assumed throughout that the treatment variable is a dichotomy. Actually any type of treatment variable is possible: multilevel variable, factorial combinations of two treatment variables, or an intervally measured treatment variable.

The effect of an intervention need not be immediate and constant (McCleary & Hay, 1980). Table 7.6 illustrates a number of possible coding schemes of the treatment variable. The first might be called a step change, because there is an immediate, constant,

---

[8] A latent-variable and multiple-indicator approach to time-series analysis is also possible in theory. Analytic work on this topic deserves exploration.

Table 7.6. *Patterns of interventions effects*

| Effect | Pre-treatment | | | | | | Post-treatment | | | |
|---|---|---|---|---|---|---|---|---|---|---|
| Step | 0 | 0 | 0 | 0 | 0 | 1 | 1 | 1 | 1 | 1 |
| Delay | 0 | 0 | 0 | 0 | 0 | 0 | 0 | 1 | 1 | 1 |
| One shot | 0 | 0 | 0 | 0 | 0 | 1 | 0 | 0 | 0 | 0 |
| Exponential decay | 0 | 0 | 0 | 0 | 0 | 1 | 1/2 | 1/4 | 1/8 | 1/16 |
| Geometric decay | 0 | 0 | 0 | 0 | 0 | 1 | 1/2 | 1/3 | 1/4 | 1/5 |
| Cummulating | 0 | 0 | 0 | 0 | 0 | 1 | 2 | 3 | 4 | 5 |
| Asymptoting | 0 | 0 | 0 | 0 | 0 | 1/16 | 1/8 | 1/4 | 1/2 | 1 |

and persistent effect. The next pattern, the delay, is just like the step pattern but there is a delay of two units of time between implementation of the treatment and its effects. In the one-shot pattern, the intervention has an effect that immediately disappears. The next four patterns show decay or increasing effects over time.

*Multiple units.* Very often there is more than one unit for which time-series data are available. The presence of such multiple units greatly enhances the internal validity of the design by enabling us to see if controlling for time adequately controls for an unknown assignment variable. For instance, Ross and Campbell (1968) used neighboring states to evaluate the effectiveness of the Connecticut crackdown on speeding. With these comparison states, one can estimate the effect on the nonexistent crackdown in those states. If a pseudotreatment effect also occurred in those states, then the "effect" would not be due to the crackdown but to some other factor, such as the weather.

A multiple-unit design may include units for which the occasion of the onset of the treatment is different. For instance, Parker, Campbell, Cook, Katzman, and Butler-Paisley (1971) investigated the effect of the introduction of television into various communities. Because the year in which television was introduced varied across communities, they could rule out the hypothesis that historical changes were confounded with the introduction of television.

### Power

There are two aspects of the time-series design that have interesting implications for power. First, because the time series usually contains data that are highly aggregated across persons and time itself, the relationships between variables tend to be greater than they would be if the variables were not aggregated. In Chapter 4 we discussed the fact that variables at the aggregate level typically correlate more highly than individual level variables. Such large correlations act as a two edge sword in terms of power. They can increase power because more variation in the outcome variable is explained. But power is decreased because the predictor variables are collinear. So the net effect of aggregation on power is uncertain.

The second point is that for certain models of serial dependency, power does not behave as we would expect it to. Ordinarily, as sample size gets very large, power approaches one. However, for a first-difference, first-order, moving-average model, as sample sizes increase, power approaches some value less than one. How much less than one depends on the size of the moving-average coefficient (Glass et al., 1975).

### Conclusion

The analysis of time-series data is seriously complicated by the problem of serial dependency. Detecting the pattern of dependency is complicated by the fact that there are a multitude of models of serial dependency, and cycles and trends can create spurious autocorrelation. A further complication arises because social science time series are often too short to allow for a precise identification of the model. Even once the pattern of autocorrelation is diagnosed, the estimation stage is not simple, because a transformation is required.

In order to accumulate a reasonable number of postintervention observations, the researcher is often forced literally to sit around and wait years. It would seem that the primary applications of the design in social research are retrospective, archival studies. Oddly enough, even though the design was developed primarily for applied research, most of the current interest in it is for basic research. For instance, a recent book edited by Kratochwill (1978) extensively discusses its use in behavior modification.

Many of the statistics and procedures of time-series analysis are unique to this design. Researchers will have to find specialized computer programs to analyze their data (McCleary & Hay, 1980). They should realize that these programs may use alternative statistics and procedures instead of the ones we have described. Those methods may be more complex than those we have discussed. We have presented only an introduction to the topic.

We should not lose sight of the fact that although most of this chapter was devoted to the problem of, and the solution for, serial dependency, a more serious issue remains. Typically the reason why the intervention is turned on and off is solely a matter of speculation. The assignment variable is both unknown and unmeasured. We can hope that its effects on the outcome measure are mediated through time, but this is only a hope. It does not seem likely to us that forces that bring about a social change increase in a simply linear fashion over time. Bias in the estimates of treatment effects is a neglected topic in time-series designs. From our point of view, it is at least as large a problem as bias in the standard errors arising from serial dependency.

# 8

# Miscellaneous designs and issues

Not every research project fits neatly into a prepackaged design. The choice of design should be guided by the scope of the problem and limitations of resources rather than by convention or habit. The first half of this chapter explores four designs not covered in the previous chapters. There are also a number of issues that crosscut the design of the research. The second half of the chapter considers these miscellaneous issues.

### Miscellaneous designs

The first two designs that we discuss are variants of the nonequivalent control group design. The first, the changing treatment design, allows for changes in subjects' status on the treatment variable. The second, the age cohort design, matches subjects on their age. The next two designs involve only a treatment group that is pretested and posttested. The patched-up design involves different cohorts of subjects all of whom receive the same treatment. The value-added approach attempts to model a growth curve over time.

### *Changing treatment design*

For many real-world treatments a person's status on the treatment changes over time. Being unemployed, undergoing psychotherapy, receiving welfare, and being married are all treatments that we enter and leave over time. Consider the study by Cohn (1978) that examined the effects of unemployment on self-esteem. In 1968–9 persons' employment status and various social variables were measured. The subjects were remeasured a year later and most subjects' employment status remained the same. However, some

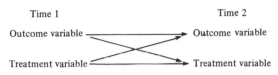

Figure 8.1. Regression model for the changing treatment design.

became unemployed and others gained employment during the year. There are then four groups of subjects:

1 Persons employed at both times (*EE*)
2 Persons unemployed at both times (*UU*)
3 Persons who became unemployed (*EU*)
4 Persons who gained employment (*UE*)

The letters *E* and *U* refer to employed and unemployed, respectively, while the first letter refers to status at time 1 and the second to status at time 2. Such a design is very similar to the nonequivalent control group design, but here the treatment variable changes over time. We shall discuss two different analysis strategies for this design that parallel the two analysis strategies for the nonequivalent control group design in Chapter 6.

*Regression adjustment.* Perhaps the most natural model for this design is shown in Figure 8.1. The treatment variable at time 1 is presumed to cause the outcome variable at time 2 and the outcome variable at time 1 is presumed to be an assignment variable for the treatment at time 2. The estimate of the treatment effect is obtained by the regression of the outcome variable at time 2 on the treatment and outcome variables at time 1. Such a strategy is virtually identical to the regression adjustment procedure described in Chapter 6 for the nonequivalent control group design. The only difference is that here the treatment variable changes over time.

The various considerations that we raised in Chapter 6 about this analysis are relevant here. In particular, it is necessary to adjust for measurement error in the time 1 outcome variable. This adjustment is necessary because the true outcome at time 1, rather than the measured outcome, needs to be controlled. As we saw earlier, this can be accomplished by adjusting the time 1 measure for unreliability via a reliability correction. The more complicated but more general solution of structural modeling is possible when there are multiple measures of the time 1 outcome construct.

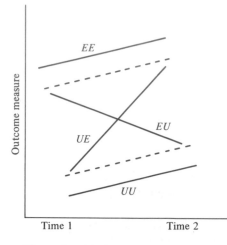

Figure 8.2. Idealized pattern of means for the changing treatment design ($E$ = employed; $U$ = unemployed; order refers to time).

If there are three occasions of measurement, there are two estimates of the treatment effect: the effect of the time 1 treatment variable on the time 2 outcome variable and the effect of the time 2 treatment variable on the time 3 outcome variable. These two estimates can be pooled through generalized least squares, as described by Hannan and Young (1977).

*Change analysis.* The change score analysis described in Chapter 6 cannot be simply extended to the "changing treatment variable" design. We stated there that for the nonequivalent control group design, change score analysis is plausible only when the assignment variable is unchanging. However, for the changing treatment design we know that subjects are entering and leaving the treatment. One must then presume that the assignment variable itself has changed and that changes in it have brought about changes in the treatment variable.

In Figure 8.2 we have graphed hypothetical means from a changing treatment design. To simplify the discussion, the graph has no discernible treatment effect over time. The top and bottom lines are for those persons whose treatment status does not change, that is, those who remain employed or unemployed. As we did in discussing the change score analysis in Chapter 6, we have assumed that in the absence of any treatment effect, the difference between

Table 8.1. *Means for various cells of an age cohort design*

|  | Age at pretesting | | | | | |
|  | 5 | | 6 | | 7 | |
|  | Treated | Untreated | Treated | Untreated | Treated | Untreated |
| Pretest | 99.0 | 100.9 | 104.2 | 103.9 | 108.1 | 107.7 |
| Posttest | 113.4 | 105.8 | 115.6 | 109.3 | 121.0 | 113.0 |

the two groups (*EE* and *UU*) is constant over time. Thus, the persons who do not change on the treatment variable can be analyzed as if they were part of the nonequivalent control group design, if stationarity can be assumed.

The remaining subjects are those whose treatment status changes. These groups are designated as *EU* and *UE* (*E* = employed, *U* = unemployed), where the first term designates time 1 and the second time 2. For these subjects the assignment variable has presumably changed, because persons have changed treatments. In Figure 8.2 we have connected the two employed means and the two unemployed means from the *EU* and *UE* groups by two dashed lines. We assume that these two dashed lines are parallel, that is, the "growth" rates for the two groups are equal. This analysis assumes that the effects of the assignment variable at time 1 on both the treatment and outcome variables at time 1 are the same as those respective effects at time 2. Such a stationarity assumption is similar but more complex than the stationarity assumption that was made in Chapter 6 for change score analysis.[1] Analytically, given this assumption, the change score analogue of data from those whose treatment status varies over time is as follows: One averages across time the scores of the *EU* group and likewise one averages the scores across time of the *UE* group. The null hypothesis of no treatment effect is tested by testing if the two means of the average scores from the two groups are equal.

We are then proposing a two-part analysis. The first is a change analysis as was described in Chapter 6 on the persons whose treatment status does not change. The second looks at the "changers." As was discussed in Chapter 6, one should consider possible

[1] It can be shown that in the case of an intervally measured treatment variable, one generalization of this strategy is cross-lagged panel correlation analysis (Kenny, 1975, 1981).

transformations of the outcome variable in order to meet the assumptions for both of these analyses. As explained in that chapter, variance-stabilizing transformations increase the probability of obtaining an interpretable result.

### Age cohort design

As we saw in Chapter 6, a major threat to the internal validity in the nonequivalent control group design is the interaction of selection and maturation. One way to control for this interaction is to employ an *age cohort design.* In most studies subjects are heterogeneous in age.[2] This is what is exploited by an age cohort design.

Table 8.1 presents an example of the design. Subjects 5, 6, and 7 years of age are pretested and 1 year later are posttested. Thus, the subjects who were pretested at age 5 are 6-year-olds when posttested; those who were pretested at age 6 are age 7 when posttested; and those who were pretested at age 7 are age 8 when posttested. Table 8.2 is a rearrangement of some of the data in Table 8.1. Data from those who are 6 years old when tested (those pretested at age 6 and those posttested at age 6) are grouped together as well as those who are 7 years old (those pretested at age 7 and those posttested at age 7). Not included in Table 8.2 are the pretest data of the 5-year-olds and the posttest data of the 8-year-olds, because no 5-year-olds were posttested and no 8-year-olds were pretested. The treatment-versus-control column heading of Table 8.2 refers to whether the child entered the treatment program or not. The pretest-versus-posttest row heading refers to the point in time at which the data were taken.

The logic of the age cohort design is as follows: Considering the 6-year-olds, if there were no treatment effects, then the row effect in Table 8.2 would measure the effect of testing and history, because pretest data are compared to posttest data. If again there were no treatment effects, the column effect would measure the effect of selection, because treated data are compared to untreated data. However, if there were a treatment effect, then the mean for the posttest–treated subjects would be too high to be explained simply by the row and column main effects. Treatment effects are then indicated by a row (pretest vs. posttest) by column (treatment vs.

---

[2] Although years from birth is the usual way in which age is measured in this design, it can be measured in other ways. For instance, in a study of pregnant women, the appropriate age measure might be month of pregnancy.

Table 8.2. *Specific comparisons of the age cohort design*

|  | Treated | Untreated |
| --- | --- | --- |
| 6-year-olds |  |  |
| Pretest | 104.2 | 103.9 |
| Posttest | 113.4 | 105.8 |
| 7-year-olds |  |  |
| Pretest | 108.1 | 107.7 |
| Posttest | 115.6 | 109.3 |

control) interaction. Such an analysis can be performed separately on the 6- and 7-year-olds.

There are three important features of the age cohort design that deserve special mention. First, the pretest data of the youngest children and the posttest data of the oldest children cannot be analyzed by the design. Thus, some data are lost. Second, the analyses of the 6- and 7-year-olds are not independent. The pretest scores of the 6-year-olds and the posttest scores of the 7-year-olds come from the same children and so the two analyses are not independent. This particular type of nonindependence (see the discussion later in this chapter) does not increase the chances of finding consistent treatment effects across age groups, rather, it decreases them. Third, although the design is longitudinal, it does not exploit this fact. All comparisons are between different subjects rather than within the same subjects as in a longitudinal design. Thus the usual increases in power afforded by having longitudinal data are lost in this analysis. Although one can and should control for other covariates, one cannot control for pretest status.

Although the design makes good intuitive sense, it still makes assumptions about the assignment variable. There are two ways in which the age cohort design can yield internally valid results. First, if age is the assignment variable, then its effects are controlled by the design because the effect of the assignment variable (age) is controlled. Second, the conditions that permit change score analysis that were discussed in Chapter 6 also result in unbiased estimates for the age cohort design. The age cohort design has one strength over the nonequivalent control group design, which is that the selection by maturation hypothesis is ruled out. Because the age cohort design separately analyzes pre- and posttests from subjects who are the same age, differential maturation is not a problem. However, the age cohort design does presume that the effects of the unknown assignment variable are the same on the pretest and the posttest for subjects of the same age. This is virtually the same assumption that was made in Chapter 6 for change score analysis. Except for the fact that age and its interaction with selection are controlled, the assumptions of the age cohort design are no more plausible than they are for a change score analysis of the nonequivalent control group design.[3]

### Patched-up design

Schools, hospitals, prisons, as well as other institutions are repeatedly admitting and treating groups of persons, and we frequently want to know how these institutions affect the lives of their clients or victims, as the case may be. One common way to answer this question is to measure groups of persons or cohorts as they enter the institution and as they leave. Campbell and Stanley (1963) refer to this design as the recurrent institutional cycle design or the patched-up design. We shall use the latter term. In Table 8.3 hypothetical results from the design are presented. Four cohorts enter a management training program from 1981 through 1984. Only post-treatment data are available for the first cohort and pre-treatment data for the last cohort. The middle two cohorts provide complete data. Typically for the patched-up design, the occasion of the post-treatment and pre-treatment measures of adjacent cohorts is not simultaneous.

Table 8.3 presents an idealized pattern of results for the patched-up design. For the two cohorts with complete data, the post-treatment means are about two units higher than the pre-treatment means: 10.2 versus 8.1 for the 1982 cohort, and 10.4 versus 8.3 for the 1983 cohort. The results of these longitudinal comparisons are suggestive of a treatment effect. Comparing within years, there is again evidence of a treatment effect of approximately two units for 1982 (10.3 vs. 8.1), for 1983 (10.2 vs. 8.3), and for 1984 (10.4 vs. 8.2).

There are four problems with the patched-up design. The first is

---

[3] Essentially this analysis matches subjects on age. In order to execute such a matching, age, which is a continuous variable, must be broken up into discrete categories (in our example, years). The choice of the category width will affect the success of the matching strategy (Rubin, 1973).

Table 8.3. *Hypothetical means from a patched-up design*

| | Year of measurement | | |
|---|---|---|---|
| Cohort | 1982 | 1983 | 1984 |
| 1981 | 10.3 | | |
| 1982 | 8.1 | 10.2 | |
| 1983 | | 8.3 | 10.4 |
| 1984 | | | 8.2 |

testing. The change in trainees' performance might not be due to the treatment but only to the effect of testing. Campbell and Stanley (1963) recommend randomly splitting in half the 1982 and 1983 cohorts and pretesting half and not pretesting the other half. Any post-treatment difference between these two groups would indicate testing effects.

Regression toward the mean is also a problem in this design. If subjects are selected into the program because they are extreme (either overprivileged or underprivileged), then we would expect their post-treatment mean to be different from their pre-treatment because of regression toward the mean. One solution to this problem is to avoid using selection schemes that pick extreme scorers.

Maturation is probably the most serious threat to the internal validity of the patched-up design. The trainees are a year older at the time of the posttest than they were at the time of the pretest. In some very special cases maturation may not be plausible. For instance, if for the variables under study we have good reasons to believe that the trainees would not change or the interval between pre- and posttest measures is short, maturation may not be plausible. Alternatively, it may be possible to control for maturation by employing a modified version of the age cohort design or by using the value-added analysis that we discuss in the next section.

Some have claimed that history is not a serious problem for the patched-up design. Because pre- and post-treatment measurements are made at approximately the same point in time, the within-time comparisons control for the effect of history. However, the within-time comparisons are confounded with cohort differences. It is possible (if not plausible) to concoct an explanation of the means of Table 8.3 in terms of the combined effects of history and cohort. Imagine that one of the goals of the management trainee program is to increase racial tolerance. The means in Table 8.3 could be explained in terms of the combined effects of cohort and history. The cohort effect would be that over time the company recruited increasingly less tolerant trainees, explaining the within-year differences. As a society, people are becoming more tolerant, which would explain the over-time differences.[4]

We believe that the two most serious threats to the design are maturation and regression toward the mean. There is no general solution to these two problems beyond finding an untreated comparison group. This would turn the patched-up design into a nonequivalent control group design.

### Value-added approach

To some observers the elaborate methods we have presented to measure treatment effects might seem far too complicated and unnecessary. Why could we not simply project an individual's growth and then see whether the treatment stunts or accelerates the growth curve? For instance, for a nutrition program, a model of change in physical height could be used to predict change. In a similar way, why could we not more carefully understand the growth pattern of the phenomena of interest and use that as a model of growth? In other words, why could we not model the process of maturation?

Such a strategy has been pursued most vigorously by Bryk and Weisberg (Bryk & Weisberg, 1976, 1977; Strenio, Bryk, & Weisberg, 1977) in their *value-added* approach. For each treated subject they attempt to measure how much the treatment adds onto his or her outcome score. The actual mechanics of the procedure are beyond the scope of this book, but the crux of the approach is that they view growth to be a function of two systematic components. These are the rate of growth (or how fast people grow) and the onset of growth (or when people start growing). To these systematic components they add a random component. They have allowed the growth rate to be either a linear function or a negative exponential function.

For instance, Bryk and Weisberg (1976) applied their analysis to

---

[4] Adam (1978) has shown that the combined effects of cohort and history are confounded with the effect of maturation. Because maturation is confounded with treatment, the combined effects of cohort and history are confounded with treatment effects.

an evaluation of Planned Variation in Head Start. They assumed a relatively simple model of growth. From the pretest data they measured the effect of age on the pretest controlling for a series of covariates. Such a procedure assumes that all subjects begin growing at the same time, grow at the same rate, and grow in a linear fashion.

Although we see much merit and promise in the long-run possibilities of the value-added approach, we are somewhat less optimistic about its present usefulness for the following two reasons. First, to plot a growth curve we need to have the same units of measurement across time. For instance, for height, inches or centimeters would be used. In *social* research, however, the choice of the units of measurement is not so clear. For variables on which subjects are growing, different tests are needed for different ages or else serious ceiling or floor effects would result. Calibrating the units of measurement of different tests is not a simple problem. Even if exactly the same test were used at two or more times, spurious "growth" would result due to a testing effect. The units of measurement problem is a difficult but not impossible challenge. More work is clearly needed.

Second, the bulk of the Bryk-Weisberg growth models are deterministic. That is, time brings about patterned changes that may vary across individuals but nonetheless are driven by time. Although such models may be valid for the growth of height or weight for which there are both a large genetic component and stable environmental causes, we believe that the development of social and intellectual skills must leave room for a changing environment. We would hope that future developments of growth models for social variables would be less deterministic.

### Miscellaneous issues

We have saved a number of issues for discussion until now. These issues are relevant for all the designs we have discussed. We discuss four different issues. The first two concern threats to internal validity. The confusing topic of regression toward the mean is explained. Next we consider the difficult question of the effect of mortality on the internal validity of conclusions. We then discuss two issues that affect conclusion validity. These topics are independence and the unit of analysis.

### Regression toward the mean

Because the topic of regression toward the mean can be very confusing, it is useful to consider it in some detail. Much of the discussion that follows is based on the excellent article by Furby (1973).

The definition of regression toward the mean is that, on the average, persons with extreme scores on a given variable (i.e., extreme in terms of standard deviation units) are not as extreme when measured on some other variable. All parts of the definition are essential, and the failure to consider each necessarily leads to confusion. To simplify presentation, the two variables to be considered are a pretest and a posttest of some measure, but this in no way limits the applicability of our discussion.

First, regression to the mean refers not to each and every individual but to an average. Not all individuals regress to the mean; only the typical individual does. Quite a few individuals may regress away from the mean, but this regression away is canceled out by the regression toward the mean of the remaining individuals.

Second, regression toward the mean refers to standard deviation units. The *untransformed* or raw unit of measurement might not exhibit regression. The old adage that "the rich get richer and the poor get poorer" seems to fly in the face of the regression toward the mean concept, because extreme scores are becoming even more extreme over time. But if the rich get richer and the poor get poorer, then the variability of income must be increasing over time. Once the measures are put into standard deviation units (or the variances are made equal over time), we shall find that the rich are getting *relatively* poorer and the poor are getting *relatively* richer. Regression to the mean still holds, even though *absolutely* the rich may have more money and the poor less. Extreme scores on a variable do not regress over time toward the mean of *that* variable; rather, a person whose score is extreme in terms of standard deviation units regresses toward zero when measured on another variable in standard deviation units.

An important aspect of regression toward the mean is that change (when each variable is measured in standard deviation units) is negatively correlated with initial status. In other words, the posttest minus the pretest (both variables standardized) cannot correlate positively with the pretest.

The amount of regression toward the mean is solely a function of the pretest–posttest correlation. If the correlation is one, there is no regression toward the mean, because there is no relative change. If it is zero, there is complete regression toward the mean, because the predicted score for each subject is the mean. (If it is negative, there is regression past the mean.) Errors of measurement exacerbate regression toward the mean. As will be shown in Chapter 9, the effect of random measurement error is to lower correlations. Because the correlation between the pretest and the posttest determines the amount of regression, and because greater amounts of measurement error (*unreliability*) lower correlations, measurement error magnifies regression toward the mean. However, because test–retest correlations are less than one for other reasons besides unreliability (e.g., real relative change), *unreliability is not the only reason for regression toward the mean.*

When there are multiple populations, the pattern of regression toward the mean can be complicated. As defined, regression toward the mean refers to the average score. Not each and every individual moves toward the mean, only the average. For instance, consider the example of intelligence test scores from a school for the retarded. If somehow the scores of the staff and the students were mixed together, we would *not* expect the average IQ of the staff to regress down toward the overall mean or the average IQ of the students to regress up toward the overall mean. Rather, we would expect the staff scores to regress toward their mean and the student scores to regress toward their mean. Although there is still regression toward the mean, it is more accurate to state that regression toward the mean occurs within the population of staff scores and within the population of student scores.

In sum, regression toward the mean refers to the average individual (not each individual) and to standard scores (not raw scores). The magnitude of regression toward the mean depends on the test–retest correlation. Given multiple populations, the pattern of regression toward the mean can be complex.

### Mortality

An applied research program takes place over a period of months or years. During the interim the subjects relocate, drop out of the program, graduate, are promoted, refuse to be tested, or, in the most extreme case of mortality, die.[5] Mortality is a problem that

---

[5] There are two different types of subject mortality. First, there is mortality from the study altogether; e.g., subjects move. Second, there is mortality from the treatment; e.g. subjects

researchers should count on. Unfortunately, we can offer no simple solutions to this problem.

Mortality is often an important outcome of an intervention. For instance, Murphy and Appel (1977) extensively analyzed the effect of computer-aided instruction on dropping out of courses in Chicago community colleges. Because the dropout rate is normally relatively high (approximately 35%), an intervention that increased the probability of remaining in a class would be a major success even if it did not improve performance.

For most applied studies the dropout rate is not the central outcome. The presence of mortality creates problems of internal validity. For instance, in a drug program all the individuals who are treated unsuccessfully could be urged to leave the program. If only the outcomes of the successfully treated are analyzed, treatment effects will be overestimated. One approach to the problem of mortality is to assume that the biasing effects of mortality in the treatment and comparison groups are the same. The researcher compares the dropout *rate* in both groups and tests to see if they are the same. However, even if no difference in dropout rate between conditions is found, mortality could still be a problem. It might well be that persons drop out of the treated and untreated groups at the same rate but for different reasons. For instance, for an adolescent counseling program, it could happen that equal proportions of treatment and comparison subjects drop out. However, it may be that among treated subjects, those who drop out do so because they have been successfully treated (i.e., they no longer need counseling), whereas in the comparison group the subjects who drop out are incorrigible. So, although equal dropout rates for the groups may be heartening, mortality may still pose a problem.

Besides comparing dropout rates, we might also compare those who drop out with those who do not on the covariates that were measured prior to dropout. An analysis is set up in which the covariates are each regressed upon the treatment variable and upon a variable that indicates whether or not a subject dropped out. Mortality is a threat to internal validity whenever the dropping-out variable interacts with the treatment variable. So finding out that subjects from low socioeconomic backgrounds were more likely to drop out of all treatment conditions would not necessarily be alarming, at least in terms of internal validity. But if this effect were

drop out of the program, but they may still remain accessible for measurement. It is important that researchers try to follow up this latter group.

stronger in the treatment condition than in the comparison condition, we should worry. Socioeconomic status is then acting as an assignment variable and should be controlled in the outcome analysis.

### Independence

In Chapter 4 we pointed out that the failure to have independent units can bias the estimate of the standard error of the treatment effect. Independence refers to uncorrelated residuals in the regression equation. The usual presumption is that a violation of the independence assumption makes the estimate of error variance too small, resulting in too large an $F$- or $t$-test. Too small an estimate of error results in too *liberal* a test and too many Type I errors. As we shall see, bias in the estimate of error variance can occasionally create too many Type II errors.

Violation of the independence assumption can come about in many different ways. First, there is the case of serial dependency (reviewed extensively in Chapter 7). For time-series data, adjacent observations tend to be more highly correlated than observations separated far in time. Another form of nonindependence is spatial dependency. Observations adjacent in space are more similar than those far apart. For example in a study of a city's day-care centers, we would expect that centers that are geographically close would be more similar than those far apart.

Besides serial and spatial dependency, nonindependence can arise because of social reasons. In natural settings persons are not kept physically separated and isolated. Rather, they communicate with each other, provide mutual assistance, imitate each other's behavior, and occasionally compete with one another. Given these social processes, it is not valid to treat the data as a set of independent replications. A related problem is that interventions are typically embedded in a social setting. The norms and atmosphere of that setting make the scores of subjects more alike than would be the scores of subjects from different settings.

The design of the research can also create problems of nonindependence. In social research a subject may have a "partner." The linkage with the partner can be a natural one, as in the case of husbands and wives or roommates, or it can be created by the researcher, as in the case of matched pairs of persons brought together to interact. If ignored in the analysis, the presence of partners (or triples or even larger groups) violates the independence assumption. As discussed in the next section, this violation can also be viewed as a unit of analysis problem.

To illustrate the different effects of nonindependence on the standard error, we shall consider a hypothetical study of the effects of marriage counseling on two outcome variables. The treatment is marriage counseling versus no marriage counseling; the two dependent measures are the individual's satisfaction with the marriage and the amount of housework done by each individual. There are two possible ways of delivering the treatment. We could assign both members of the couple to a treatment condition (the couple as the unit of assignment), or we could assign one member of the couple to the treatment and let the other serve as comparison (the individual as the unit of assignment). To simplify matters we assume in each case that assignment is done randomly.

Almost certainly a husband's score is correlated with his wife's score. The correlation would be positive for the satisfaction measure (if one member is satisfied, so is the other) and negative for the housework measure (if one person does most of the work, the other does less). Because the scores of the couple are correlated and therefore not independent, we cannot treat each person as an independent replication in the statistical analysis. Although we can and should include couple in the statistical analysis, it is instructive to consider the effect of ignoring couple on the standard error.

When couples are the unit of assignment, the estimate of the treatment effect involves a comparison of treated and untreated couples. However, looking within a treatment group, observations are not independent, because the husband and wife are both in the same group. We have then a biased estimate of the variation within treatment groups because of nonindependence. The variation is underestimated when the correlation between spouses is positive, as in the case of the satisfaction measure. To understand this better, consider the case in which husbands and wives totally agree on how satisfied they are in their marriages. In such a case the variation of subjects within treatment groups is deflated because married partners have identical scores. In a sense there are twice as many degrees of freedom as there ought to be. When the correlation is negative, the error term is inflated, because the scores within groups are dissimilar.

If individuals are the unit of assignment, for the satisfaction measure the estimate of error is too large. Persons within each

Table 8.4. *The effect of nonindependence on whether the test of the treatment is too liberal (too many Type I errors) or too conservative (too few Type I errors)*

| Nonindependence | Residuals correlated | |
|---|---|---|
| | Positively (satisfaction) | Negatively (housework) |
| Within treatment groups (couples assigned to treatment) | Liberal | Conservative |
| Between treatment groups (persons assigned to treatments) | Conservative | Liberal |

treatment group are not married to each other, whereas the comparison of treatment groups involves persons who are married to each other. Given the positive correlation for satisfaction, we would expect the treated and untreated means to be relatively similar, but this fact is not taken into account in the error term. If we examined the housework-dependent variable, the estimate of the error is too small. The treatment means would be negatively correlated, whereas the error term ignores this.

Table 8.4 summarizes the effects of type of nonindependence and the direction of the correlation of the outcome variable. The row heading refers to the type of nonindependence, which can either be within treatment groups or between treatment groups. *Within-treatment-group* nonindependence refers to contamination or linkages between persons who are in the same treatment. Thus the correlated observations are in the same treatment group. *Between-treatment-group* nonindependence refers to contamination or linkages between subjects who are in different treatment groups. Thus the correlated observations are in different treatment groups. Within a single experiment, both types of nonindependence are possible depending on what treatment variable we look at. For instance, for the marriage counseling example, couples might be assigned to either receive the treatment or not. For this treatment variable there is nonindependence within the treatment group, because the correlated observations are in the same treatment group. However, if sex of subject was looked at as a "treatment," then observations would be nonindependent between treatment groups, because the correlation is between persons of different sexes. Thus, within the same experiment, the standard error for one effect can be inflated whereas for another effect it can be deflated.

For the interrupted time-series design that we discussed in Chapter 7, nonindependence is a major problem. Table 8.4 can clarify the direction of bias for that design. It is reasonable to assume that the largest autocorrelations are those with the shortest lags. If such is the case and if the first set of observations are untreated and the next set of observations are treated, then the bulk of the nonindependence is within treatment groups, because adjacent observations are likely to be in the same treatment group. However, if the treatment is given to even-numbered time points and withheld from odd ones, the bulk of the nonindependence is between treatment groups. The sign of the autocorrelation coupled with the type of nonindependence determines the direction of bias in the standard error.

A violation of the independence assumption results in biased estimates of error variance. To solve this problem one needs to understand the process that generated correlated observations and take that process into account in the statistical analysis. This may mean transforming the data as in time-series analysis, or it may mean including new factors in the analysis, such as couple.

Before we leave the topic of nonindependence, we should note that it should not be viewed solely as a nuisance problem that invalidates standard tests of significance. For certain problems the pattern of nonindependence is the very topic of study. For instance, if we are interested in social networks, the diffusion of innovation, or classroom effects, the structure of nonindependence in the data specifies the social process.

### Unit of analysis

In Chapter 4 we discussed the issue of the *unit of analysis,* that is, the unit of the *statistical* analysis. We pointed out that the appropriate unit of analysis is usually the unit of assignment.

The unit-of-analysis question in social research is actually three very different but related questions that unfortunately get tangled together. To determine the unit of analysis we need to answer three different questions: *generalization, compositional effects,* and *independence.* Let us consider a hypothetical study to help us differentiate the three questions. Imagine a national survey of 100 day-care centers from which ten children in each day-care center are measured. The researcher wishes to measure the effect of government subsidy versus no government subsidy and the effect of the child's sex on social development. The question is what should be the unit of analysis: the child or the day-care center.

*Generalization* refers to the effect of subsidy on *what,* the child or day-care center. Although the child may seem to be the natural unit of generalization, there may be good reasons for preferring generalization at the level of the center. Subsidies are given to centers, not to children. Moreover, the subsidy is spent by the center, and its effect is presumably on all the children and not just some. For the effect of sex, it may seem that the only level of generalization is the child. However, it may be that sex has its effect through the sex ratio of the day-care center. In centers with high proportions of boys, the staffs have a certain orientation; whereas in those centers with high proportions of girls, the staffs act differently. Generalization at the center level is a more reasonable option to consider than might at first be thought.

*Compositional effects* refer to the fact that individuals have been placed into the different day-care centers in a nonrandom fashion. The children in the different centers may differ in terms of age, parental background, and the like. The different day-care centers are composed of different types of persons. Because the subsidies are given to the center and the centers differ in terms of their composition, the individual level of analysis is not appropriate. If the child were the unit of analysis, then compositional differences would be confounded with the treatment variable. The presence of compositional effects then raises questions concerning the unit of analysis.

*Independence* is the most neglected aspect of the unit of analysis-related questions. In day-care centers, children, hopefully, are not isolated in cells. Rather, they interact and mutually influence one another. When children's scores are correlated, the basic analysis model we have presented is not valid. Given nonindependent observations, the appropriate unit of analysis is the center.

*If one wishes to generalize at the level of the day-care center, or is worried about either the presence of compositional effects or nonindependence, one should treat the day-care center as the unit of analysis.* However, the costs in terms of conclusion validity may be prohibitive. For our example, if the individual is the unit of analysis, there are about 1,000 degrees of freedom, whereas if the

Table 8.5. *Analysis-of-variance table for a hierarchically nested design*

| Source of variance | Mean Square | Degrees of freedom |
|---|---|---|
| Treatments ($T$) | $MS_T$ | 1 |
| Centers within treatments ($C$) | $MS_C$ | 98 |
| Subjects within centers within treatments ($S$) | $MS_S$ | 900 |

center is the unit, the degrees of freedom are about 100. It would be well worth the time and effort to determine if the individual could be used as the unit of analysis, even if one assumes that there are nonindependence or compositional effects. One can evaluate empirically whether compositional effects and nonindependence prohibit an analysis at the individual level in the following way.

Table 8.5 is an analysis-of-variance table for the hypothetical day-care center design. The design is said to be hierarchically nested (Winer, 1971). Centers are nested within treatments and subjects are nested within centers. If the center is the appropriate unit of analysis, then the correct $F$-ratio for examining treatment effects is $MS_T/MS_C$. If the individual is to be used as the unit of analysis, then the appropriate error term is the pooled error term of subjects and centers, which is

$$\frac{df_S MS_S + df_C MS_C}{df_S + df_C}$$

We shall refer to this as the *pooled error term*. In order to use this pooled error term, we need to test for compositional effects and lack of independence. This can be done by computing the $F$-ratio of $MS_C/MS_S$. If nonsignificant it indicates that, regardless of the unit of generalization, we can use the pooled error term (Anderson & Ager, 1978).

This strategy is useful when we have a hierarchically nested design with assignment at the level of the center. The reader is urged to consult statistical textbooks in choosing error terms for other designs.

In practice, one often cannot use the group or center as the unit of analysis even if that is the desired level of generalization and even if compositional effects and nonindependence are likely. There may just be too few degrees of freedom to employ such a strategy.

### Conclusion

In this chapter we considered four different designs. Two of the designs are in some sense variants of the nonequivalent control group design: the age cohort design and the changing treatment design. The age cohort design is useful if age is the assignment variable or if a large selection by maturation interaction is a likely threat to internal validity. The changing treatment variable design can be analyzed by procedures described in Chapter 6 with some slight modifications. We also considered the patched-up design and found it to be lacking in internal validity. We then considered the value-added analysis, where treatment estimates are derived by projecting growth curves.

We explored two factors that affect internal validity, regression toward the mean and subject mortality, and two factors that affect conclusion validity, independence and unit of analysis. An understanding of these factors should aid the researcher in designing and analyzing applied social research.

# 9

# The post-only correlational design

Applied social researchers are frequently asked to evaluate a social intervention or program after it has taken place. Usually, in such cases, the researcher gathers data only after the treatment has been administered, collecting information simultaneously on outcomes, background characteristics of the subjects, and treatment. From such cross-sectional data the researcher is faced with the difficult task of making causal inferences about the impact of the social intervention. Research conducted in this manner employs what we call a *post-only correlational design*.

In a more formal sense, this research design is very much like the nonequivalent control group design discussed in Chapter 6, except that longitudinal data or pre-treatment measures are not available. In both this design and the nonequivalent control group design, various groups of subjects receive different treatments. In neither design are subjects assigned randomly to treatment conditions, and the assignment rule is unknown. Hence we expect them to differ even in the absence of treatment effects. Unlike the nonequivalent control group design, however, post-only correlational designs do not include pre-treatment measures through which we might attempt to control for the unknown assignment variable. In post-only correlational designs, inferences about the unknown assignment rule must be made on the basis of data collected after subjects have been exposed to the treatment. We have seen in Chapter 6 that it is very difficult to control adequately for an unknown assignment rule when we are able to gather pre-treatment data. Not surprisingly, when we only have post-treatment data, adequate control is all the more difficult. In the absence of pre-treatment measures, any given post-treatment variable can be seen as potentially reflecting both the assignment rule as well as treatment effects. In correlational designs, a variable that is one researcher's outcome variable

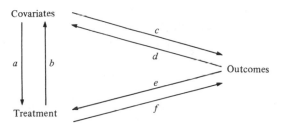

Figure 9.1. Causal effects in the post-only correlation design.

of interest may be another researcher's covariate. The distinction between outcome variables and covariates is not provided by time of measurement, but rather must be derived theoretically.

As if the problem of adequately controlling for the unknown assignment rule were not enough, designs of the post-only correlational sort may also be handicapped by the researcher's inability to assess the exact treatment level or combination received by a subject. If the researcher appears on the scene well after the conclusion of the treatment, he or she may be forced to gather information about treatment conditions from the recollections of the subjects. Thus there may be error in the measurement of treatment variables, a situation that we have not met in the designs discussed thus far. Further, if treatment information is gathered from the subjects' own recollections, it may be that the errors in those recollections are systematic; that is, they may be affected both by the assignment variable and by the treatment. Causal inference in the presence of such systematic errors becomes much more difficult.

The design is thus characterized by an unknown assignment rule and by cross-sectional post-only data. As a result, the underlying model of causal effects between the treatment, the outcome, and covariates may be as complex as that depicted in Figure 9.1. What we wish to estimate in this model is the causal arrow $f$ representing the effect of the treatment on the outcome. The covariates represent the researcher's attempt to control for the unknown assignment rule (causal arrow $a$). These need to be controlled because they are related to the outcome in the absence of treatment effects (causal arrows $c$ and $d$). We measure all three types of variables concurrently, and hence the covariates may be influenced by both the treatment (arrow $b$) and the outcome (arrow $d$). In addition, the outcome may influence the measurement of treatment when treatment information is gathered from subjects' recollections (arrow *e*). The estimation of all of these effects simultaneously is simply not possible from cross-sectional data. Hence a number of simplifying assumptions must be made. Because the conclusions of such an analysis are heavily dependent on the simplifying assumptions, post-only correlational designs are most useful as exploratory, hypothesis-generating research designs. The causal inferences from such designs remain plausible hypotheses until tested more rigorously, if such is possible.

Although the post-only correlational design presents substantial threats to internal validity, such a design may have high construct validity. This benefit derives from the fact that data are cross-sectional rather than longitudinal, thus permitting the researcher to examine more easily many diverse populations and treatment combinations. Longitudinal designs are almost always plagued by dropout rates: Those who are successfully reinterviewed differ from those who are not. Gathering data at only one time avoids this problem.

At this point, it may be helpful to illustrate the problems and advantages of post-only correlational designs by presenting a well-known example. Following this example we turn our attention to the analysis of post-only correlational data.

## The *Equality of Educational Opportunity* report

Perhaps the best-known and most massive example of a post-only correlational research design is the *Equality of Educational Opportunity* (*EEO*) report prepared by James S. Coleman and colleagues (1966). Mandated by an act of Congress to be completed within a year, this study sought to assess, among other things, the factors that influence primary and secondary educational achievement throughout the United States. A massive test battery and questionnaire were administered to more than six hundred thousand school children, and the characteristics of their schools, teachers, and peers were recorded. In essence, the treatments to be evaluated were the many, many different combinations of teacher, school, and peer characteristics. The researchers sought to assess the extent to which each of these affected achievement. Clearly, students in these different learning settings might be expected to differ in a variety of ways, hence we might expect outcome differences in the absence of treatment effects. However, all data were gathered post-treatment. The study thus exhibits the two characteristics of a post-only correlational study: an unknown assignment rule and cross-sectional rather than longitudinal data.

The richness and detail of the data that were collected by Coleman and his colleagues demonstrate the advantages of employing a post only correlational design. For purposes of describing and documenting the schooling process in America, these data are unmatched. No quasi-experimental design would have yielded information as rich and as informative, given the time restrictions under which the study was conducted.

At the same time, when it comes to making causal inferences about the effects of schooling, the disadvantages of a post-only correlational design become apparent. Suppose that we wanted to estimate the causal effects of some school characteristic (e.g., size of library) on verbal achievement, controlling for differences in students' background (e.g., socioeconomic status of family). Threats to the validity of such causal inferences arise from the following sources:

1   As in the nonequivalent control group design, controlling for socioeconomic status of family may be inadequate to the extent that the true assignment variable is not reflected in it or is reflected with error. The estimated effect of library size may then be biased.

2   Because socioeconomic status is measured after the treatment rather than before, it is conceivable that measures of it may be affected by the treatment. For instance, socioeconomic status was measured in part by the presence of reading materials in the home (e.g., newspapers, magazines, books, encyclopedia). It is conceivable that the presence of a large school library may induce families to have more reading materials around the house. To the extent that the treatment affects the "background" variable, controlling for it will cause us to underestimate treatment effects.

3   Just as the treatment may exert a causal effect on the supposed background variable, so too the outcome can have such an effect. To use the preceding example, it is conceivable that school library size may induce higher student verbal achievement, which would encourage parents to purchase books or an encyclopedia for home use. If such is the case, then the "background" variable is not causally prior to the outcome and hence should not be controlled in estimating treatment effects.

Because of these problems and others, the causal conclusions of Coleman and his colleagues concerning schooling effects have been criticized (e.g., Bowles & Levin, 1968; Bridge, Judd, & Moock, 1979; Cain & Watts, 1970). Nevertheless, if the data are looked at descriptively and predictively, they are unmatched. No other sort of research design could have so completely and so quickly described schooling in America.

### Classic analysis of the post-only correlational design

Multiple regression is traditionally used to analyze post-only correlational data. The usual regression equation is some variant of the following:

$$Y = b_0 + \sum_i b_{1i} Z_i + \sum_j b_{2j} X_j + e$$

where $Y$ is some outcome variable, covariates are represented by $Z_i$, and the treatment variables by $X_j$. Residual variation in $Y$ is labeled $e$. The $b$'s are regression coefficients to be estimated. If multiple outcomes are assessed, typically a separate regression equation is computed for each. Various multiplicative interactions may be included in the regression equation. Such interactions would typically be between pairs of the treatment variables, or between a treatment variable and a covariate. An interaction between two treatment variables assesses whether the effect of one treatment variable depends on the level of another. A treatment variable by covariate interaction tests whether a treatment effect varies with the background characteristics of the subjects.

The various partial regression coefficients for the treatment variables $(b_{2j})$ are estimates of the treatment effects and are the basis of interpretation. With interactive effects, the hierarchical analysis procedure that was presented in Chapter 5 is recommended. Specifically, a regression equation is computed with all of the highest-order interactions that are theoretically justified. The equation is then recalculated dropping out any of the highest-order terms that are nonsignificant. If all of them are nonsignificant, then the equation is recomputed, dropping out nonsignificant predictors at the next highest level. This hierarchical procedure continues until all of the highest-order interactions or effects that remain in the equation are significant. The resulting equation can then be graphed or tabled for ease of interpretation.

In the past, estimates of the treatment effect other than the partial regression coefficients have occasionally been used. For instance, a number of researchers have calculated the "additional variance explained" when a treatment variable is added to a regression equation in which the outcome has been regressed on the covariates (e.g., Coleman et al., 1966; Wolf, 1978). This increment in $R_2$ or explained variance results from a hierarchical regression procedure in which terms are sequentially *added* to the equation, rather than sequentially *deleted,* as we have advocated. Interpretation of the increment to variance explained is more cumbersome and, we think, less desirable than interpreting the partial regression coefficient for the treatment. As we have repeatedly seen, the regression coefficient for a dummy-coded treatment variable is the difference between the treatment and comparison group means on the outcome, adjusting for whatever covariates are included.

### Sources of bias in the classic analysis

There are a number of potential sources of bias in the estimate of treatment effects under the classic regression analysis: bias arising from measurement error; bias resulting from variables that cause the outcome and are correlated with the treatment but that are omitted from the analysis; and bias resulting from nonrecursive or feedback causal processes. Each of these is discussed below.

#### *Bias resulting from measurement error*

It is sometimes not realized that measurement error in variables frequently biases regression coefficients. Although measurement error has been briefly discussed previously in this volume, especially errors in the pretest in Chapter 6, a more complete analysis has been postponed until now.

The usual psychometric model for measuring any construct is that the measured variable contains both the "true" score and error:

$$X = T + E$$

where $X$ is the measured variable, $T$ is the true score, and $E$ is error. It is normally assumed that $E$ is uncorrelated with $T$ and with all other variables. From this assumption, it follows that the variance of $X$ equals the sum of the variances of $T$ and $E$, or

$$\sigma_X^2 = \sigma_T^2 + \sigma_E^2$$

The ratio of the true score variance to the total variance ($\sigma_T^2/\sigma_X^2$) is known as the reliability of $X$ ($r_{XX}$). In classic psychometric theory, then, the reliability of a variable is the percentage of variance that is explained by the true score construct. The correlation between the true score and the variable is the square root of the reliability:

$$r_{XT} = \sqrt{\frac{\sigma_T^2}{\sigma_X^2}}$$

When $X$, containing measurement error, is correlated with some other variable $Y$, which we assume to be error-free, the resulting correlation, $r_{XY}$, can be shown to equal the correlation between the true score of $X$ and $Y$ times the square root of the reliability of $X$. In equation form,

$$r_{XY} = r_{TY}r_{TX}$$

where $X$ is the observed variable, $T$ is its true score, and $Y$ is an error-free variable. To the extent that the correlation between $X$ and $T$ is less than one, the observed correlation, $r_{XY}$, will underestimate what the correlation would be if $X$ were measured without error.

With measurement error in both $X$ and $Y$, the observed correlation between the two is smaller than what would be the correlation between true scores. Frequently, correlations are corrected for measurement error in both variables by using the standard *correction for attenuation:*

$$\frac{r_{XY}}{\sqrt{r_{XX}r_{YY}}}$$

where $r_{XX}$ and $r_{YY}$ are the respective reliabilities.

The regression coefficient that results when $Y$ is regressed on $X$ may also be affected by measurement error. If $X$ is measured with error but $Y$ is not, the regression coefficient, $b_{YX}$ ($Y$ the criterion, $X$ the predictor) is closer to zero than it would be if $X$ were measured without error. If there is measurement error in $Y$ but not in $X$, the observed regression coefficient is not attenuated. If both variables are standardized and the standardized regression coefficient, $\beta_{YX}$, is calculated, error in either the predictor, $X$, or the criterion, $Y$, attenuates the coefficient. Again the extent of attenuation is determined by the square root of the reliabilities of the observed variables.

When the regression equation incorporates more than two

predictor variables, the biasing effects of measurement error become more complex. Suppose that we had a three-variable model with one outcome, $Y$, one treatment variable, $X$, and one covariate, $Z$. We wish to evaluate the effects of error in $X$, $Y$, and $Z$ on the regression coefficient for the treatment, $b_{YX.Z}$. If we have error in $Y$, but in neither $X$ nor $Z$, the regression coefficient for treatment is unbiased. In the standardized case, the standardized regression coefficient, $\beta_{YX.Z}$ is attenuated to the extent that $Y$ is unreliable. If there is measurement error in $X$, the treatment variable, but in neither $Y$ nor $Z$, both the unstandardized regression coefficient, $b_{YX.Z}$, and its standardized counterpart are attenuated. Perhaps the most surprising case is when there is measurement error in $Z$, the covariate, but in neither $X$ nor $Y$. Measurement error in $Z$ can cause us to overestimate the treatment effect (whether standardized or not), to underestimate it, or, very infrequently, to estimate it without bias. The presence and direction of bias can be shown to depend on a relationship between the bivariate correlations. We tend to overestimate treatment effects with error in $Z$ when

$$r_{YX} < \frac{r_{YZ}}{r_{XZ}}$$

When the direction of this inequality is reversed, we tend to underestimate the treatment effect.[1] If $r_{YX}$ equals $r_{YZ}/r_{XZ}$, no bias results from errors in $Z$.

It is likely to be the case that many, if not all, of the variables that we measure contain error. When using unstandardized regression coefficients, errors in the criterion do not lead to bias. Researchers should still strive, of course, for reliable outcome variables, because criterion measurement error decreases power. Measurement error in the predictor variables has an uncertain effect on the regression coefficients, because there are multiple sources of bias. Error in a given predictor leads to the relative attenuation of its effect. That effect, however, is also biased by errors in all other predictors, and the direction of that bias is not systematic. The total bias from all sources is therefore a complex function of the unknown reliabilities of the variables and the correlations among them. This depressing conclusion becomes even more depressing when we realize that the classic psychometric assumption of random measurement error is unlikely to hold. Measurement error in one variable is likely to be correlated with error in others.

[1] A proof of this is given by Judd (1980).

Figure 9.2. An omitted variable ($Z$) that is correlated with the treatment ($X$) but does not cause the outcome ($Y$).

### Bias resulting from omitted variables

An infinite number of variables are omitted from every regression equation. The absence of these variables from a regression equation can both affect the power of tests of treatment effects and can also result in bias in the estimate of these effects. In order to clarify the effect of omitted variables, they should be divided into four types.

*Type 1: omitted variables that are uncorrelated with both the treatment and the outcome.* Such a variable is superfluous, because it shares no variance with the other variables in the system. Including it results in a loss of power. If, for instance, sex of subject is uncorrelated with either treatment or outcome, we shall lose statistical power by including it in the analysis because there will then be fewer degrees of freedom that remain for error.

*Type 2: omitted variables that are correlated with the treatment but that exert no causal effect on the outcome.* Such a variable, $Z$, is depicted in Figure 9.2. Entering $Z$ into the regression equation of $Y$ on $X$ results in a substantial loss of power. An example of such a situation is found in a regression-discontinuity design in which the pretest measure, used to determine assignment, is uncorrelated with the outcome variable. Controlling for such a pretest results in a loss of power, because it is collinear with the treatment. It does not increase internal validity, because it is uncorrelated with the outcome.

*Type 3: omitted variables that are correlated with the outcome but not with the treatment.* Including such omitted variables in the regression equation will increase the power of the test of treatment effects. In essence this is the rationale for analysis of covariance *in randomized experiments.* There, because of random assignment, the covariate is uncorrelated on the average with the

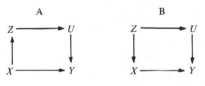

Figure 9.3. Models of an omitted variable (Z) that is correlated with both the treatment and the outcome.

treatment. Omitted variables that are correlated with the outcome but not with the treatment can also be used quite profitably in correlational designs to increase power.

*Type 4: omitted variables that are correlated with the treatment and also with the outcome when treatment is controlled.* There are two models for potential omitted variables that fall under this fourth category. These two models are depicted in Figure 9.3. In these models, $Z$ is the omitted variable that is correlated with residual variation in $Y$ ($U$) when $X$ is controlled. In model A of Figure 9.3, the omitted variable $Z$ is affected by the treatment. In model B of Figure 9.3, the omitted variable affects the treatment.

If $Z$ is omitted from the regression equation in which treatment effects are estimated, omitted variables that are caused by the treatment (as in Figure 9.3A) do not lead to bias in the estimate of the effect of treatment on outcome. However, if the omitted variable is one that causes the treatment (as in Figure 9.3B), serious bias will result when that omitted variable is correlated with residual variation in $Y$.[2]

An example will illustrate the difference in the status of the two models of Figure 9.3. Suppose that a researcher was interested in the effect of different teacher–student ratios in day-care centers on the development of reading aptitude in the children enrolled. It is reasonable to expect that relatively well-to-do families are more likely to send their children to day-care centers with high teacher–student ratios. We would also expect that children from well-to-do families would do better on the outcome measure of reading readiness than children from poorer backgrounds, in the absence of treatment effects. In our usual language, wealth or status of family constitutes, at least in part, the assignment variable. It causes

[2] In Figure 9.3B, the omitted variable, $Z$, affects $U$. In fact, whenever the omitted $Z$ is correlated with $U$ and causes $X$, bias results.

assignment to treatment (as in Figure 9.3B) and is also related to the outcome. Bias in the estimate of the treatment effect results if this omitted variable is not controlled.

Suppose that there was a causal effect of teacher–student ratio even when the assignment variable was controlled. It is undoubtedly the case that the teacher–student ratio affects the process of interaction in the day care. For instance, it affects the amount of individual attention given to children, which in turn is likely to affect reading readiness. In this case, the researcher would not be in error in concluding that student–teacher ratio affects reading readiness, even if the variable, individual attention, was omitted from the analysis.

In conclusion, there is a single type of omitted variable that threatens internal validity: a variable that causes the treatment and is correlated with the outcome when treatment is controlled. Although conclusion validity is affected by other types of omitted variables, internal validity is not.

*Construct validity of the omitted variable.* We can differentiate within the single type of omitted variable that results in bias by examining the similarity between the constructs represented by the omitted variable and the treatment. At one extreme, the omitted variable represents a completely distinct construct from that which is measured by the treatment variable. At the other extreme, the constructs of both the treatment and the omitted variable are identical. In between these extremes, the constructs represented by the omitted and treatment variables are similar or related conceptually, but are not identical. These relatively abstract distinctions are explained in the following paragraphs.

At one extreme, the omitted variable and the treatment represent completely different constructs. For instance, parents' wealth determines if children can attend a day-care center with a high teacher–student ratio. Here, wealth and teacher–student ratio are clearly different constructs. This extreme illustrates what is usually the case with an omitted assignment variable. If that assignment variable is correlated with the outcome in the absence of treatment effects, it needs to be controlled in the analysis.

Between the two extremes the omitted variable may represent in part the treatment construct, but in other ways it does not. For example, it may be that we are unable to measure the treatment variable that we would like to. Instead, we find another variable that is similar to it and that appears as a proxy for it. The effect of the proxy variable will only approximate the effect of the true treatment, and thus bias results. For instance, the size of a school library has often been included in studies of factors that affect educational achievement. The true treatment construct in such cases is usually not the size of the library itself but rather the school administration's commitment toward spending money on educational materials. That commitment, which is the omitted variable, is assumed to be unmeasurable, and so a proxy variable takes its place in the regression analysis. A good proxy variable is one that represents as closely as possible the omitted true treatment construct. We then make inferences, on the basis of the analysis of the proxy variable, about the hypothetical effect of the omitted treatment for which we have only a proxy. In a formal sense, the estimated effect of the proxy variable, number of books in library, is biased when the construct for which it is a proxy is omitted from the analysis. In other words, if we manipulated the number of books in some school library, we would probably not expect to find changes in achievement unless we also manipulated the omitted theoretical construct for which it is a proxy. If we realize, however, that the included treatment variable is merely a proxy for an omitted true treatment, then cautious interpretations of results can be made.

Proxy variables are variables that are included in an analysis because they represent at least in part the omitted theoretical construct that is of major interest. Thus we assume that proxy variables measure the omitted construct with error. In the case of proxy variables, this error is assumed to be both random as well as systematic. That is, the proxy variable reflects not only the theoretical construct of interest, but also other constructs as well. Its departures from the theoretical construct of interest are not simply random.

If the included treatment variable measures *only* the theoretical construct of interest but contains in addition random error, then it is not a proxy variable; rather, it is an *indicator* of the construct with less than perfect reliability. Such a situation defines the other extreme for biasing omitted variables. The variable that is included in the regression analysis is an imperfect measure of the omitted true construct, but imperfect only through random, rather than systematic, departures. We have already discussed the fact that measurement error in variables that are included in regression analysis results in bias. It should now be apparent that, in fact, bias

Figure 9.4. Model with disturbance ($U$) of outcome correlated with the treatment.

from measurement error is just one example of bias in regression analysis caused by omitted variables. In the case of measurement error, the omitted variable is the construct.

There is really only one source of bias in multiple regression estimation. Prior to this point, we talked about bias due to the omission of the assignment variable, and bias from measurement error. In fact, in both cases, the bias results because a variable that causes the measured treatment and is correlated with the outcome has been omitted from the analysis. One convenient way of thinking about the biasing effects of omitted variables is to refer to all of the unmeasured sources of variation in the outcome as if they were a single variable. This single variable is called the disturbance or residual of the outcome. In models where bias is present, the treatment is correlated with this disturbance. Such a situation is portrayed in Figure 9.4, where $U$, the disturbance of $Y$, refers to all of the unmeasured causes of the outcome $Y$. In this model some part of this disturbance is related to the treatment variable $X$. As we have explained, this part of $U$ may range from the omitted assignment variable to the true score treatment construct. Regression analysis always yields biased estimates of the effect of $X$ on $Y$ when the true causal model is such that the disturbance of $Y$ is correlated with $X$.

### Bias resulting from reciprocal causation

In the introductory section of this chapter, we argued that because treatments and outcomes are measured concurrently in the post-only correlational design, it may be that the measured treatment is both a cause and an effect of the outcome. In other words, the true causal model for this design is as in Figure 9.5. In this model, we have two disturbances, $U_x$ and $U_y$, because both variables are effects as well as causes. In other words, in the case of each variable we

Figure 9.5. Model with reciprocal causation between treatment and outcome.

can refer to the other variable as one of its causes and we can also specify a disturbance that represents all the rest of its causes.

If we used multiple regression to estimate the causal effects of the system depicted in Figure 9.5, our estimates would be biased for the fundamental reason we have already identified: Each cause is in turn and in part correlated with the disturbance to the other variable. For instance, the causal effect of $X$ on $Y$ is biased when estimated by multiple regression. Because $U_y$ is a cause of $Y$, which in turn causes $X$, $U_y$ and $X$ are correlated. Hence, we cannot estimate the effect of $X$ on $Y$ without bias, because the unmeasured disturbance of $Y$ is also a cause of $X$. Similarly, multiple regression would yield a biased estimate of the effect of $Y$ on $X$, because $Y$ is also affected by the disturbance to $X$, $U_x$.

### Summary of problems in classic analysis

In this section we have dealt with three sources of bias in the use of multiple regression to estimate causal effects in the post-only correlational design. The first source is the inevitable presence of measurement error. The second source of bias is due to omitted variables that cause the treatment and are correlated with the outcome when treatment is controlled. Finally, we discussed how the presence of reciprocal causation in the post-only design leads to biased estimates of causal effects. Although we have presented each of these three sources of bias separately, we have argued that in fact they all derive from one underlying problem: Multiple regression yields biased causal estimates when the unmeasured causes of an outcome, that is, its disturbance, are correlated with the treatment. In the case of measurement error, the unmeasured cause of the outcome that also causes the measured treatment is the "true" treatment. In the case of reciprocal causation, the disturbance to the outcome exerts a mediated causal effect on the treatment, mediated by the outcome itself.

To go beyond the classic analysis of the post-only correlational design, and to eliminate its inevitable biases, we need to use an analytic procedure that eliminates the fundamental problem that is the stumbling block of multiple regression. In other words, we need a procedure that estimates causal effects even when we allow the disturbance of the outcome to be correlated with the causes of that outcome. Such a procedure would alleviate the sources of bias that we have discussed, because they all result from this same fundamental problem.

### Analysis of complexities of the post-only correlational design

In the following pages two procedures are described that can generate unbiased estimates of treatment effects in the presence of measurement error in the treatment, omitted variables, and reciprocal causation. These procedures allow us to estimate the effects even when the treatment variable is correlated with the unmeasured disturbance of the outcome. Although these procedures overcome the fundamental problem in the use of multiple regression, they in turn make other assumptions that may make their use problematic. We discuss these in the course of our exposition of the techniques.

#### *Two-stage least squares*

Because the problem in the use of multiple regression is that the treatment is correlated with the outcome's disturbance, one strategy to overcome this problem might be to assess effects of just that part of the treatment variable that is *uncorrelated* with the disturbance. Exactly this rationale lies behind the procedure known as two-stage least squares (2SLS). As the name implies, there are two steps involved in two-stage least-squares analysis. In the first step, we attempt to identify variation in the treatment that is uncorrelated with the disturbance. In the second stage, multiple regression is used to regress the outcome on just that portion of the treatment that the first stage has identified as uncorrelated with the disturbance.

In Figure 9.6 a causal model is depicted in which $X$, the treatment, is a cause of $Y$; $U$ is the disturbance of $Y$ and is correlated with $X$. The reason for the correlation could be that the assignment variable is omitted or that the treatment is measured with error. The variables $Z_1$ and $Z_2$ are called *instrumental variables,* or instruments, and have the following properties:

1  They do not have any direct effect on $Y$.
2  They are uncorrelated with the disturbance $U$.
3  They are correlated with the treatment variable, $X$.

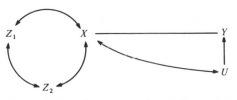

Figure 9.6. An instrumental variable model in which $X$ is correlated with $Y$'s disturbance.

To use two-stage least squares to estimate the effect of $X$ on $Y$ in this model, the first step is to regress $X$ on $Z_1$ and $Z_2$ in order to derive predicted values for $X$:

$$\hat{X} = b_0 + b_1 Z_1 + b_2 Z_2$$

where $\hat{X}$ is the predicted value of $X$ given the ordinary least-squares coefficients $b_0$, $b_1$, and $b_2$. Because this $\hat{X}$ is a linear combination of $Z_1$ and $Z_2$, and because these instruments are in turn uncorrelated with $U$, $\hat{X}$ is therefore itself uncorrelated with the disturbance $U$. In other words, through the regression of $X$ on $Z_1$ and $Z_2$ we have generated a new variable,[3] $\hat{X}$, which is by definition uncorrelated with $U$. In the second step of two-stage least squares, $Y$ is regressed on $\hat{X}$. Because this new variable $\hat{X}$ is uncorrelated with the disturbance $U$, its regression coefficient is an unbiased estimate of its effect on $Y$.

Although two-stage least squares can yield unbiased effects estimates in cases such as Figure 9.6, it should be apparent that the quality of the estimates depends heavily on meeting the assumptions behind the instruments. In other words, it is strictly necessary that the instruments are neither a direct cause of $Y$ nor correlated with its disturbance $U$. If these assumptions are violated, then the causal model is misspecified, and the resulting effects estimates will be substantially biased. Unfortunately there is no sure empirical procedure for defining variables that meet the assumptions of good instruments. The assumptions ultimately rest on strong theory.

We have only provided an introduction to the use of two-stage least-squares estimation. Before using this technique, we strongly

---

[3] When $Z_1$ and $Z_2$ are uncorrelated with $X$, the "variable" $\hat{X}$ will have zero variance. In such a case, if $Y$ were regressed on $\hat{X}$, the coefficient for $\hat{X}$ would be undefined. This is why it is essential that the instrumental variables be correlated with $X$.

encourage the reader to consult more detailed treatments (James & Singh, 1978; Wonnacott & Wonnacott, 1970).

In an analogous procedure to that used for estimating effects in the case of Figure 9.6, two-stage least squares can be used to estimate effects in models involving reciprocal causation. The procedure is slightly more complicated because each of the variables involved in the reciprocal causation is correlated with the other dependent variable's disturbance. Therefore at least one instrumental variable is needed for each variable involved in the causal feedback loop. In addition, the first stage in the two-stage least-squares procedure needs to be conducted on each of the variables in the feedback loop.

Figure 9.7 will be used to illustrate the application of two-stage least squares to reciprocal causation models. In this model we wish to estimate the effects of $X_1$, $X_2$, and $Y_2$ on $Y_1$ and of $X_2$, $X_3$, and $Y_1$ on $Y_2$. In other words, we wish to estimate the coefficients of the following *structural equations:*

$$Y_1 = b_{01} + b_{11}X_1 + b_{21}X_2 + b_{31}Y_2 + U_1$$

$$Y_2 = b_{02} + b_{12}X_2 + b_{22}X_3 + b_{32}Y_1 + U_2$$

(These structural equations are *not* multiple regression equations. In these equations the coefficients represent *true* causal effects, which we have seen are estimated with bias when multiple regression is used.)

Just as in the analysis of models with omitted variables, the first stage in the two-stage analysis of reciprocal causation models is to regress $Y_1$ and $Y_2$ on the variables that are uncorrelated with the two disturbances, that is, on $X_1$, $X_2$, and $X_3$. In the model of Figure 9.7, these first-stage regressions would take the form

$$\hat{Y}_1 = b_{03} + b_{13}X_1 + b_{23}X_2 + b_{33}X_3$$

$$\hat{Y}_2 = b_{04} + b_{14}X_1 + b_{24}X_2 + b_{34}X_3$$

These first-stage equations that are calculated using ordinary multiple regression are frequently referred to as *reduced-form equations.* They indicate the anticipated change in each of the $Y$'s expected from a unit change in each of the $X$'s, whether that change is a direct causal effect or mediated through the other $Y$ variable. In other words, they essentially ignore the reciprocal causation between the $Y$'s and estimate total effects of $X$'s on $Y$'s. These

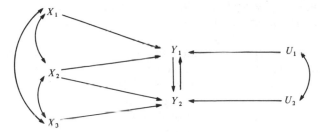

Figure 9.7. A reciprocal causation model with instrumental variables.

reduced-form coefficients are unbiased using multiple regression because all $X$'s are uncorrelated with the disturbances, $U_1$ and $U_2$, by definition.

In the second stage of analysis, the structural equations are estimated using multiple regression, substituting the predicted $Y$'s, $\hat{Y}_1$ and $\hat{Y}_2$, as predictors in the regression equation. Thus $Y_1$ in Figure 9.7 would be regressed on $X_1$, $X_2$, and $\hat{Y}_2$ and $Y_2$ would be regressed on $X_2$, $X_3$, and $\hat{Y}_1$. The resulting coefficients are unbiased estimates of the causal coefficients because each of the predictors in a given equation are uncorrelated with the disturbance of the criterion. Thus, $\hat{Y}_2$ is uncorrelated with $U_1$. Likewise, $\hat{Y}_1$ is uncorrelated with $U_2$.

The choice of instrumental variables in reciprocal causation models is crucial to the success of two-stage estimation. In Figure 9.7, $X_1$ is an instrument for $Y_1$ in estimating its effect on $Y_2$. $X_3$ is an instrument for $Y_2$. These instruments must be chosen on strong theoretical grounds to meet the following criteria:

1  The variable must not appear in the structural equation that contains as a predictor the variable for which it is an instrument;
2  The variable must be uncorrelated with the disturbances to all variables involved in the feedback loop; and
3  It must exert a fairly substantial direct effect on the variable for which it is an instrument.

If assumptions 1 and 2 concerning the instruments do not hold, the model has been misspecified and serious bias in the estimates results. If assumption 3 does not hold, the analysis is imprecise. Again the reader is urged to consult the more detailed treatments cited earlier.

### General approach to estimating linear structural equation models

In recent years there has been considerable effort devoted by a group of statisticians toward developing a general, unified technique for estimating causal models. Karl Jöreskog and Dag Sörbom (1978) in particular have developed an analytic procedure to estimate causal effects in structural equation models. This procedure can be used instead of the estimation techniques discussed in the chapter to this point. In addition, it substantially extends these techniques by integrating reliability assessment into the estimation of the causal model. We have referred to this procedure in earlier chapters without going into detail. At this point, more extended discussion is appropriate.

When we were discussing measurement error earlier in this chapter, we stated that researchers sometimes correct correlations for attenuation before estimating causal effects. The problem with such a strategy is that it separates the measurement model or the reliability estimation procedure from the causal model or the estimation of causal coefficients. In fact, it is possible to integrate the two, to estimate both the measurement and the causal or structural models simultaneously.

The approach of Jöreskog and Sörbom integrates the estimation of the measurement and structural models by making use of *multiple indicators* of unmeasured or latent constructs. The method assumes that all measured variables are indicators of unmeasured constructs. For instance, suppose that we measured the treatments received by a subject population in various ways. We might be interested in the effect of teachers' experience on achievement. We might measure the treatment construct both by asking teachers how long they have taught and by checking school records. In essence we would then have two indicators of the latent treatment construct, both of which probably contain some error of measurement. Likewise, we might have multiple indicators or measures of the outcome construct: a verbal achievement test, a grade-point average, and a mathematics achievement test. Finally, we might believe that treatment assignment was produced by a socioeconomic status construct for which we have only very imperfect measures such as reported parents' education, type of neighborhood, and so forth. The causal model among constructs (the effect of experience on achievement controlling for socioeconomic status of student) and the measurement models for the latent constructs are illustrated in Figure 9.8.

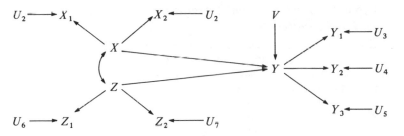

Figure 9.8. A multiple-indicator structural model.

In this figure, $X$ is the unmeasured treatment construct for which we have two indicators, $X_1$ and $X_2$. Each of these indicators is caused both by the construct and by error or residual variation, $U_1$ and $U_2$. This describes the measurement or reliability model for the latent treatment construct $X$. The standardized coefficients of the effects of $X$ on $X_1$ and on $X_2$ are the square root of the reliabilities of those variables. Likewise, there are similar measurement models for the latent outcome measure $Y$ (three indicators: $Y_1$, $Y_2$, and $Y_3$, each of which has residual variation, $U_3$ through $U_5$) and for the socioeconomic status construct $Z$ (two indicators: $Z_1$ and $Z_2$, each having residual or error variation, $U_6$ and $U_7$). In addition to these measurement models, Figure 9.8 depicts a causal model among the latent constructs $X$, $Y$, and $Z$. In this causal model $X$ and $Z$ cause the latent outcome $Y$. In addition, there is a disturbance ($V$) to this latent outcome.

The information used to estimate the coefficients of the model, both the measurement or reliability coefficients and the causal coefficients among latent constructs, consists of the twenty-one bivariate correlations among the seven indicators, and each of their variances. If this is sufficient information to estimate the coefficients of the model,[4] an iterative procedure is used to estimate the coefficients. Greatly oversimplified, this procedure starts with approximations of values for the coefficients and determines what the correlation matrix between indicators should be given those starting coefficients. It then modifies the coefficient estimates to yield closer approximations to the observed correlation matrix. The

[4] This condition of sufficient information is traditionally called the *identification* issue in econometrics and structural modeling. By itself, determining if causal models are identified is a complex endeavor, independent of the complexity of estimation. The reader is encouraged to consult Blalock (1969), Duncan (1975), and Kenny (1979) for discussions of identification.

Table 9.1. *Variances and correlations of indicators for model of Figure 9.9*

|        | Variances | $X_1$ | $X_2$ | $Z_1$ | $Z_2$ | $Y_1$ | $Y_2$ |
|--------|-----------|-------|-------|-------|-------|-------|-------|
| $X_1$  | 11.90     |       |       |       |       |       |       |
| $X_2$  | 13.54     | .846  |       |       |       |       |       |
| $Z_1$  | 24.50     | .290  | .297  |       |       |       |       |
| $Z_2$  | 1.46      | .313  | .320  | .623  |       |       |       |
| $Y_1$  | 10.43     | .158  | .162  | .205  | .221  |       |       |
| $Y_2$  | 3.10      | .150  | .153  | .194  | .209  | .800  |       |
| $Y_3$  | 15.13     | .126  | .128  | .163  | .176  | .672  | .635  |

result of the iterations is a set of coefficient estimates that minimize a weighted discrepancy between the observed correlation matrix and that predicted by the model. Commonly, the discrepancy is minimized in such a way to provide what are called *maximum-likelihood* parameter estimates. In Table 9.1, a hypothetical correlation matrix for the example we presented in Figure 9.8 is given, together with the variances of the variables. In Figure 9.9, the maximum-likelihood parameter estimates are given.

The causal parameters that are given in Figure 9.9 can be interpreted much like regression coefficients are interpreted, with the added complexity that they refer to the effects of latent or unmeasured variables. Thus the treatment effect in Figure 9.9 is .08, the effect of $X$ on $Y$. We interpret this effect just as we would interpret an unstandardized regression coefficient: A one-unit change in $X$ produces a .08 unit change in $Y$. The added complexity in interpretation with latent constructs is that the metrics or scales for the latent variables depend on the measurement models. The usual approach is to set the metric of each construct equal to the metric of one of its indicators, by fixing the effect of the construct on that indicator at unity. For instance, the effect of $X$ on $X_1$, has been set to one.

It may happen that the correlation matrix contains more information than is required to derive the estimated coefficients. In this case, the additional information in the matrix provides a set of consistency tests that enable us to determine if the model that has been constructed is consistent with the observed correlation matrix. For instance, it might be in our Figure 9.8 that $Y_1$ and $Y_3$ (verbal

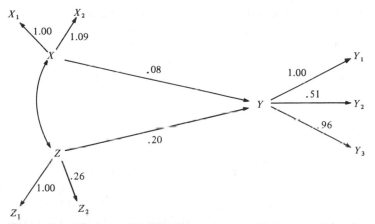

Figure 9.9. Maximum-likelihood structural coefficients resulting from data on Table 9.1 (disturbance variances omitted).

and mathematics achievement tests) measure something different than $Y_2$ (grade-point average). In other words, all three may not be indicators of the same underlying construct, and a more correctly specified model might include two latent outcome constructs, the first having indicators $Y_1$ and $Y_3$, the second having the unique indicator $Y_2$. These two latent outcome constructs might show quite different treatment effects.

The ability to test for possible misspecification of the model is a great advantage of this multiple-indicator estimation procedure over those that do not make use of multiple indicators. In addition, the procedure essentially subsumes all of the analytic procedures we have described in this chapter and elsewhere in this book. If we have single error-free indicators of constructs in a recursive model with the disturbance uncorrelated with predictor variables, maximum-likelihood coefficients are identical to those that multiple regression yields. Likewise, models such as that depicted in Figure 9.6 involving omitted variables can be estimated by the procedure. Like two-stage least squares, at least one instrumental variable is necessary for each independent variable that is correlated with the disturbance. If such instruments are lacking, the observed correlation matrix will not contain sufficient information to derive the coefficients. Thus, although this procedure can be used to estimate the coefficients of models with omitted variables, it solves the omitted-variable problem in an identical manner to two-stage least squares: by the inclusion of instrumental variables. Given instrumental variables, we can estimate structural coefficients either through a two-stage least-squares procedure or through this general procedure. The general procedure can also be used to estimate the coefficients of models involving reciprocal causation, such as that depicted in Figure 9.7, again assuming the presence of instrumental variables.

Because the procedure integrates the measurement and the causal or structural models, it becomes possible to include latent constructs in causal models that are not of theoretical interest in and of themselves, but rather that represent systematic sources of error in our measures. Earlier we discussed the distressing possibility that errors of measurement in two or more variables may be correlated. For instance, if we measured the same three variables at two time points, it is likely that factors that result in errors in the measures at time 1 also result in errors at time 2. By specifying such common sources of errors in our measures as latent constructs, we can estimate structural coefficients even allowing correlated errors of measurement, *if sufficient information is contained in the correlation matrix.*

Given the advantages of a multiple-indicator approach to measurement error, an overall test of model misspecification, and the generality of the procedure, some might wonder why all other, more traditional data analytic procedures continue to be used. In fact, however, there are some disadvantages in this general approach for estimating structural coefficients.

The first disadvantage is its complexity. In the preceding paragraphs we have only hinted at the complexity of the procedure. For relatively simple analysis tasks, where, for instance, measurement error is expected to be small and random, the procedure may well be inefficient.

The second major disadvantage is that the maximum-likelihood estimation procedure assumes that all variables share a multivariate normal distribution. It is unfortunate that the robustness of this assumption is at present unknown. Thus deviations from this assumption may possibly result in substantial estimation biases.

Despite these disadvantages, it is clear to us that this procedure is a major analytic advance and will be used with increasing frequency in social research. The inevitable presence of measurement error in social research makes its advantages substantial. A multiple-indicator approach to error and the simultaneous assessment of both measurement and causal models render this procedure clearly superior to others currently in use. The interested reader is referred to more advanced texts for details on how these procedures can be used (e.g., Bentler, 1980; Jöreskog & Sörbom, 1979; Kenny, 1979).

### Summary and conclusion

The post-only correlational design is one that is relatively easy to implement. The researcher needs only to gather data at one point in time from a variety of different subjects, some of whom received the treatment of interest and some of whom did not. In a formal sense, the design is defined by an unknown assignment rule and cross-sectional data.

Because of the ease with which correlational data can be gathered, the detail of descriptive information can be impressive. The *Equality of Educational Opportunity* report (Coleman et al., 1966) bears witness to this fact. At the same time, the absence of longitudinal or pre-treatment data renders causal inference about the effects of treatments quite tenuous. To estimate unbiased treatment effects, one must attempt to control for the variable(s) that determined treatment assignment using post-treatment data. In Chapter 6 we discussed the difficulties in attempting to control for an unknown assignment rule with pre-treatment measures. When we have only post-treatment data, the problem is all the more difficult. It is quite unlikely that bias-free estimates of treatment effects will result when this design is used. On the other hand, for other purposes, the design is unexcelled.

The classic analysis for correlational designs employs multiple regression to estimate treatment effects. To reduce bias, a number of covariates are generally included in the regression equation to approximate control for the unknown assignment rule. As we have argued earlier, a hierarchical regression procedure is advocated, in which nonsignificant higher-order interactions are systematically deleted and the regression equation recomputed.

Three different sources of bias in this classic regression analysis were identified: measurement error, omitted variables, and nonrecursive causal processes. In fact, all three are variants on a single type of misspecification. Regression analysis estimates causal effects with bias whenever the disturbance of the outcome is correlated with the included predictor variables.

Two related estimation procedures were discussed that can be used to overcome this fundamental misspecification problem. First, two-stage least squares can be used to estimate the effects of that part of the various predictors that is uncorrelated with the disturbance to the dependent variable. Such a procedure necessitates instrumental variables. Meeting the assumptions that are the basis of such variables may be quite difficult. The second estimation procedure that was discussed was a general structural model estimation procedure generating maximum-likelihood parameter estimates. This general technique has a number of distinct advantages over others that have been discussed previously. First, given sufficient information, an overall goodness-of-fit test is conducted that can indicate possible misspecifications in the model. Second, reliability estimation is integrated into the estimation of causal effects, given multiple indicators of latent constructs, so that bias from measurement error ceases to be a problem. Finally, the estimation procedure is amazingly flexible, providing the researcher with a single procedure for estimating all of the models discussed earlier in the chapter.

# 10
## Further probing of applied research data

Our primary emphasis in the previous nine chapters has been on the estimation of treatment effects. In this chapter we move beyond the measurement of a program's effectiveness and examine various ways to probe the analyses. We first consider what some have called *process analysis*. Instead of testing only if the treatment causes the outcome variable, we set forth an explicit causal chain. For instance, day' care may cause reduced parent–child interaction, which may in turn cause reduced dependence, which may in turn cause greater intellectual creativity. A process analysis moves beyond a simple input–output analysis to a careful analysis of *how* the treatment affects the outcome variable. Another side of process analysis focuses on *who* is especially helped by the intervention. For instance, day care may have a stronger effect on children whose social development is poor to begin with.

Process probes are usually done by the original or primary investigator. Secondary analysis refers to the work of a second researcher who reanalyzes the data set. The role of a second researcher is to evaluate the claims of the primary researcher. Secondary analysis plays a crucial role in the evaluation of applied social research.

Finally, after a series of studies have been done to examine the effect of a treatment, the results need to be combined in some manner. This task has been called *meta-analysis* by Glass (1976). Recent development of quantitative methods to summarize results across studies can greatly aid growth of scientific knowledge.

### Process analysis

Suppose that an investigator is studying the effect of day care on aggressive behavior. Her hypothesis is that type A day care, in which the staff intervenes rarely and lets children work out their own problems produces less aggression than a different type of day care, type B. Her rationale is that type A allows the children to manage their aggression in an interpersonal context, whereas type B prevents the children from undergoing such a learning process. Using a randomized experimental design, the investigator has determined that type A day-care centers do produce less aggressive children than type B. Although her major hypothesis is supported by the data, a number of interesting questions about the *process* still remain. First, *how* does a type A day-care center produce less aggression than a type B day-care center? Second, *for whom* is a type A day-care center better than a type B day-care center? The "how" question we shall call the issue of mediation, and the "for whom" question we shall call interaction.

### Mediation

In Figure 10.1 we have an example of a possible mediational scheme. The different types of day-care center philosophies determine the number of opportunities for interpersonal problem solving, which in turn affects the amount of aggression. Although this chain is a very simple one, we shall see that testing it is not so simple.

The model in Figure 10.1 is much more highly elaborated than the simple question of whether the treatment affects the outcome variable. Verification of the process model would give the researcher a story to tell about *how* the treatment produces change. The effect of the treatment on the outcome variable by itself gives rise to different explanations of that effect. By specifying and testing a mediational structure, we can choose among these explanations.

It may be the case that some untreated subjects receive the treatment or that some treated subjects receive varying degrees of the treatment. This may happen because of the inevitable difficulties encountered in conducting applied research. When this is the case, simple treatment comparisons ignore the varying amounts of treatment actually received. One can then use the actual amount of treatment received as a mediator of the treatment–outcome variable relationship. Including this variable enhances the construct validity of the treatment.

In order to claim mediation, the researcher must present evidence for the following three conclusions:

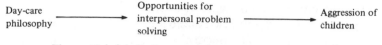

Figure 10.1. Mediation example.

Conclusion I. The treatment causes the outcome variable. Without this conclusion there can be no mediation. Too often mediational models are viewed as a fallback analysis strategy to employ when gross treatment effects are not found. This is clearly a very foolish approach, because one cannot locate a mediating process if nothing needs mediation.[1] The search for *interacting* variables, discussed in the next section, is reasonable even if there is no gross treatment effect.

Conclusion II. The treatment causes the potential mediator. If a variable is to be a mediator, it must be determined in part by the treatment variable.

Conclusion III. The mediator must cause the outcome variable controlling for the treatment. A variable is not a mediator unless it directly affects the outcome variable.

If there is evidence for these three conclusions, there is evidence for mediation. To claim that the hypothesized mediating variable explains the treatment effect, it must also be demonstrated that the effect of the treatment on the outcome variable is zero once the mediator has been controlled.

In practice, it may be very difficult to reach all three conclusions simultaneously, given noisy social science data. For instance, if the mediating chain is a long one, the treatment may have a low correlation with the outcome. Consider an intervention that is supposed to have an effect on a variable but the effect is distal, for example, the effect of antismoking advertisements on lung cancer death rate. If there are many links between a given treatment and its outcome variable, the resulting correlation between the two variables is quite low. This is so because in a causal chain the effects are multiplied through to determine the correlation. Thus if $X$ causes $Y$, $Y$ causes $Z$, and $Z$ causes $U$, and all these paths (standardized regression coefficients) are .4, then the correlation between $X$, the first element in the chain, and $U$, the last element in

[1] When we do not find treatment effects, looking at "mediating" variables may be informative in understanding why the treatment has *no* effect. First, it may be that the treatment simply never affects a critical variable known to affect the outcome. Second, it is possible, although unlikely, that the effect of the treatment variable, controlling for the mediating variable, is offset by the mediating process.

the chain, is only .064. Thus the presence of a mediational process implies that the correlation between the treatment and the outcome may not be high, resulting in low conclusion validity. Additionally, to reach the third conclusion, concerning the effect of the mediator on the outcome variable, one should treat the outcome as the criterion and the mediator and the treatment variables as predictor variables in a regression equation. However, if conclusion II holds, these two predictor variables should be highly correlated. This correlation between predictor variables, that is, multicollinearity, results in poor conclusion validity for conclusion III.

Besides conclusion validity, there are also serious problems of internal validity in testing mediation. A mediational model can be both correlational and experimental. The treatment variable may be a manipulated variable, whereas the mediating variable is always an unmanipulated variable. Although we can be reasonably confident about the causal impact of the treatment on the outcome variable ignoring the mediator, we enter uncertain grounds when we include an unmanipulated mediating variable. Measurement error in the mediator, reciprocal causation between the mediator and the outcome, and omitted variables can seriously distort the estimate of the proposed mediator's effect on the outcome variable. (See Chapter 9 for a review of these problems.) We should recognize a mediational analysis for what it really is: a correlational analysis.

The serious problems of conclusion and internal validities in mediational analysis should not deter us from such a strategy. The identification of a mediator aids us in establishing the construct validity of the treatment. Because a mediational model tells how the treatment works, we can much better understand what the treatment is and how to improve its effectiveness.

The actual mechanics of a mediational analysis vary somewhat depending on the design of the research. However, because we have presented a general regression model for the analysis of social research designs, we can make a number of points that apply to all mediational analyses.

To test conclusion I, one should *ignore* the mediator and estimate the treatment effect. Conclusion II can be tested by performing an analysis similar to that proposed for conclusion I. This time the mediator is the dependent variable in the regression equation. For conclusion III, the analysis for conclusion I is repeated, but the mediating variable is also included as a predictor in the equation.

It is interesting to note that one could employ the analysis of covariance (ANCOVA) to test a mediational hypothesis in the following way. For conclusion III, one sets up an ANCOVA with the mediator being the covariate. Conclusion III implies that the covariate has a significant effect on the outcome variable. This use of ANCOVA is very different from our previous discussion of its use in randomized experiments (Chapter 4). For a mediational analysis, the treatment causes the covariate, which was not permitted when we discussed it in Chapter 4.

The most advanced way of testing a mediational model is through the use of structural equation modeling, discussed in the previous chapter. Such an approach can evaluate the three conclusions simultaneously. Moreover, if there are multiple indicators of the mediating variable, the biasing effects of measurement error can be eliminated, as we discussed in Chapter 9. In some very special circumstances, feedback between the mediator and outcome variable can be allowed. Further discussion of a structural modeling approach to mediation is contained in Judd and Kenny (1981).

### Interaction

Let us return to our day-care example. The investigator determined that type A day care creates lower aggression than type B day care and that opportunities for interpersonal problem solving seem to mediate this effect. Suppose that you are an administrator who is considering changing your emphasis from type B to type A. You would probably want to know if this effect would hold for the children in your program as well. You would then be very curious about whether the results of the original study held for the entire sample or whether the effect was true only for a subsample, say, boys. In other words, you wish to know *for whom* does the treatment work. Statistically this question is one of interaction.[2]

The search for such interactions is often not conducted as carefully as the major analysis. Consider two less than optimal strategies for finding interactions. First, after all analyses have been completed, the sample is broken into discrete subgroups and the treatment effect is measured for each group. These effects are then compared and differences among them are thought to indicate interactions. There are various problems with this approach. First,

---

[2] In certain literatures, variables that interact with a treatment are called moderator variables. We prefer the term interacting variables, because "moderating" implies that the treatment effect is reduced.

because treatment effects are tested separately for each subgroup, the error estimates are not pooled. Because the degrees of freedom for error are then less than an overall test of interaction, conclusion validity is relatively low. Second, there is not a direct test of whether the treatment effect varies across groups. This second point is important. Suppose the researcher finds that the treatment works for males but there is not a significant difference for females. He or she cannot conclude that the program worked better for males. Such a hypothesis should be tested directly as a treatment by sex interaction. To illustrate the folly of not testing the interaction directly, consider a treatment effect of 4.0 for males and 5.0 for females. It is conceivable that the treatment effect for males is significant whereas that for females is not, even though the treatment effect for males is smaller! This could happen if either there are few females in the study or the error variance for females is high.

A second inefficient analysis strategy for investigating interaction is to analyze only the treated subjects. The researcher conducts an analysis to determine which subjects changed the most. For instance, using a design with a pretest, the researcher would measure change (either raw or covariate adjusted) and then see which variables predict it. If, for example, age were a significant positive predictor of change, then it might be argued that older children benefited more from the program than younger children. This strategy suffers from the same flaw as that of the previous strategy. It fails to *explicitly* compare change in the treated subjects with change in the control subjects.

Consider the study by Bossé, Garvey, and Costa (1980) of the effect of quitting smoking on weight gain. They were interested in determining what types of ex-smokers gain weight. One strategy would be to investigate persons who have recently quit smoking and determine what factors predict weight gain. In addition, however, Bossé et al. looked at weight gain of smokers who did not quit. They found that ex-smokers of high-tar cigarettes gained more weight after quitting than ex-smokers of low-tar cigarettes. However, smokers of high-tar cigarettes who did not quit gained no more weight than low-tar smokers. If weight gain had been associated to the same extent with tar content among continuing smokers, the researchers could not have concluded that cigarette tar caused differential weight gain after quitting cigarettes. A comparison

Table 10.1. *Flu shot example*

| Age | Treatment | |
|---|---|---|
| | A | B |
| Under 70 | 4.72 | 6.19 |
| | (.212)[a] | (.162) |
| Over 70 | 9.83 | 18.31 |
| | (.102) | (.055) |

[a] 1/(number of days).

group is needed to measure not only treatment effects but also differential treatment effects.

We thus urge the researcher to check for interacting variables by explicitly testing interaction terms. The product terms that we and others have recommended may seem awkward at first. However, they are essential and readily interpretable given the following recommendations (see also Chapter 5). First, the product term should be created after first subtracting from each component its mean or median. This substantially reduces collinearity between each of the components and the interaction term as well as makes the regression coefficients for the components more interpretable. Second, one should test interactions hierarchically and omit from the model those that are not significant. Third, to aid interpretation, the results of the interaction should be graphed or tabled.

Occasionally an analysis will reveal *too many* interactions. Because interactions are generally less parsimonious accounts of the data than main effects, one might consider approaches that reduce variance due to interactions. Consider a hypothetical study in which the subjects were sent a notice that they could receive a free flu shot. The treatment variable is two different ways of informing persons of the shot, and the outcome variable is the number of days between receiving the notice and coming in for the flu shot. Suppose that the researcher obtained the results as depicted in Table 10.1. The treatment effect seems larger for older respondents; in other words, treatment and age seem to interact. However, this may be deceptive. Let us create a new outcome variable, the speed with which a person came in for the flu shot after receiving the notice (speed =

one divided by the number of days). The means for this transformed outcome measure are presented in parentheses in Table 10.1. The treatment effects on this transformed variable are about the same for the two age groups. There is then no interaction. Thus we can sometimes remove "interactions" by transforming the outcome variable. When are transformations recommended? The principle of parsimony by itself implies that we should prefer the analysis that has the fewest interaction terms. In some cases, however, one might transform away one's most interesting results. In addition, transformation may result in an uninterpretable metric for the outcome variable. Practical guides to transformation are provided by Mosteller and Tukey (1977).

### Secondary analysis

It is becoming increasingly common that, for large-scale evaluations, a second set of researchers reanalyze the data collected by the original researcher. This is called *secondary analysis* or secondary evaluation (Cook, 1974), with the first researcher being called the *primary analyst* and the reanalyzer the *secondary analyst*. Examples of secondary analysis are the Elashoff and Snow (1971) reanalysis of the Rosenthal and Jacobson (1968) "Pygmalion" study, the Cook, Appleton, Conner, Schaffer, Tamkin, and Weber (1975) reanalysis of the Ball and Bogatz (1970) evaluation of *Sesame Street,* and the Smith (1972) partial reanalysis of the Coleman report (Coleman et al., 1966).

Secondary analysis may seem like an unusual enterprise to the basic researcher. Basic researchers often feel a proprietary relationship toward their data. The usual mechanisms for criticism of basic research, such as editorial review and replication, may not, however, be efficient mechanisms for the criticism of applied social research. The results of applied research are often not published in journals, and the cost of replication may be prohibitive. Because the potential applications from applied social research are so consequential, careful scrutiny of conclusions is essential. The process of secondary analysis is one way of providing such scrutiny.

The task of the secondary analyst is much easier than that of the primary analyst. First, his or her analysis questions can be answered at a leisurely pace, whereas the primary analyst must meet deadline after deadline. Second, the primary analyst has already had to make tough decisions, whereas the secondary analyst need only reevaluate the answers. Third, the primary analyst usually must not only analyze the data but also maintain a small (or large) organization of coders, interviewers, computer programmers, and the like. Most secondary analysts can proceed without such an organization. It is thus no small wonder that the secondary analyst's report looks so much more polished than the primary researcher's.

The role of the secondary analyst has often been that of a critic. It is difficult to imagine that any secondary analyst would have the courage to tell the funding agency that, after spending many thousands of dollars, he or she could find nothing wrong with the original report. Almost by necessity, the secondary analyst will search out every mistake, no matter how minor.

To perform a secondary analysis, the researcher must first obtain access to the data. Some secondary analyses can be performed just on the basis of information in the original report. Because the basic input for virtually all statistical techniques is a correlation or a covariance matrix, one can reanalyze published research reports using the primary researchers' own methods or alternative methods if those matrices are presented. Even if they are not, we may be able to reconstruct them from the original report. Occasionally one may need more information than is contained in the original report. This requires the assistance of the primary analyst. One could write the researcher and try to obtain the necessary results. Obviously, any frivolous and needlessly burdensome requests should be avoided. Reasonable requests made to reasonable investigators are honored. Primary investigators have the obligation to release their data to responsible secondary analysts.

There are three different types of secondary analysis.

*Type I.* The first type of secondary analysis is the *exact* reanalysis of the data as was done by the primary investigator. The purpose of this is not so much to check the honesty of the primary investigator, but to determine if the primary and the secondary investigator have the same data. Moreover, the replication of the analysis elucidates the many unreported decisions that the primary investigator made, for example, how missing data were treated, how composites were formed, what covariates were used in the analysis. Fortunately, to date most secondary analysts have been able to replicate the primary analyst's results exactly. One major exception is the finding that two variables of the Coleman report were mislabeled (Smith, 1972).

*Type II.* The second type of secondary analysis is to use a different method to answer the primary researcher's question. Included in this type would be tests of the assumptions of the primary investigator. For instance, Elashoff and Snow (1971) found very extreme intelligence test scores in the Rosenthal and Jacobson (1968) study, which to some extent invalidated their use of analysis of variance. Reanalyses also include more powerful and sensitive analyses of the primary researcher's hypothesis. For instance, Cook et al. (1975) used many different analysis strategies to evaluate the effects of *Sesame Street.*

*Type III.* The third type of secondary analysis has been to use the data in order to test a new hypothesis. For instance, Cook et al. (1975) asked whether disadvantaged children learned more from *Sesame Street* than advantaged children, whereas the primary analysts, Ball and Bogatz (1970), were content to ask only whether disadvantaged children learned. It is this last type of secondary analysis that has proved to be most informative. The first two types of questions usually only confirm the original researcher's results, whereas this third type can extend and refine the original conclusions or can answer new questions that never occurred to the primary investigator.

Cook and Gruder (1978) have argued that secondary analysis should parallel in time the primary analysis. This would allow secondary researchers to communicate to the primary researchers any problems they see in the study. Then the primary researchers could make the necessary changes that they see fit to make. Also, if the secondary researchers wished to pose a different question from that of the primary researchers, they might be able to entice the primary researchers to measure the necessary variables, oversample one group, or add another comparison group.

## Combining the results across studies

In the past few years there has been considerable interest in quantitative literature reviews (Rosenthal, 1980). We are all familiar with qualitative reviews that verbally describe studies. The only quantitative aspect of such reviews is the "nose count," for example, five studies in one direction, two in the opposite direction, and twenty, no effects. A quantitative review evaluates the literature more formally. We shall present three different approaches to

Table 10.2. *Results of five hypothetical studies*

| Study | t | df | df/(df − 2) | Z |
|---|---|---|---|---|
| 1 | 2.05 | 40 | 1.053 | 1.996 |
| 2 | 1.43 | 20 | 1.111 | 1.393 |
| 3 | .79 | 32 | 1.067 | .786 |
| 4 | 1.36 | 180 | 1.011 | 1.357 |
| 5 | − .45 | 18 | 1.125 | − .449 |
| Sum | 5.18 | 290 | 5.367 | 5.083 |

quantitative reviews. The first is the combining of $p$ values across studies. The second is combining measures of effect size of each study. The third approach is the most formal and relies on Bayesian methods.

### Combining p *values*

One coarse measure of a treatment effect is the *one-tailed* $p$ value associated with its inferential statistic. One can summarize the studies by combining their $p$ values. Doing this may result in stronger conclusions than the studies individually. For instance, if an investigator did one study and obtained $p = .06$ and a second $p = .09$, their combined probability would be very small even though neither study is statistically significant by itself. Rosenthal (1978) presents a series of methods for combining probabilities, two of which will be briefly outlined. The two methods we present are fairly simple and do not suffer from the drawbacks of other methods discussed by Rosenthal. In Table 10.2 we present the results from five hypothetical studies investigating the same phenomenon.

*Adding* t*'s.* In each study we assume that there is a *one-tailed* $t$ statistic associated with the treatment effect. We can combine these to yield a standard normal deviate or, as it is commonly called, a $Z$ score, under the null hypothesis of no effect. The equation for combining the $t$'s across studies is

$$Z = \frac{\Sigma t}{\sqrt{\Sigma[df/(df - 2)]}}$$

The numerator is simply the sum of the *t* statistics. When a study yields a result *not* in the predicted direction, the *t* should be negative, but still one-tailed. The denominator sums the degrees of freedom for each study divided by the degrees of freedom less two. For the example in Table 10.2, we obtain

$$\frac{5.18}{\sqrt{^{40}/_{38} + {}^{20}/_{18} + {}^{32}/_{30} + {}^{180}/_{178} + {}^{18}/_{16}}} = 2.236$$

This *Z* has a one-tailed *p* value of .0127.

*Weighted Z's.* The above procedure treats all studies equally. One might wish to weight them differentially. We can choose to weight studies by different criteria that indicate validity. For instance, we could create an "internal validity" scale much in the way that Bernstein and Freeman (1975) did. Alternatively, we might evaluate the construct validity of each study and judge the degree to which a study successfully operationalized the relevant constructs. Weighting by measures of internal or construct validity may be called weighting by quality. Glass (1976) has questioned such procedures, and Taveggia (1974) has shown at least in one instance that the results of a "good" study are no different from the results of a "bad" study. Finally, one could weight each study by its conclusion validity. The most direct procedure for doing this is to weight by degrees of freedom.[3]

Before the weighted *Z* statistic can be computed, one must transform the one-tailed *t* statistic from each study to a *Z* statistic. This is done by determining the exact one-tailed *p* value of the *t* statistic and finding the corresponding *Z* statistic for that value. This always results in a *Z* value that is less than the *t* in absolute value. Wallace (1959) gives an approximation that should be generally serviceable:

$$Z = t\left(1 - \frac{t^2}{4df}\right)$$

This approximation tends to be conservative (i.e., produces a *Z* too close to zero) when the degrees of freedom are few. These *Z* values

---

[3] Some other weighting strategy is probably more optimal than weighting by degrees of freedom if the aim is to maximize power.

are weighted and then combined by the following formula:

$$\frac{\Sigma w_i Z_i}{\sqrt{\Sigma w_i^2}}$$

where the $w_i$ are the weights for study $i$ (e.g., the degrees of freedom). The numerator takes each $Z$ and multiplies it by its weight and sums across these products. The denominator is the square root of the sum of squared weights. The result of this formula is a $Z$ statistic with an associated $p$ value. For our example, using Wallace's approximation and using the degrees of freedom as weights, we would obtain

$$\frac{369.03}{\sqrt{35,748}} = 1.952$$

from the results of Table 10.2. This $Z$ has a one-tailed $p$ value of .0255. This method produces a "less significant" result than the method of adding $t$'s in our particular example because of the heavy weight given to the one study that has 180 degrees of freedom.

*Averaging effect sizes.* Rosenthal (1978) concludes with the warning that combining $p$ values only tells the researcher whether the effect across studies is significant. Because virtually every treatment has an effect no matter how trivial, and because combining across studies increases conclusion validity, we ought to expect the combined probabilities of a large number of studies to be significant. What we want, then, is not only the combined $p$ value but the average size of the treatment effect as well. A measure of the treatment effect is in principle not affected by sample size, whereas a $p$ value is.

We need to compute the effect size for each study and average them across studies. The best known example of this method is that of Smith and Glass (1977). For some 833 outcome studies of psychotherapy, they measured the *effect size* using a modified version of Cohen's (1969) measure $d$,

$$\frac{\overline{Y}_E - \overline{Y}_C}{s}$$

where $\overline{Y}_E$ is the mean for the treated subjects, $\overline{Y}_C$ is the control mean, and *s* is the pooled within-group standard deviation.[4] Smith and Glass (1977) found that the average effect size was .68, indicating that persons who received psychotherapy were .68 standard deviations better off than those who did not receive psychotherapy. An effect size or *d* of .68 corresponds to a .32 correlation between psychotherapy and the outcome.

The results of studies can be combined by computing the mean or median of the effect sizes across studies. One can take the mean effect size and test whether it is significantly different from zero by the following equation

$$t_{N-1} = \frac{\overline{d}\sqrt{N}}{s_d}$$

where $t_{N-1}$ is a *t* statistic with $N - 1$ degrees of freedom, $N$ is the number of studies, $\overline{d}$ is the average effect size, and $s_d$ is the standard deviation of the effect sizes. This *t*-test has much less power than a combined probability. It is therefore sensible only when $N$ is large. One can also test whether effect sizes vary across studies in meaningful ways. For instance, Smith and Glass found that psychotherapy changed the outcome of anxiety the largest amount ($\overline{d} = .97$) and changed the outcome of school or work achievement the least ($\overline{d} = .31$).

*Bayesian methods.* When the measures of the outcome variable are roughly equivalent across studies, it may be possible to combine results more formally. Consider a study by Schmidt and Hunter (1977) on the use of intelligence tests to predict job performance for general clerks. Most studies showed a nonsignificant correlation between intelligence and job performance. Instead of combining probabilities or effect sizes, Schmidt and Hunter took a different tack. They argued that the correlation between intelligence and later job performance was a function of the true correla-

---

[4] Frequently we have only a *t* statistic for the treatment effect instead of the means. To derive Cohen's *d* from the *t* statistic,

$$d = t \sqrt{(1/N_1) + (1/N_2)}$$

the equation can be used, where *N* refers to the respective sizes of the treatment groups. Deriving *d* when covariates or other treatment variables are present becomes more complicated. In such cases the *d* for a dichotomous treatment variable (dummy coded) equals that variable's unstandardized regression coefficient divided by the square root of the mean square error from the regression equation. The *t* for that regression coefficient should not be used to derive the effect size.

tion, restriction of range in the intelligence test, and unreliability in the measure of job performance. Restriction of range refers to the fact that the standard deviation of intelligence varied with study. Using a complex approach based on Bayesian principles, they estimated the population correlation between intelligence and job performance to be .67. Even though their method predicted such a large correlation between the two variables, it also explained why most studies yielded a nonsignificant correlation. The interested reader is urged to consult Schmidt and Hunter for details.

The choice of the procedure for combining results may be less important than other issues. Let us consider three of these. First, there is the file-drawer problem. A large effect across a combined set of studies may be due to the fact that studies that obtained no significant effect were never published but were deposited in a file drawer. Rosenthal (1979) provides at least a partial answer to this problem. A second problem is that many primary researchers do not present enough detail to provide input for the formulas to combine results. Too often, if a result is nonsignificant, only that fact is mentioned and the *t*-value is omitted. Berman (1981) gives a detailed account of the problems and pitfalls of combining results when researchers fail to present sufficient results. Third, researchers may not employ *t* statistics but may use $\chi^2$ or *F* or a nonparametric statistic. Rosenthal (1978) provides some guide to this problem, but in many cases the researcher must be quite ingenious to apply the relevant formulas.

### Conclusion

The analysis of applied data should not end with an *F* or a *t* statistic. The results can be probed in useful ways. First, the primary researcher may investigate how the effect works and for whom. Second, another researcher may reanalyze the data to provide answers to new questions. Finally, the study itself may serve as a single data point in a study of studies.

# 11
# Conclusion

Our original intention in writing this book was to present a set of discrete chapters on different applied research designs and their analyses. However, it soon became apparent to us that much of what we had to say consisted of themes or ideas that ran across designs. All of the designs we have discussed represent variants on certain central design themes. Likewise, in the analysis of these designs there are certain fundamental problems that appear again and again. In this concluding chapter, it is our intention to discuss these common issues of design and analysis.

### Fundamental analysis issues

We started in Chapter 2 by outlining the fundamental analysis model that has been used throughout. In its basic form this model is quite straightforward. Multiple regression is used to estimate the treatment effect by regressing the outcome measure on the treatment variable. To obtain an unbiased estimate of the treatment effect, we need to control for the assignment variable in this analysis if the assignment variable is correlated with the outcome in the absence of treatment effects.

The most important result from this general analysis model is the treatment effect estimate. This treatment effect estimate is an unstandardized partial regression coefficient. As we saw in Chapters 4 and 6, this regression coefficient represents the difference in the mean outcomes between the treatment and control groups, adjusting for the assignment variable. In and of itself, this effect estimate is a meaningful piece of information, independent of the inferential statistics associated with it. It provides us with our best expectation concerning the magnitude of the treatment effect in terms of the actual metric of the outcome variable rather than

220

relative to the variation in the sample on which the research was conducted. It should generally be reported in all research reports.

In the application of this general model to the analysis of data from any of the designs we have discussed, three important issues are encountered. The first issue is the accuracy of the treatment effect estimate. We have given the name *bias* to this problem and discussed it repeatedly. The second issue concerns how "noisy" or reliable the estimate of the treatment effect is, regardless of the presence or absence of bias. This issue has been referred to as the *precision* of our test. The third issue concerns our ability to estimate the noise or reliability of the estimate of the treatment effect. This last issue, one of bias in the estimate of the reliability of the treatment effect, has been discussed repeatedly under the assumption of *independence* of observations. In the following paragraphs these three issues are briefly reviewed.

Bias results when the assignment variable is not controlled in the analysis, if the assignment variable is related to the outcome in the absence of treatment effects. The strength of randomized experiments lies in the fact that the assignment variable, a random one, is known on the average to be uncorrelated with the outcome. In designs like the regression discontinuity design, where the assignment variable is known, bias can be eliminated as long as the correct functional form for the assignment variable–outcome variable relationship is specified. Eliminating bias is the fundamental problem whenever the assignment variable is unknown, as in the nonequivalent control group design. In such cases, we can never be sure that we have adequately controlled for the unknown assignment variable. We have therefore recommended that multiple adjustment strategies be employed in attempting to remove bias. Although we have focused on the problem of serial dependency in the interrupted time-series design, the problem of bias is just as large, if not larger, there as it is in the nonequivalent control group design. We use time to control for what is frequently an unknown assignment rule. To the extent that time is a poor proxy for the rule, the estimate of treatment effects is biased. Finally, in the post-only correlational design, the assignment rule is unknown and attempts to remove bias are likely to be unsuccessful.

Even if our estimate of the treatment effect, the unstandardized partial regression coefficient, is unbiased, it may not be very reliable. To define the reliability of the treatment effect estimate, we need to think of exact replications of the research. To the extent that the treatment effect estimates vary across these replications, its reliability is low. More formally, the reliability is the standard error of the treatment effect estimate. When the treatment effect estimate is unreliable, the research has relatively low conclusion validity and we may decide that the treatment exerts no effect when in fact it is effective. In Chapter 3 we discussed factors that affect the reliability or precision of the estimated treatment effect. Likewise, in all of the designs that we have examined we have reminded the reader of analysis decisions that affect the precision of the treatment effect estimate.

The analysis strategy that underlies the basic analysis model is the equivalent of analysis of covariance, translated into a multiple regression format. This equivalence was demonstrated in Chapter 4. Analysis of covariance simultaneously has effects on both the bias problem and the precision problem. If we know the assignment variable and use it as the covariate, then its primary function as the covariate is to remove bias. At the same time, however, to the extent that it is correlated with the outcome, it improves the precision with which the treatment effect is estimated. In other cases, especially in randomized experiments, we use covariates with the sole intention of improving the precision of the treatment effect estimate. Inevitably, however, unless there is absolutely no relationship between the covariate and the treatment variable, some adjustment results from the inclusion of the covariate.

The third issue in the analysis of applied research designs concerns our ability to estimate the reliability of the treatment effect estimate (i.e., its error variance). Whereas the second issue refers to the relative magnitude of that reliability in theory, this third issue concerns our ability in practice to estimate its magnitude without bias. Tests of the statistical significance of the treatment effect assume that we have the correct estimate of its reliability. To the extent that our estimate of its magnitude is biased, we are prone to make either Type I or Type II conclusion errors. Bias in the estimate of error variance is a completely separate issue from bias in the estimate of treatment effects. The former sort of bias affects conclusion validity; the latter threatens internal validity. As we have discussed extensively in Chapters 4, 7, and 8, the major source of bias in the estimate of error variance derives from inappropriate assumptions concerning the independence of observations. In Chapter 7 a type of nonindependence, *serial dependency,* was identified and a substantial part of the chapter was devoted to corrections that must be made to overcome serial dependency. As we saw in Chapter 8, the problem of nonindependence or of serial dependency can cause us either to have more confidence in our treatment effect estimate than we should, or it can lead us to underestimate the reliability of the treatment effect estimate.

### Fundamental design issues

Just as the analyses of applied research designs are variants on a general analysis model, so, too, the research designs themselves can be seen as variants on certain central notions of research design. Thus, rather than seeing these research designs as a diverse and discrete set, it becomes possible to relate them to each other along a small set of fundamental dimensions.

In Chapter 2 we argued that the minimal requirement for purposes of internal validity is the presence of both treatment and comparison observations. Unless we have some set of observations that are recorded under the treatment condition and another set under a nontreatment condition, we have no hope of estimating the treatment effect. Given that we do have observations in both treated and comparison conditions, either we can observe the same units in all treatment conditions or the data in different treatment conditions may be derived from different units. In the language of experimental design, between-treatment comparisons can be made either between units or within units. For instance, if we were assessing the effects of some particular drug, either we could observe all patients with and without the drug (within-unit comparisons), or we could assign one group of subjects to receive the drug and the other not to (between-unit comparisons). A third type of "design," an inadequate one from the point of view of internal validity, does not permit between-treatment comparisons, because it gathers observations from only a single treatment condition. In this type, there is no estimate of the treatment effect. In summary, research designs either assess the treatment effect by comparisons between units or within units, or no between-treatment comparisons are made.

Just as between-treatment comparisons are necessary to estimate treatment effects, so it is necessary to gather more than a single observation within each of the treatment conditions in order to estimate the reliability or precision of the treatment effect estimate. In the extreme, if we have only one observation in each treatment condition, we have no estimate of within-condition variation and, hence, we are unable to calculate the statistical significance of the observed treatment effect. Multiple observations within treatments, or replications, can be gathered either within or between units. That is, within each of the various treatments, we can observe the same unit repeatedly (within-unit replication), or we can observe multiple units (between-unit replication). In some designs we may do both: Observations within treatment conditions may be gathered from more than a single unit, but, in addition, each unit may be observed multiple times.

In addition to the basis for between-condition comparisons and for within-condition replications, we can differentiate between research designs by an old and familiar factor: the nature of the assignment variable. For our purposes, it has been important to distinguish three types of assignment variables – a random one, a known but nonrandom one, and an unknown one. Whenever treatment comparisons are made, the nature of the assignment variable has, of course, profound implications for internal validity and analysis. When there is only a single treatment from which observations are gathered, there is by definition no assignment variable.

If we take each of these dimensions that differentiate research designs and form all possible combinations, as in Table 11.1, we come up with a set of research designs that subsume those discussed in this book. Although all of the designs in this set are possible, they differ in their informativeness or utility. They also differ in the frequency with which they are used.

In the next few pages we discuss the specific research designs that constitute the cells of this table. Before doing so, it may be helpful again to review the difference between the rows and columns of the table. The columns represent the ways in which we may take multiple observations *within* any given treatment: We may observe the same subject multiple times, or we may observe different subjects, or we may have only a single observation per condition. The rows of Table 11.1 refer both to the nature of *between*-condition comparisons and to the type of assignment variable. Between-condition comparisons can be made either within subjects or between subjects, or they may not be made at all. The assignment variable describes the rule by which observations are assigned to treatment conditions when between-condition comparisons are made.

The most frequently encountered social research designs involve

Table 11.1. *Basic social research designs*

| Between-condition comparisons | Assignment variable | Within-condition replications | | |
|---|---|---|---|---|
| | | Between units | Within units | None |
| Between units | Random | 1 | 8 | 15 |
| | Known | 2 | 9 | 16 |
| | Unknown | 3 | 10 | 17 |
| Within units | Random | 4 | 11 | 18 |
| | Known | 5 | 12 | 19 |
| | Unknown | 6 | 13 | 20 |
| None | | 7 | 14 | 21 |

observing different subjects or units a single time in the different treatments of interest, as in cells 1, 2, and 3 of Table 11.1. In other words, units are nested within treatments and, hence, between-condition comparisons are made between units. At the same time, within any treatment condition, the outcomes from a number of units are likely to be measured. Hence, within-treatment replications are likewise between units.

Most randomized experiments involve between-unit comparisons and between-unit replications. Likewise, the regression discontinuity design, the nonequivalent control group design, and the post-only correlational design are typically of this form. These designs, however, differ from each other on the third design factor, that is, the nature of the assignment rule. Randomized experiments, of course, employ a random assignment rule (cell 1). The regression discontinuity design employs a known assignment rule (cell 2). And both the nonequivalent control group design and the post-only correlational design have an unknown assignment rule (cell 3). To distinguish between these last two designs, it is necessary to introduce a fourth design factor: the presence of a pretest or pretreatment measure. In the nonequivalent control group design a pretest is gathered. In a correlational design the data are exclusively cross-sectional.

When within-treatment replications are between units, but treatment comparisons are made within units, repeated measurement designs result (cells 4, 5, and 6). In these designs, every unit or subject is observed a single time under each of the treatment conditions. In other words, treatments are crossed with subjects. These designs, which are relatively uncommon in applied social research, are discussed in Chapter 4.

In the final cell of the first column of Table 11.1 (cell 7), we have a design in which there are *no* comparisons between conditions and yet there are replications between units. In other words, there is only a single treatment with observations from multiple units in that group. With no treatment comparisons, of course, this sort of design is susceptible to nearly all of the threats to internal validity. Nevertheless, such a design is used surprisingly frequently. For instance, if we want to evaluate a course in a college, students who are enrolled in the course are typically asked what they thought of it. In spite of the absence of any meaningful comparison group, the responses in such an evaluation are usually considered by themselves to be a valid indicator of the quality of the course.

In the second column of Table 11.1, replications within treatments are within units. In other words, the same unit, be it a person, a classroom, a family, or whatever, is observed multiple times in any given treatment condition. Strictly speaking, only a single unit is observed in each of the treatment conditions.

Cells 8, 9, and 10 depict designs that involve treatment comparisons between units with within-unit replications. These designs are relatively uninteresting, because, with only a single unit in every condition, the type of assignment rule is essentially irrelevant. Under a random assignment rule, we have a randomized experiment, but, with only one unit per condition, unit differences are confounded with treatment effects. The same is true with a known or an unknown assignment rule.

The designs of cells 11, 12, and 13 of Table 11.1 are variations on the interrupted time-series design that was discussed in Chapter 7. In these designs, a single unit is observed repeatedly within conditions, and between-condition comparisons are also made within that same unit. As we saw in Chapter 7, the assignment variable refers to the rule for deciding whether any observation is treated or not. A random assignment rule is one in which the unit goes into and out of any given treatment on a random basis. Frequently time serves as the known assignment rule in these designs. In such a case, it is known before any observations are taken at what point in time or in what order the unit will be in each treatment. Most frequently, the true assignment variable is unknown. The unit receives the treatments in a given order, but we do not know exactly what determined the order.

The design of cell 14 is one in which there is only a single treatment condition and a single unit is repeatedly observed in that condition. Just as in the design of cell 7, the absence of a control group makes this design an especially poor one from the point of view of internal validity. The design is frequently used in an informal way, particularly for diagnostic purposes. Suppose that we want to diagnose why a particular individual seems to be having trouble keeping a job. It makes sense, as a start, simply to observe that individual repeatedly on the job in order to get a sense of what the problem might be.

The third column in Table 11.1 (cells 15 through 21) defines a series of designs in which there is no variation within conditions because only a single observation is made in each. In these designs, as long as we make treatment comparisons, the treatment effect can be estimated. Unfortunately, however, without replications we are unable to estimate the reliability of that estimate. In spite of this serious deficiency, these designs can be quite useful in a sort of heuristic manner, if our goal is to formulate hypotheses for more systematic research.

Our purpose in dwelling upon Table 11.1 and its three research design factors is to clarify how various design decisions affect both the research validities discussed in Chapter 3 as well as the three analysis issues that we identified in the first section of this chapter.

Internal validity is of course dependent on making treatment comparisons. Regardless of whether those comparisons are between or within units, without a treatment and a comparison group, at the minimum, we have no estimate of the treatment effect.

As we have said throughout the book, the distinctions among assignment variables are also crucial for internal validity. With a random assignment rule we can have confidence that the treatment effect is estimated without bias. With a known assignment variable, such confidence is possible as long as we know the functional form of the relationship between the assignment variable and the outcome. With an unknown assignment variable, confidence that bias has been avoided is severely reduced. Having a pretest helps some, but even here the distinct possibility of bias remains.

Replications within treatment conditions are necessary so that we can calculate the reliability of the treatment effect estimate. In other words, if we have a design without replications, we have no conclusion validity. In statistical terms, we have no within-condition variation with which to compare the between-condition difference.

Assuming that we have replications within treatment conditions, we then want to know if we can assess the reliability of the observed treatment effect without bias. As we discussed in Chapter 8, we are likely to misestimate the reliability of the treatment effect whenever observations are not independent of each other, either within treatment conditions or between treatment conditions, that is, whenever multiple observations are taken from the same unit. Such misestimation can increase the chances of either Type I or Type II conclusion errors, depending on the conditions that were identified in Chapter 8. There we also suggested that whenever nonindependence of observations is a threat, whether in the interrupted time-series design or elsewhere, data adjustments or transformations are necessary to eliminate bias in the estimate of the reliability of the treatment effect. Occasionally, changes in the unit or level of analysis can also alleviate nonindependence problems.

### Final comment

Just as we believe that there are common threads that run across the designs and analyses discussed in this book, so we believe that none of these designs or analysis strategies is sufficient by itself. They are all subject to errors. Different designs are better for some purposes than are others. Likewise, different analyses of the same design are better for some purposes than are others. No single design, nor any single analysis, is the choice across occasions and research problems. Flexibility and replication are required if we are to have confidence in our results. Flexibility and replication are required both within and across research studies. Within any given study, we have urged the reader to analyze the resulting data in more than a single way. Thus, for instance, we have recommended the simultaneous use of different adjustment strategies in the nonequivalent control group design, and we have encouraged different approaches within the same interrupted time-series design to alleviate the problem of serial dependency. Between studies, we encourage researchers to use different designs, with different strengths, to look at the same research problem. Initially, for purposes of hypothesis formation, a descriptive correlational study may be most appropriate. A randomized experiment may then be best to gain confidence in the hypothesized treatment effect. Then, a quasi-experimental research design may be appropriate to increase both the construct and the external validities of the experimental work. Such a multifaceted approach has the best chance of reaching conclusions that are valid.

Our fundamental goal in writing this book has been to maximize the validity of applied social research. We feel that we have highlighted the issues of construct and conclusion validities that have been too often ignored with unfortunate consequences. Moreover, we feel that we have presented an honest, if somewhat pessimistic, appraisal of the internal validity of the various research designs. This problem of potential bias seems to raise its head nearly everywhere. In spite of that, however, we do believe that well-conducted applied social research is invaluable. Only through such research can we begin to assess whether social interventions are effective. Both caution and flexibility are necessary resources to the researcher. To the extent that this book gives those resources to the reader, we shall judge it to have accomplished our goal.

# Supplementary reading

## 2. The basic evaluation model

Cohen, J., & Cohen, P. *Applied multiple regression/correlation analysis for the behavioral sciences*. Hillsdale, N.J.: L. Erlbaum Associates, 1975.

Wonnacott, R. J., & Wonnacott, T. H. *Econometrics*. New York: Wiley, 1970.

## 3. Validity in social research

Campbell, D. T., & Fiske, D. W. Convergent and discriminant validation by the multitrait-multimethod matrix. *Psychological Bulletin,* 1959, *56,* 81–105.

Campbell, D. T., & Stanley, J. C. *Experimental and quasi-experimental designs for research*. Chicago: Rand McNally, 1963.

Cook, T. D., & Campbell, D. T. *Quasi-experimentation: design and analysis issues for field settings*. Chicago: Rand McNally, 1979, chap. 2.

Cronbach, L. J., & Meehl, P. E. Construct validity in psychological tests. *Psychological Bulletin,* 1955, *52,* 281–302.

## 4. Randomized experiments

Cochran, W. G., & Cox, G. M. *Experimental designs* (2nd ed.) New York: Wiley, 1957.

Cohen, J. Multiple regression as a general data-analytic system. *Psychological Bulletin,* 1968, *70,* 426–43.

Fennessey, J. The general linear model. *American Journal of Sociology,* 1968, *74,* 1–28.

Riecken, H. W., & Boruch, R. F. *Social experimentation: a method for planning and evaluating social intervention*. New York: Academic Press, 1974.

## 5. The regression discontinuity design

Overall, J. E., & Woodward, J. A. Nonrandom assignment and the analysis of covariance. *Psychological Bulletin,* 1977, *84,* 588–94.

Rubin, D. B. Assignment to treatment group on the basis of a covariate. *Journal of Educational Statistics,* 1977, *2,* 1–26.

Thistlethwaite, D. L., & Campbell, D. T. Regression-discontinuity analysis: an alternative to the ex post facto experiment. *Journal of Educational Psychology,* 1960, *51,* 309–17.

### 6. The nonequivalent control group design

Bryk, A. S., & Weisberg, H. I. Use of the nonequivalent control group design when subjects are growing. *Psychological Bulletin*, 1977, *85*, 950–62.

Reichardt, C. S. The statistical analysis of data from nonequivalent group designs. In T. D. Cook & D. T. Campbell (Eds.), *Quasi-experimentation: design and analysis issues for field settings*. Chicago: Rand McNally, 1979.

Sörbom, D. An alternative to the methodology for analysis of covariance. *Psychometrika*, 1978, *43*, 381–96.

### 7. The interrupted time-series design

Gottman, J. M. *Time series analysis for the behavioral sciences*. Cambridge: Cambridge University Press, 1981.

McCleary, R., & Hay, R. A. *Applied time series analysis*. Beverly Hills, Calif.: Sage, 1980.

### 8. Miscellaneous designs and issues

Bryk, A. S., & Weisberg, H. I. Value-added analysis: a dynamic approach to the estimation of treatment effects. *Journal of Educational Statistics*, 1976, *1*, 127–55.

Furby, L. Interpreting regression toward the mean in developmental research. *Developmental Psychology*, 1973, *8*, 172–9.

### 9 The post-only correlational design

Bentler, P. M. Multivariate analysis with latent variables: causal modeling. *Annual Review of Psychology*, 1980, *31*, 419–56.

Duncan, O. D. *Introduction to structural equation models*. New York: Academic Press, 1975.

James, L. R., & Singh, B. K. An introduction to the logic, assumptions, and basic analytic procedures of two-stage least squares. *Psychological Bulletin*, 1978, *85*, 1104–23.

Kenny, D. A. *Correlation and causality*. New York: Wiley-Interscience, 1979.

### 10. Further probing of applied research data

Cook, T. D. The potential and limitations of secondary research. In M. W. Apple, M. J. Subkoviak, & H. S. Lufler, Jr. (Eds.), *Educational evaluation: analysis and responsibility*. Berkeley, Calif.: McCutchan, 1974.

Judd, C. M., & Kenny, D. A. *Process analysis: estimating mediation in treatment evaluation. Evaluation Review*, 1981.

Rosenthal, R. (Ed.) *New directions for methodology of behavioral science: quantitative assessment of research domains*. San Francisco: Jossey-Bass, 1981.

# References

Adam, J. Sequential strategies and the separation of age, cohort, and time-of-measurement contributions to developmental data. *Psychological Bulletin,* 1978, *85,* 1309–16.

Alwin, D. F. Approaches to the interpretation of relationships in the multitrait-multimethod matrix. In H. L. Costner (Ed.), *Sociological methodology 1973–1974.* San Francisco: Jossey-Bass, 1974.

Anderson, L. R., & Ager, J. W. Analysis of variance in small group research. *Personality and Social Psychology Bulletin,* 1978, *4,* 341-5.

Anderson, N. H. Cognitive algebra. In L. Berkowitz (Ed.), *Advances in experimental social psychology* (Vol. 7). New York: Academic Press, 1974.

Ball, S., & Bogatz, G. A. *The first year of Sesame Street: an evaluation.* Princeton, N.J.: Educational Testing Service, 1970.

Barker, P., & Pelavin, S. *Concerning scores and scale transformations in standardized achievement tests, their accuracy and dependability for individual and aggregation: the case of MAT 70.* Rand Corporation WN-9161-NIE, September 1975.

Bentler, P. M. Multivariate analysis with latent variables: causal modeling. *Annual Review of Psychology,* 1980, *31,* 419–56.

Berman, J. S. *Social bases of psychotherapy.* New York: Oxford University Press, 1981.

Bernstein, I. N., & Freeman, H. E. *Academic and entrepreneurial research: the consequences of diversity in federal evaluation studies.* New York: Russell Sage, 1975.

Blalock, H. M. *Theory construction: from verbal to mathematical formulations.* Englewood Cliffs, N.J.: Prentice-Hall, 1969.

Bossé, R., Garvey, A. J., & Costa, P. T. Predictors of weight change following smoking cessation. *International Journal of the Addictions,* 1980, *15,* 969–91.

Bowles, S. S., & Levin, H. M. The determinants of scholastic achievement – an appraisal of some recent evidence. *Journal of Human Resources,* 1968, *3,* 393–400.

Box, G. E. P., & Jenkins, G. M. *Time-series analysis: forcasting and control.* San Francisco: Holden-Day, 1970.

232

Bridge, R. G., Judd, C. M., & Moock, P. R. *The determinants of educational outcomes: the impact of families, peers, teachers, and schools.* Cambridge, Mass.: Ballinger, 1979.

Bridge, R. G., Reeder, L. G., Kanouse, D., Kinder, D. R., Nagy, V. T., & Judd, C. M. Interviewing changes attitudes – sometimes. *Public Opinion Quarterly,* 1977, *41,* 56–64.

Bryk, A. S. *An investigation of the effectiveness of alternative statistical adjustment strategies in the analysis of quasi-experimental growth data.* Unpublished doctoral dissertation, Harvard University, 1977.

Bryk, A. S., & Weisberg, H. I. Value-added analysis: a dynamic approach to the estimation of treatment effects. *Journal of Educational Statistics,* 1976, *1,* 127–55.

Use of the nonequivalent control group design when subjects are growing. *Psychological Bulletin,* 1977, *85,* 950–62.

Cain, G. G., & Watts, H. W. Problems in making policy inferences from the Coleman Report. *American Sociological Review,* 1970, *35,* 228–42.

Campbell, D. T. *The effect of college on students: proposing a quasi-experimental approach.* Research report, Northwestern University, 1967.

Reforms as experiments. *American Psychologist,* 1969, *24,* 409–29.

Campbell, D. T., & Boruch, R. F. Making the case for randomized assignment to treatments by considering the alternatives: six ways in which quasi-experimental evaluations tend to underestimate effects. In C. A. Bennett & A. A. Lumsdaine (Eds.), *Evaluation and experiment: some critical issues in assessing social programs.* New York: Academic Press, 1975.

Campbell, D. T., & Erlebacher, A. E. How regression artifacts in quasi-experimental evaluations can mistakenly make compensatory education look harmful. In J. Hellmuth (Ed.), *Compensatory education: a national debate,* Vol. 3, *Disadvantaged child.* New York: Brunner/Mazel, 1970.

Campbell, D. T., & Fiske, D. W. Convergent and discriminant validation by the multitrait-multimethod matrix. *Psychological Bulletin,* 1959, *56,* 81–105.

Campbell, D. T., & Stanley, J. C. *Experimental and quasi-experimental designs for research.* Chicago: Rand McNally, 1963.

Cochran, W. G., & Cox, G. M. *Experimental designs* (2nd ed.). New York: Wiley, 1957.

Cohen, J. Multiple regression as a general data-analytic system. *Psychological Bulletin,* 1968, *70,* 426–43.

*Statistical power analysis for the behavioral sciences.* New York: Academic Press, 1969.

Partialed products *are* interactions; partialed powers *are* curve components. *Psychological Bulletin,* 1978, *85,* 858–66.

Cohen, J., & Cohen, P. *Applied multiple regression/correlation analysis for the behavioral sciences.* Hillsdale, N.J.: L. Erlbaum Associates, 1975.

Cohn, R. M. The effect of employment status on self-attitudes. *Social Psychology,* 1978, *41,* 81–93.

Coleman, J. S., Campbell, E. Q., Hobson, C. F., McPartland, J., Mood, A. M.,

Weinfeld, F. D., & York, R. L. *Equality of educational opportunity.* Washington, D.C.: U.S. Department of H.E.W., Office of Education, 1966.

Cook, T. D. The potential and limitations of secondary research. In M. W. Apple, M. J. Subkoviak, & H. S. Lufler, Jr. (Eds.), *Educational evaluation: analysis and responsibility.* Berkeley, Calif.: McCutchan, 1974.

Cook, T. D., Appleton, H., Conner, R., Schaffer, A., Tamkin, G., & Weber, S. J. *"Sesame Street" revisited: a case study in evaluation research.* New York: Russell Sage, 1975.

Cook, T. D., & Campbell, D. T. *Quasi-experimentation: design and analysis issues for field settings.* Chicago: Rand McNally, 1979.

Cook, T. D., & Gruder, C. L. Metaevaluation research. *Evaluation Quarterly,* 1978, *2,* 5–51.

Cronbach, L. J. *Essentials of psychological testing* (3rd ed.). New York: Harper & Row, 1970.

Cronbach, L. J., & Furby, L. How we should measure "change" – or should we? *Psychological Bulletin,* 1970, *74,* 68–80.

Cronbach, L. J., & Meehl, P. E. Construct validity in psychological tests. *Psychological Bulletin,* 1955, *52,* 281–302.

Dawes, R. M. The robust beauty of improper linear models in decision making. *American Psychologist,* 1979, *34,* 571–82.

Deutsch, M., & Collins, M. E. *Interracial housing.* Minneapolis: University of Minnesota Press, 1951.

Deutsch, S. J., & Alt, F. B. The effect of Massachusetts' gun control law on gun-related crimes in the city of Boston. *Evaluation Quarterly,* 1977, *1,* 543–68.

Director, S. M. *Underadjustment bias in the quasi-experimental evaluation of manpower training.* Unpublished doctoral dissertation, Northwestern University, 1974.

Duncan, O. D. *Introduction to structural equation models.* New York: Academic Press, 1975.

Edwards, W., Guttentag, M., & Snapper, K. A decision theoretic approach to evaluation research. In E. L. Streuning & M. Guttentag (Eds.), *Handbook of evaluation research* (Vol. 1). Beverly Hills, Calif.: Sage Publications, 1975.

Elashoff, J. D., & Snow, R. E. *Pygmalion reconsidered.* Worthington, Ohio: Charles A. Jones, 1971.

Feldt, L. S. A comparison of the precision of three experimental designs employing a concomitant variable. *Psychometrika,* 1958, *23,* 335–53.

Fennessey, J. The general linear model. *American Journal of Sociology,* 1968, *74,* 1–28.

Furby, L. Interpreting regression toward the mean in developmental research. *Developmental Psychology,* 1973, *8,* 172–9.

Gilbert, J. P., Light, R. J., & Mosteller, F. Assessing social interventions: an empirical base for policy. In C. A. Bennett & A. A. Lumsdaine (Eds.), *Evaluation and experiment: some critical issues in assessing social programs.* New York: Academic Press, 1975.

Glass, G. V. Primary, secondary and meta-analysis of research. *Educational Researcher,* 1976, *5,* 3–8.

Glass, G. V., Willson, V. L., & Gottman, J. M. *Design and analysis of time series experiments.* Boulder: Colorado Associated University Press, 1975.

Goldberger, A. S. *Selection bias in evaluating treatment effects: some formal illustrations* (Discussion Paper 123–72). Madison: University of Wisconsin, Institute for Research on Poverty, June 1972.

Goodman, L. Some alternatives to ecological correlation. *American Journal of Sociology,* 1959, *64,* 610–25.

Gottman, J. M. *Time series analysis for the behavioral sciences.* Cambridge: Cambridge University Press, 1981.

Gottman, J. M., & Glass, G. V. Analysis of interrupted time-series experiments. In T. R. Kratochwill (Ed.), *Single subject research.* New York: Academic Press, 1978.

Hammond, J. Two sources of error in ecological correlations. *American Sociological Review,* 1973, *38,* 764–77.

Hannan, M. T., & Young, A. A. Estimation in panel models: results on pooling cross-sections and time series. In D. R. Heise (Ed.), *Sociological methodology 1977.* San Francisco: Jossey-Bass, 1977.

Hardin, E., & Borus, M. E. *The economic benefits and costs of retraining.* Lexington, Mass.: D.C. Heath, 1971.

Harris, R. J. *A primer of multivariate statistics.* New York: Academic Press, 1975.

Hibbs, D. A., Jr. Problems of statistical estimation and causal inference in time series regression models. In H. L. Costner (Ed.), *Sociological methodology 1973–74.* San Francisco: Jossey-Bass, 1974.

James, L. R., & Singh, B. K. An introduction to the logic, assumptions, and basic analytic procedures of two-stage least squares. *Psychological Bulletin,* 1978, *85,* 1104–23.

Jöreskog, K. G., & Sörbom, D. *LISREL: analysis of linear structural relationships by the method of maximum likelihood.* Chicago: National Educational Resources, 1978.

*Advances in factor analysis.* Cambridge, Mass.: Abt Associates, 1979.

Judd, C. M. Bias resulting from random errors of measurement in multiple regression. Unpublished paper, Harvard University, 1980.

Judd, C. M., & Kenny, D. A. *Process analysis: estimating mediation in treatment evaluation. Evaluation Review,* 1981.

Kenny, D. A. Cross-lagged panel correlation: a test for spuriousness. *Psychological Bulletin,* 1975, *82,* 887–903.

*Correlation and causality.* New York: Wiley-Interscience, 1979.

A comment on Rogosa (1980). Unpublished manuscript, 1981.

Kenny, D. A., & Cohen, S. H. A reexamination of selection and growth processes in the nonequivalent control group design. In K. Schuessler (Ed.), *Sociological methodology 1980.* San Francisco: Jossey-Bass, 1980.

Kratochwill, T. R. *Single subject research.* New York: Academic Press, 1978.

Lazarsfeld, P. F., & Reitz, J. G. *An introduction to applied sociology.* New York: Elsevier, 1975.

Maccoby, N., & Farquhar, J. W. Communication for health: unselling heart disease. *Journal of Communication,* 1975, *25,* 114–26.

McCain, L. J., & McCleary, R. The statistical analysis of the simple interrupted time series quasi-experiment. In T. D. Cook & D. T. Campbell (Eds.), *Quasi-experimentation: design and analysis issues for field settings.* Chicago: Rand McNally, 1979.

McCleary, R., & Hay, R. A. *Applied time series analysis.* Beverly Hills, Calif.: Sage, 1980.

Meier, P. The biggest public health experiment ever: the 1954 field trial of the Salk poliomyelitic vaccine. In J. M. Tanur, F. Mosteller, W. Kruskal, R. Link, R. Pieters, & G. Rising (Eds.), *Statistics: a guide to the unknown.* San Francisco: Holden-Day, 1972.

Mosteller, F., & Tukey, J. W. *Data analysis and regression.* Reading, Mass.: Addison-Wesley, 1977.

Murphy, R. T., & Appel, L. R. *Evaluation of the PLATO IV computer-based education system in the community college.* Princeton, N.J.: Educational Testing Service, 1977.

Nunnally, J. C. *Psychometric theory* (2nd ed.). New York: McGraw-Hill, 1978.

Overall, J. E., & Woodward, J. A. Nonrandom assignment and the analysis of covariance. *Psychological Bulletin,* 1977, *84,* 588–94.

Parker, E. B., Campbell, D. T., Cook, T. D., Katzman, N., & Butler-Paisley, M. Time-series analysis of effects of television on library circulation. Unpublished paper, Northwestern University, 1971.

Rees, A. The graduated work incentive experiment: an overview of the labor-supply results. *Journal of Human Resources,* 1974, *9,* 158–80.

Reichardt, C. S. The statistical analysis of data from nonequivalent group designs. In T. D. Cook & D. T. Campbell (Eds.), *Quasi-experimentation: design and analysis issues for field settings.* Chicago: Rand McNally, 1979.

Riecken, H. W., & Boruch, R. F. *Social experimentation: a method for planning and evaluating social intervention.* New York: Academic Press, 1974.

Robinson, W. S. Ecological correlations and the behavior of individuals. *American Sociological Review,* 1950, *15,* 351–7.

Rosenthal, R. *Experimenter effects in behavioral research.* New York: Irvington, 1976.

   Combining the results of independent studies. *Psychological Bulletin,* 1978, *85,* 185–93.

   The "file drawer problem" and tolerance for null results. *Psychological Bulletin,* 1979, *86,* 638–41.

Rosenthal, R. (Ed.) *New directions for methodology of behavioral science: quantitative assessment of research domains.* San Francisco: Jossey-Bass, 1980.

Rosenthal, R., & Jacobson, L. *Pygmalion in the classroom: teacher expectation* and pupils' intellectual development. New York: Holt, Rinehart, and Winston, 1968.

Rosenthal, R., & Rosnow, R. L. *Artifact in behavioral research.* New York: Academic Press, 1969.

Rosenthal, R., & Rubin, D. B. Interpersonal expectancy effects: the first 345 studies. *The Behavioral and Brain Sciences,* 1978, *3,* 377–415.

Ross, H. L., & Campbell, D. T. The Connecticut speed crackdown: a study of the effects of legal change. In H. L. Ross (Ed.), *Perspectives on the social order: readings in sociology.* New York: McGraw-Hill, 1968.

Ross, H. L., Campbell, D. T., & Glass, G. V. Determining the effects of a legal reform: the British "breathanalyzer" crackdown of 1967. *American Behavioral Scientist,* 1970, *13,* 493–509.

Rubin, D. B. The use of matched sampling and regression adjustment to remove bias in observational studies. *Biometrics,* 1973, *29,* 185–203.

Assignment to treatment group on the basis of a covariate. *Journal of Educational Statistics,* 1977, *2,* 1–26.

Schmidt, F. L., & Hunter, J. E. Development of a general solution to the problem of validity generalization. *Journal of Applied Psychology,* 1977, *62,* 529–40.

Scriven, M. Evaluation perspectives and procedures. In J. W. Popham (Ed.), *Evaluation in education: current application.* Berkeley, Calif.: McCutchan, 1974.

Seaver, W. B., & Quarton, R. J. *Social reinforcement of excellence: dean's list and academic achievement.* Paper presented at the 44th Annual Meeting of the Eastern Psychological Association, Washington, D.C., May 1973.

Smith, M. *Equality of educational opportunity:* the basic findings reconsidered. In F. Mosteller & D. P. Moynihan (Eds.), *On equality of educational opportunity.* New York: Vintage, 1972.

Smith, M. L., & Glass, G. V. Meta-analysis of psychotherapy outcome studies. *American Psychologist,* 1977, *32,* 752–60.

Sörbom, D. An alternative to the methodology for analysis of covariance. *Psychometrika,* 1978, *43,* 381–96.

Staw, B. M. Attitudinal and behavioral consequences of changing a major organizational reward: a natural field experiment. *Journal of Personality and Social Psychology,* 1974, *29,* 742–51.

Strenio, J., Bryk, A. S., & Weisberg, H. I. *An individualized growth model perspective for evaluating educational programs.* Proceedings of the 1977 Annual Meeting of the American Statistical Association, Chicago, 1977.

Sudman, S. *Applied sampling.* New York: Academic Press, 1976.

Taveggia, T. C. Resolving research controversy through empirical cumulation: toward reliable sociological knowledge. *Sociological Methods and Research,* 1974, *2,* 395–407.

Thistlethwaite, D. L., & Campbell, D. T. Regression-discontinuity analysis: an alternative to the ex post facto experiment. *Journal of Educational Psychology,* 1960, *51,* 309–17.

Wallace, D. L. Bounds on normal approximations to student's and the chi-square distributions. *Annals of Mathematical Statistics,* 1959, *30,* 1121–30.

Warner, R. M. Periodic rhythms in conversational speech. *Language and Speech,* 1979, *22,* 381–96.

Winer, B. J. *Statistical principles in experimental design.* New York: McGraw-Hill, 1971.

Wolf, R. *Achievement in America.* New York: Teachers College Press, 1978.

Wonnacott, R. J., & Wonnacott, T. H. *Econometrics.* New York: Wiley, 1970.

# Index

239